FEEDING FRENZY

Trial lawyers, the media, politicians and corporate adversaries:

Inside the Ford-Firestone crisis

By

Jon F. Harmon

Eloquent Books
New York, New York

Eloquent Books
An imprint of AEG Publishing Group
845 Third Avenue, 6th Floor - 6016
New York, NY 10022
www.eloquentbooks.com

ISBN: 978-1-60860-731-0

Printed in the United States of America

Book Design: Roger Hayes

DEDICATION

To Mary, the love of my life, and to our four boys, Michael, Tim, Jeff and Dan; too many hours missed through the many months of this terrible crisis, time we could have been together.

To my Mother who taught me a love of reading and writing; to my Father who taught me to think logically and to demand sound thinking from others.

ACKNOWLEDGMENTS

I began to write this book in the summer of 2001 with Ford's crisis communications work still ongoing. Not long afterward, the September 11 terrorist attacks forever changed our world and I put aside the draft I had started. Instead, I used my spare time to work on the four personal journals I was writing simultaneously for my four sons. In the wake of 9/11, they seemed more important. About the same time, I had begun to wonder if it was possible for me to publish an even-handed account of the Firestone tire crisis. With hundreds of lawsuits pending against Ford for rollover accidents mostly involving the Explorer, I knew Ford's corporate lawyers would not want me to publish an inside account of the Firestone-Ford tire fiasco. As long as I worked at the company, I couldn't publish such a book.

I left Ford in February 2007 after a 23-year career and with no regrets. I had experienced and led just about every facet of communications – corporate public affairs, strategic communications and product public relations. It was time to begin the next chapter of my career. And it was time to write this book. I had completed much of the work when I was recruited to lead the global PR team at Navistar International Corp. and soon found myself too busy to finish the writing project.

When I left Navistar in early 2009, I vowed to finally complete this work. Events in the news spoke to its continued relevance. The domestic auto industry had cratered. A spectacular run-up in oil prices led to $4.50 / gallon gasoline (and $5.50 / gallon diesel) by the summer of 2008 and all but shut down sales of fuel-thirsty trucks and SUVs. And though fuel prices soon began to recede, the worse was yet to come. The credit crisis that brought down Lehman Bros. on Sept. 15, 2008 spread throughout the world of lending. Without available credit, auto sales virtually dried up. Even Toyota announced it would lose more then a billion dollars in 2008 – its first loss in 70 years. The CEOs of the three Detroit automakers traveled to Washington to appeal to Congress for emergency loan guarantees. Congress (and the editorial pages of newspapers across the country) had no sympathy for the Detroit Three. They were particularly scornful of the Big Three executives' use of corporate jets to travel to Washington to ask for the "bailout." (In fact, each of the three automakers subsequently announced plans to sell off their corporate jets. Meanwhile, successful plaintiff lawyers – who've enriched themselves suing big corporations – continue to own and operate private jets to better scamper about the country chasing ambulances. But don't look for these lawyers to relinquish their well-crafted image as "Davids" fighting against injustices perpetrated by the "Goliath" automakers.)

It was with a sense of déjà vu that I watched the television reports showing the automaker CEOs enduring caustic lectures from career politicians, people who by and large had never run a business and had less than a stellar record of managing other people's money. It is so much easier to criticize than to do, to second-guess than to make difficult, real-time decisions when faced with complicated, intertwined problems and incomplete information.

I continue to believe in the future of Ford, despite the excruciatingly hard times it currently faces, and know first-hand of the hard work and good intentions of the product designers, development engineers, vehicle dynamics experts, safety analysts and all the others who are all too easily impugned by grand-standing Congressmen – or by trial lawyers spinning conspiracy stories to juries and journalists of a callous company knowingly sacrificing safety for profit.

In many ways this book is a more thoughtful and useful work than it would have been had it been published in the immediate aftermath of the tire mess. With the benefit of nearly eight years of hindsight and reflection, I could focus on aspects that have sustainable relevance and application to the public relations professional, and skip or pass over quickly less significant events.

My thanks to Tom Baughman for the insights that inform the conclusions at the end of Chapter 10. And a special thank you to Keith Bradsher, Jason Vines and Jill Bratina for their perceptive and provocative comments that shape the Epilogue.

I look forward to readers joining the conversation about the practice of crisis communication on the author's blog, Force for Good Communications, at: http://forceforgoodcom.com/

I also want to acknowledge the leadership of David Scott, who served as Ford's vice president of Public Affairs for 13 years beginning in 1985. David set the bar high for those on his staff, requiring integrity, honesty and modesty in all our communications. I learned so much from him and from the great bosses I worked for over the years at Ford – Hal Watts, Ed Lintz, Jim Bright, Mary Joseph, Bonnie Townsend, Jim Vella, Ray Day.

While I wasn't able to mention by name in the text of this book all the great and dedicated people on Ford's Tire Team throughout the crisis, I'd like to acknowledge three who were always there to help answer my questions even with so much on their plates: truck engineer Andy Vandecaveye, customer service executive Joe Bradley, and a lawyer with a warm heart, Tom Falahee. Plus three others from Public Affairs: video and event producer Corryl Parr, broadcast news manager Nancy Branstetter-McCauley, and Ford Communications Network's leader Terry Bresnihan.

And, of course, Donna Thomas, who helped keep me sane during this crazy time. Ken Zino had hired Donna to be his administrative assistant in early August 2000; her first day at Ford was the day before we flew off to Washington for the big recall announcement. When Zino and I returned to Dearborn, we took up "temporary" residence in the Glass House. Zino moved his laptop and three-ring binders to a small desk in Jason's executive office on the 12th floor. I moved to an open office on the 10th floor with the corporate Public Affairs people. I found a nearby cube for Donna who had spent the past few days outside Zino's regular office in Ford's Product Development Center with nothing to do. She became my right hand. I routinely gave Donna impossible assignments, such as to take my hand-scratched notes and completely rework a massive PowerPoint presentation before my review with Executive Vice President Richard Parry-Jones 30 minutes later, while I took a stack of messages from her and returned calls to journalists on immediate deadline. That was life during the tire crisis. I sometimes miss it.

CONTENTS

PREFACE

"Lying makes a problem part of the future; truth makes a problem part of the past."

- *College and professional basketball coach Rick Pitino, author of* Lead to Succeed

* * *

For generations, the automobile has captured the public imagination like no other product. For good and for bad, the auto's impact on society, the economy and the environment has been immense. It's not surprising then that the auto business is the most closely followed industry in America. A dedicated press corps chronicles the accomplishments and missteps of the auto companies, charts monthly sales totals and quarterly earnings or losses, and reviews current and up-coming products. Glossy enthusiast magazine "buff books" feature lavish photo spreads from distant drives of the hottest new cars; local newspapers include less colorful product drive reviews and ask-the-mechanic columns. Auto analysts forecast the companies' financial performance for Wall Street investment banks and institutional investors. Safety advocates and environmental activists keep the automakers in their cross hairs, and not coincidentally, so does a cottage industry of trial lawyers. Elected leaders find political advantage in pillorying or in praising auto executives depending on the shifting winds of public opinion.

Change is constant. The auto business is particularly unforgiving to the analyst or historian who confidently projects the future based on

xi

the successes and failures of today. Automotive history is replete with ups and downs, comebacks and downfalls, many unexpected and surprising. The mighty have a way of falling, and falling hard. And sometimes the fallen get back up when everyone has counted them out.

More than two decades ago, Pulitzer prize-winning author David Halberstam sounded a wakeup call to American industry in his study of contrast between a chronically under-performing Ford Motor Company and a rising star in Nissan. Funny thing, though; by the time *The Reckoning*[1] was published in 1986, Ford was the hottest automaker in the world, buoyed by the success of its new flagship, the Taurus. Meanwhile, Nissan was beginning to stumble badly with product failures and poor financial results. In subsequent years, the fortunes of the two companies would reverse again and then yet again.

As *Feeding Frenzy* goes to print in the summer of 2009, two-thirds of the former "Big Three" American automakers are in bankruptcy court, having fallen victim to a succession of body blows, many of them self-inflicted. Bad management decisions over many years rendered the companies overly reliant on pickup trucks and sport utilities, and noncompetitive in a car market dominated by Japanese and Korean automakers. Record gasoline prices that peaked the previous summer at $4.50 a gallon all but killed the market for trucks and SUVs. Meanwhile, the escalation of the subprime mortgage mess led to a pervasive credit crisis that choked off the availability of funds for would-be auto customers looking to finance or lease. And all that begat the global economic downturn that has come to be known as the "Worst Recession Since the Great Depression."

In the capital-intensive business of auto manufacturing, a lack of sales leads to a breathtakingly rapid burn of cash reserves. Without billions of dollars in bailout loans from the Federal government, General Motors and Chrysler would have been dissolved. Even with the bailouts, both companies fell into bankruptcy protection, hoping to shed enough debt obligations to emerge as smaller, humbler enterprises capable of succeeding in the aftermath of the recession. It will be a difficult road. The two companies' already poor reputations have been further tarnished by the unpopular bailouts. Countless potential customers simply will not consider buying a GM or Chrysler vehicle.

Unlike its cross-town rivals, Ford Motor Company has weathered the storms without a government bailout. Ford management had the foresight two years earlier to prepare for a deep economic downturn, prudently mortgaging assets – including factories, office buildings and even the Blue Oval trademark itself – to bank more than $20 billion in cash and liquidity, an ultimate "rainy day" fund that it has relied on through unrelenting downpours.

Ford has struggled along with every other automaker to survive the economic meltdown. But the company seems strategically poised to succeed when automobile customers return to dealerships in robust numbers. Ford will have a stronger product lineup than GM or Chrysler, having moved more nimbly to develop fuel-efficient vehicles. It already has a significant quality advantage. Indeed, in many quality measurements, Ford has equaled or surpassed Japanese stalwarts Toyota and Honda.

If Ford does indeed return to robust profitability, it will have overcome the legacy of a devastating crisis in many ways unprecedented in the long history of American business. In the year 2000, when this book's story begins, Ford was riding a wave of success that seemingly had it on a glide path to surpass mighty General Motors as the world's top-selling automaker. Then a terrible, prolonged corporate crisis derailed Ford's momentum so completely it would spend the entire decade trying to implement one turn-around plan after another.

And yet it could have been far worse.

The crisis could have destroyed Ford Motor Company. Left unchallenged, the unceasing accusations of trial lawyers would have forever painted Ford in the prevailing conventional wisdom as criminally culpable and utterly disdainful of human loss and suffering. At the dawn of an age of instant information sharing, such a characterization would have been a corporate death sentence. *Feeding Frenzy* details the imperfect work of a team of communications professionals at Ford determined to achieve balance and fairness in the deluge of media coverage swamping the company. They rewrote the rules of crisis communication along the way.

It was the biggest and longest running business story of the year 2000. It was the first major corporate crisis of the 21st century and an instant case study in crisis communications. But it also was a heart-wrenching story of many personal accounts of human tragedy in the wake of sudden, unpredictable rollover accidents. It was the story of engineers and safety analysts, struggling to understand the cause of the accidents and to prevent their reoccurrence. And, too, it was the story of politicians and lawyers, scrambling to position themselves advantageously in the public turmoil that followed.

This is a story of a bitter dispute between Ford Motor Company and its largest tire supplier, Firestone, and the severing of the companies' 97-year-old relationship that began with two great American industrialist friends, Henry Ford and Harvey Firestone.

This book focuses on crisis communications. It examines an unprecedented media feeding frenzy, particularly in those breathless 14 weeks that started a week before the massive Firestone tire recall in August 2000 and didn't stop until the intriguing drama of hanging chads in Florida in a contested Presidential election finally pushed tires off the front pages of American newspapers. It attempts to draw meaningful lessons from this unprecedented communications melee, while examining the dynamic of the corporate communicator and the news media during a long, evolving crisis. This work provides the reader with a ringside seat on the Ford crisis communications team during a most fascinating and wrenching corporate conflict.

* * *

Contemporary studies in crisis communications management still often focus on two incidents that are seen as bookends as the correct and incorrect way to handle a sudden catastrophic corporate problem: the Johnson & Johnson Tylenol recall of 1982 and the Exxon Valdez oil spill disaster of 1989. In the case of the Tylenol poisonings, the company is said to have acted swiftly and courageously in voluntarily recalling its product, communicating effectively, then re-introducing Tylenol in tamper-resistant packaging, leading ultimately to an increase in its market share. And in the case of the Valdez oil spill, Exxon is depicted as being slow to act, indecisive and callous, stonewalling and recalcitrant, only stepping up to its full respon-sibilities to the Alaskan environment after being skewered in the court of public opinion and seeing its corporate reputation suffer. White hat versus black hat. Skilled versus inept.

The complex Ford-Firestone dispute has multiple players and multiple acts and it does not lend itself to such simplistic pronouncements. And that is precisely why the serious student of crisis communications management will find it to be a more fertile ground for analysis and debate.

Additionally, as the new millennium's first major crisis communications case study, it features a media dynamic profoundly different from the situations of earlier decades. The management teams at Johnson & Johnson and Exxon did not have to deal with mass media with instant deadlines. (Neither, of course, did Ford during the days of the Pinto fires in the early 1970s, another crisis often studied.) The rise of CNN, CNBC, MSNBC and other 'round-the-clock television news networks, along with the Internet sites of the major daily newspapers, have profoundly changed the business of journalism. In the intense competition among these many news organizations to quickly advance a big story a little bit further, speed is often valued over accuracy and balance. Extremely short deadlines lead to sound-bite journalism in which a company placed on the defensive is fundamentally at a severe disadvantage. It is simply not possible to persuasively explain several technical points about a vehicle's driving characteristics, let alone reference two or three relevant safety statistics in the eight-second bite a CBS producer has allocated to the auto company in a two-and-a-half minute piece already packaged with emotionally powerful footage of a grieving widow, a flipped-over vehicle and a sound bite from a "safety advocate" insisting that "The Explorer is inherently and dangerously unstable by design." **The deck is stacked against the corporation. It cannot hope to receive a fair hearing in this venue of the court of public opinion. This out-of-balance dynamic, most pronounced in modern television journalism, has led to the recent rise of media-savvy trial lawyer resource groups whose livelihood depends on the daily promotion of product horror stories and criticism of corporations.**

* * *

Ford's communication work throughout this demanding and stressful time was not perfect but it was consistently honest and forthright. We were committed to high-integrity communication principles not only because they are the right way to work but because they are the smart way as well. We made our share of mistakes. The work chronicled in this book was conducted in real time under a barrage of media scrutiny. There was little time to think and no time to reflect. That is the nature of a crisis. Periodically, we'd read in the pile of daily clips a story quoting a "crisis communications expert" from some university or uninvolved PR agency second-guessing our work. Invariably, they were more critical than complimentary.

Although it is the prerogative of an "expert" critic to take advantage of hindsight and suggest alternative strategies and tactics that might have worked better, one should remember that it is infinitely easier to criticize than it is to execute in real time. We faced an unprecedented swarm of journalists competing with one another to be first, rather than to be most fair. Even journalists from established media often seemed more interested in baiting a source into a "gotcha quote" than in getting at an elusive and complex truth. The big television networks were the worst about this, developing nearly complete stories before asking for any input from us. Often these stories were built around a demonstrably flawed premise but had already been slotted into the evening news, and the producers expected them to air with or without a short sound bite from Ford. The so-called crisis communications experts had not earned their living in such an environment; we were blazing a new trail in a media environment that simply hadn't existed in previous major corporate crises.

Business leaders and public relations professionals reading this book undoubtedly will judge the work of the Ford communications team through a lens of hindsight and by their own personal experience. But they might also ask themselves if they are sufficiently prepared to face a similar storm of frenzied media sparked by some sudden and unpredictable corporate crisis.

This narrative of the Firestone crisis and my periodic interjection of "lessons learned" may provide useful insight into the successful practice of crisis communications. To make the discussion even more relevant in a communication age being transformed by social media and micro-communication, I have added an Epilogue for a look to the future of crisis management. In the spring of 2009, I caught up with three of the most important characters in this crisis communications case study – the talented, young agency gun who turned around Firestone's inept media relations practice before she turned 30; the indomitable, irreverent and always quotable vice president of Ford's Public Affairs staff; and the prolific *New York Times* Detroit bureau chief who attacked SUVs and especially the Explorer as if on his own personal jihad. Each of these three bigger-than-life personalities offers unique insights in the Epilogue on where the practice of crisis communications may be headed in the future.

Ford was clearly more progressive and strategic in the practice of public relations than Firestone was, at least in the opening rounds of this protracted crisis. Still, it is now obvious that we at Ford were fundamentally unprepared for a development that would become one of the hallmarks of this first major corporate crisis of the 21st century – the media-savvy plaintiff attorney. Nearly 10 years later, I can say with confidence what's coming next: **A major communications crisis surely will hatch on the Internet in a blog-storm that will engulf a corporation fundamentally unprepared for the social-media-savvy plaintiff attorney adversary network. Those who fail to heed the lessons of history, and to apply them to the new realities of a rapidly changing world, will end up as reputational road kill.**

* * *

As a business story, this is a cautionary tale about what could have been, what should have been. A Ford Motor Company that was poised to lead its industry as it once had. To be at the start of its second 100 years, perhaps, something of the leader and innovator it was throughout much of its first 100 years. As such, this story does not begin with the tire troubles that brought Ford and Firestone together to announce a massive tire recall. It begins one week before that announcement, when Ford Motor Company still owned the reputation of a winner and still dreamed of lasting greatness.

CHAPTER ONE

PRIDE BEFORE THE FALL

"I believe the distinction between a good company and a great company is this: A good company delivers excellent products and services; a great one delivers excellent products and services, and strives to make the world a better place."

- *William Clay Ford, Jr., Ford Motor Company chairman, 1999 Ford Annual Report, Letter from the Chairman.*

* * *

Annoyed. Harry J. Pearce was quite annoyed. And he wanted all the reporters in the room to know it.

The bitter tone of the General Motors news conference on August 3, 2000 spoke volumes about the public reputations of two auto companies headed in opposite directions. The GM executive, who seven years earlier had rocketed to national prominence by masterfully exposing a network television news magazine's shoddy journalism, had called this press conference seemingly with the sole purpose of declaring that he was ticked off. Pearce was annoyed at Ford Motor Company for successfully cultivating a positive reputation for environmental responsibility. And he was annoyed at the automotive journalists for failing to see that GM, as Pearce insisted, was more of an environmental leader than Ford was.

"I'm annoyed, seriously annoyed," Pearce said again. Why couldn't the journalists see, he complained, that Ford was not being "intellectually honest" as it positioned itself as "somehow the environmental leader?"[1]

It was not a shining moment for General Motors. It was especially uncomfortable for the GM public relations people who had failed to convince Pearce not to call a news conference without some semblance of news, even if he *was* annoyed. Indeed, the effect of Pearce's ranting was to draw further attention to Ford's position of leadership among auto companies on societal issues and to underscore the inability of General Motors to recognize the proper demeanor of a leader.

Veteran journalists had to be struck by the contrast from Pearce's masterful news conference seven years earlier. In 1993 GM Executive Vice President Harry Pearce had captivated a room packed with print and broadcast journalists by dramatically demonstrating how *Dateline-NBC* had rigged a series of "tests" designed to show the danger posed by the "side-saddle" gas tanks on GM pickups. Unbeknownst to its viewing audience, *Dateline* had installed underneath the test pickup truck several tiny model rocket engines. The rocket engines could be remotely ignited just after the truck had been slammed into a barrier with enough force to cause a fuel leak. If the truck leaked fuel, a quick burst of flames from the hidden rocket engines would ensure an instantaneous and furious blaze. The *Dateline* story was dramatic television and the fiery demonstration was a killer visual element that scored with its viewers. Undoubtedly, it scared many of them away from Chevrolet and GMC truck dealerships. GM engineers watching the *Dateline* program were puzzled as to what would cause the truck to ignite so quickly; some immediately suspected the test had been rigged. A team of investigators hired by GM traveled to the city where the test had been conducted and began to snoop around. It wasn't long before they found in a local junkyard the burnt remains of the pickup truck featured in the *Dateline* story. They also found charred model rocket engines still affixed to the truck's underbody. Millions of viewers who had seen the *Dateline* piece had been led to believe they had seen a controlled test of a "dangerous" truck suddenly bursting into flames in an otherwise non-life-threatening crash. The fiery spectacle they were shown had, in fact, been a carefully prepared made-for-TV stunt, Pearce said.[2]

Pearce conducted that press briefing with the dramatic demeanor of a prosecuting attorney making a closing argument in a packed courthouse. His masterful command of the news conference had accomplished its principal objectives – helping to restore the faith of GM customers in their trucks as well as forcing NBC into an embarrassing apology that would lead to the creation of new guidelines for journalistic integrity.[3] It would also make Pearce a serious contender for the top job at General Motors. Indeed, Pearce was named vice chairman and elected to GM's Board of Directors in 1996, making him effectively the second-most powerful executive at GM.[4]*

* * *

But now the journalists were anything but spellbound. At first they rolled their eyes. Then they openly snickered. Pearce's PR people stood nervously at the back of the room watching helplessly. "GM leads Ford today in truck fuel economy, both on average and on a model-by-model basis, including SUVs," Pearce growled. "General Motors will still be the leader in five years, or 10 years, or for that matter 20 years. End of story."[5]

When the news conference finally ended, journalists began to call Ford's Public Affairs people for comment. We resisted the temptation to throw further gasoline on the flames Pearce had lit. We were savvy enough to know that Ford had won this round and we would do best to take the high road, at least when we were on the record, repeating Ford's commitment to dramatically increase the fuel economy of its SUVs. Gloating would have been unbecoming for a leader.

Media undoubtedly were disappointed not to get further jabs from Ford's PR team, which was led by the ever-quotable Jason Vines. Vines had held prominent PR jobs at Chrysler and at Nissan before coming to Ford; he also had at one time earned extra money entertaining bar crowds as a standup comedian and he continued to

---

Pearce later would be diagnosed with cancer and would have to step back from the limelight, taking him out of the running for GM's top job. His August 2000 news conference was the first time he had led a news-making event since he had disclosed his bout with cancer.

3

wield a wickedly irreverent sense of humor. Journalists loved Vines because of his wit and sarcasm, his fearlessness at being quoted in difficult times as well as good ones, and for the time he always made for media, personally returning journalists' calls at all hours of day or night.

Vines was right in trusting his instincts to resist further volleys at GM this time. Media coverage focused on Pearce's unseemly demeanor. "It's always fun to see archrivals pull off the gloves and get into an old-fashioned, bare-knuckled brawl," wrote veteran auto pundit Paul Eisenstein. "A few days ago, we witnessed Harry Pearce, vice chairman of General Motors, all but foaming in frustration at having been outmaneuvered by Ford Motor Co."[6]

It was easy for Ford spokespeople to smugly take the high road in their responses to Pearce's petulance. Ford was sitting at the top of the world, posting a profit of $7.2 billion in 1999, the best year ever for any of Detroit's Big Three automakers.[7] Most of Ford's profits were generated by selling pickup trucks and SUVs, which were built on truck platforms. The Explorer alone would account for 445,000 sales in 2000 and was thought by industry analysts to be the most profitable vehicle in the world (but this was a matter of conjecture since automakers did not report profits for individual vehicle lines).[8] And Ford led all automakers on *Fortune* magazine's "Most Admired Companies" list.[9] Meanwhile, General Motors had seen its market share steadily sink from about 45 percent of all new vehicles sold in the United States in the early 1980s to less than 28 percent in 2000. Still the world's largest automaker, GM had its best-ever profit year in 1999 at $5.7 billion,[10] also relying on robust truck and SUV sales in the U.S. But those numbers paled in comparison to Ford's earnings. An *AutoFacts* report in June 1999 predicted that Ford would pass GM in total global auto sales by 2005.[11] Few of GM's product introductions in recent times had excited the marketplace, and its garish new Pontiac Aztek sport utility-van-wagon was an outright disaster, considered by many critics to be the ugliest car ever mass-produced. Thousands of GM managers compelled to drive Azteks as their company cars to help keep the factory open risked public ridicule with every trip to the supermarket.

The veteran members of Ford's Public Affairs team knew there was another good reason to refrain from gloating – a company's good fortune was notoriously fleeting in the cyclical world of the automotive industry. An automaker could be the darling of the industry one day and all-too-quickly find itself under the microscope of disapproving critics. But no one could have predicted the total reversal of fortune just ahead for Ford. Within 12 months Ford would become the "embattled" auto company with its spokespeople under siege on every conceivable front. In addition to a massive tire problem there would be reports of declining quality in many of Ford's vehicle lines, numerous product recalls, troubled launches of important new cars and trucks, market share losses and steep declines in profits, the loss of much of its advantage over competitors in assembly plant productivity, and frightening reports of Legionnaires disease at two of its facilities, as well as lawsuits from employees claiming discrimination in connection with a controversial new performance appraisal program. These problems and many others would be chronicled in a damning *BusinessWeek* cover story with the ultimate public-relations-nightmare headline: "Ford: It's Worse Than You Think."[12]

Lesson Learned: Maintain perspective. There will be times when your company seemingly can do no wrong and the media is content to chronicle your successes with glowing reviews. Don't get complacent and don't gloat about your competitors' missteps. There will also be times when bad fortune comes in droves for your company. Don't get suicidal. This too shall pass.

* * *

What had set Pearce off was the recent success of Ford's public relations efforts to position the company as a leader in addressing societal concerns. Ford was following a concerted strategy to promote a series of industry-leading actions addressing environmental and safety issues, and the strategy was working. Ford was seen as a leader in corporate citizenship. And GM was not, despite the many significant societal commitments the company had made – including a billion-dollar-plus investment in its innovative EV1 electric car. GM had introduced the EV1 to great fanfare in 1997, featuring it in commercials that suggested electric cars would soon be as common as electric toasters.[13] But only 1,100 EV1s were ever produced, more than half of which were recalled to fix a battery cable that had the potential to overheat to the point of starting a fire. GM quietly stopped production in 1999. By 2003, GM had collected all the EV1s from its lease customers and had sent the cars off to be crushed, disappointing environmentalists. GM patiently explained that it could not continue to stock replacement parts and maintain knowledgeable dealership technicians for the small number of unique, high-voltage electric cars; GM was a high-volume manufacturer better equipped to sell and service vehicle lines by the hundreds of thousands. That explanation did not stop environmental activists from crying foul. And conspiracy! Enough people found the conspiracy theories plausible for Sony Pictures to produce and release in 2006 the documentary "Who Killed the Electric Car?"[14]

* * *

A major reason Ford was making inroads in enhancing its societal reputation was the presence of its dynamic young chairman, William Clay Ford, Jr. The great-grandson of the company's founder, Bill Ford was a fly-fishing outdoorsman deeply committed to environmental responsibility. His "greenness" made other executives nervous, at Ford and at the other auto companies. Bill Ford met regularly with environmental activist "non-governmental organizations" (or NGOs) such as the Sierra Club and the Union of Concerned Scientists whose extreme positions had not engendered them to the auto industry. These groups were adversaries of the automobile (and especially critical of large, "gas-guzzling" sport utility vehicles), and were easily dismissed within the industry as wacko "tree-huggers." Bill Ford was the first auto executive to open a serious, constructive dialogue with them, resulting in considerable good will toward Ford Motor Company by a broad contingent of people who thought that protecting the Earth's environment was a good idea.

Bill Ford's support of environmental causes not only endeared him to the "green crowd," but also gave the media a high-profile personality that could put a human face on stories about hard-to-understand environmental technology. No other auto company was headed by an executive with such a genuine love of nature and commitment to environmental sustainability. If Ford Motor Company received more than its due in press coverage for its environmental announcements, Bill Ford was largely the reason.

In fact, senior members of Ford's Public Affairs team worried that Bill Ford might become known as a "one-issue" chairman. When Bill Ford was elected Chairman of the Board and Jacques Nasser named CEO in January 1999, spokespeople explained the division of responsibilities by saying, "Jac runs the company; Bill runs the Board."[15] In terms of responsibility as spokesmen, Nasser would be the top-ranking executive for operational announcements, with Bill Ford weighing in publicly only when necessary to provide strategic perspective. Bill Ford continued to champion environmental responsibility within the company but only occasionally appeared at environmental announcements to the press.

Ford Motor Company's reputation for social responsibility really took off with a series of announcements under the theme "Cleaner, Safer, Sooner." The strategy for these announcements had been developed by a Ford vice president in charge of advanced engineering and a Ford public relations director as they flew together over the Atlantic in a corporate jet one month before the 1998 Detroit auto show. Officially known as the "North American International Auto Show," the all-important Detroit show fell at the beginning of what was shaping up to be a lean, "in-between" year for Ford product news. With only a few product freshenings to promote and no concept cars with any sex appeal, there was no hope for Ford to "dominate" the news coming out of the show. More than 2,000 credentialed journalists would be covering news conferences by every automaker in the world and there were countless new vehicles and concept cars for them to write about. But "dominate the show" was precisely the objective Nasser had given his operating committee as the Detroit show drew near. The onus to deliver was squarely on the Public Affairs team.

In early December, Ford Chief Technical Officer Neil Ressler invited Ken Zino, director of Product Development Public Affairs, to join him on a trip to Cologne, Germany. Ressler's team of research scientists and engineers on both sides of the Atlantic had developed a relatively inexpensive means of reducing vehicle tailpipe emissions with a uniquely efficient exhaust catalyst and a new engine computer algorithm. With these innovations, Ford could produce vehicles that

7

would be substantially cleaner than required under the current federal emissions standards. Furthermore, the Ford breakthrough would be difficult for competitors to match, at least in the near term. Ressler wanted to announce a commitment to reduce Ford's light truck emissions to the level that passenger cars already had to meet, years ahead of any new regulatory requirement for trucks. Inspired by Bill Ford's desire for the company to become a leader among automakers in environmental performance, Ressler had been mulling over a plan for a theme of corporate responsibility. Ford would announce one action after another over the next three years to build and sustain its leadership mantle, rather than taking the traditional approach of unveiling a new and different message at each Detroit auto show. As an analytically minded engineer, Ressler wanted to develop a steady, continuous series of technical actions to answer the challenge Nasser had issued and that would be consistent with Bill Ford's vision.

As a communications executive, Zino wanted a simple message to help Ressler's technical solutions resonate with the media and with customers. Together, they sketched a plan called "Cleaner, Safer, Sooner" that called for Ford to commit to a series of actions related to the environment and safety performance of its vehicles, well ahead of any regulatory mandate. Actions that the rest of the industry would be hard pressed to follow.

At the Detroit auto show in January 1998, Nasser announced the first "Cleaner, Safer, Sooner" promise: to voluntarily certify all its sport utility vehicles, as well as its Windstar minivan, as Low Emission Vehicles (LEV in government jargon) beginning in the upcoming '99 model year. Nasser had enthusiastically endorsed the plan, especially after Ressler pointed out that Ford had a clear lead over other auto companies in the difficult art of marrying engine control logic with highly advanced exhaust catalysts that together could deliver low emissions even on a relatively fuel inefficient vehicle like a sport utility.*

---

*A vehicle would achieve LEV certification from the Environmental Protection Agency if the amount of tailpipe emissions of carbon monoxide, hydrocarbons and nitrous oxides were below certain low levels per each mile the vehicle was driven; since a bigger, heavier vehicle (such as an SUV) burned more fuel to travel that mile, it ordinarily would generate more emissions. So certifying SUVs to meet the LEV standard would require very efficient catalytic converters

GM and Chrysler executives clearly felt sand-bagged by Ford's surprise commitment. Ford should have followed standard auto industry practice, they said, of coordinating public announcements about regulatory matters through the auto industry's trade group in Washington. In other words, auto companies should stand together on regulation, not try to stand apart.[16]

One month later at the Chicago auto show, Ford was at it again, announcing a second "Cleaner, Safer, Sooner" commitment. The company said that its trucks and SUVs would meet all passenger car safety standards beginning in the '99 model year. GM and Chrysler officials were livid. "Rivals said Ford should not use sensitive safety and environment issues for one-upsmanship," reported Jim Healey in *USA Today*. "'Our vehicles are going to be clean – next year. Our vehicles are going to safe – next year. What does that say about this year? It's stupid,' griped Jason Vines, Chrysler public relations official..."[17]

Vines woke up the morning that the *USA Today* story appeared, he later told me, a little worse for wear and tear after entertaining journalists the night before. As he sipped his usual morning beverage – scalding-hot black coffee – Vines read his "stupid" quote and felt the stinging sense of regret every spokesperson occasionally experiences. He quietly slunk over to the Ford stand and found Nasser to offer an apology and his congratulations on the positive coverage Ford's announcement had garnered. Nasser good-naturedly accepted Vines' apology and wished him well. Two years later, Nasser would hire Vines to lead Ford's global Public Affairs staff.

* * *

Just as Ressler had envisioned, Ford continued to make news over the next few years, using the "Cleaner, Safer, Sooner" positioning theme. This proved to be an effective communications strategy. Media invariably mentioned the other "Cleaner, Safer, Sooner" commitments Ford had made prior to each announcement, providing greater scale than any one announcement would have had by itself. Subsequent "Cleaner, Safer, Sooner" announcements included the expansion of the LEV commitment to Ford's pickup trucks, the proliferation of side air bag systems, and the introduction of Ford's "Personal Safety System" that included seat belt pretensioners as well as weight sensors that could modify the aggressiveness of inflation in an airbag to protect children.[18]

Ford also had its promotional missteps – its "Beltminder" system of annoyingly insistent chimes that reminded drivers to buckle their safety belts failed to capture the imagination of the news media (although it did achieve the desired effect of increasing safety belt usage and in doing so was probably the greatest life-saver of any technology Ford had voluntarily adopted).[19] And GM beat Ford to the punch with an announcement of the installation of glow-in-the-dark release switches inside car trunks to allow children or others trapped inside to escape.[20]

But there was no doubt that with its environmental-championing chairman setting the tone, Ford Motor Company was well out in front of the rest of the industry. The company nurtured its new reputation for social responsibility not only through the "Cleaner, Safer, Sooner" actions but also with an increasingly candid self-assessment aimed at winning over critics and adversaries. At Ford's annual stockholder meeting in May 2000 the company released its first corporate citizenship report, "Connecting with Society." Similar to an annual report, the 98-page booklet detailed the progress the company was making against a wide variety of social responsibility actions, including tailpipe and smokestack emissions, recycling, vehicle safety ratings, and employment diversity. Although self-congratulatory in places, the report staked new ground in being open and transparent. "Transparency" wasn't just part of the jargon of the corporate social responsibility watchdogs who were a primary audience of the report; it had become an internal buzzword – reflecting a new commitment to openly discuss difficult issues. Embracing transparency in external communications to stakeholders that included critics was a tactic only undertaken by individuals and organizations confident that they were on the right path. Bill Ford and Jac Nasser clearly had instilled a sense of higher purpose in the Ford ranks.

Nowhere was this self-assured candidness more evident than on two pages toward the back of the corporate citizenship report. A section titled "Sport Utility Vehicle Case Study" outlined the social concerns posed by the rapid increase in SUV sales, noting that the SUV market had taken off with the introduction of the Ford Explorer in 1990. SUVs were less fuel-efficient than passenger cars and as such increasingly drew the ire of environmental groups worried about global warming. Ford had sold more than 750,000 SUVs in 1999, far more than any other automaker, and therefore had a responsibility to acknowledge and address the issues posed by SUVs.[21] The article included a sidebar titled "Another Point of View" featuring a quote from a Sierra Club press release:

> *At a time of mounting concern over global warming, air pollution and oil exploration in fragile wilderness areas, the gas-guzzling SUV is a rolling monument to environmental destruction... The nine-passenger (Ford) Excursion is a suburban supertanker, stretching over 19 feet in length and slurping one gallon of gasoline for every 12 miles it travels. This "suburban assault vehicle" spews as much global warming pollution into the air as two average cars.[22]*

The report immediately caused an uproar. Although it should not have been news to anyone that environmentalists were critical of SUVs, it *was* newsworthy that the leading maker of SUVs had acknowledged the criticism and given it some validity by including it in a company publication. Ford's "mega mea culpa" played particularly big in the *New York Times*, whose young Detroit bureau chief, Keith Bradsher had been conducting a one-man crusade against the sport utility vehicle. He was prolific in writing a seemingly endless string of stories that criticized SUVs for their emissions, their poor fuel economy, their generally under-utilized off-road capabilities, and their propensity to roll over in highway crashes, as well as the danger they posed to occupants of smaller cars who might get tangled in an accident with a much heavier SUV. Tall, lanky and supremely self-assured, Bradsher had surely always been the smartest kid in class. And like the brainiac in high school who never could make it with the cool kids, Bradsher and his brand of advocacy journalism were not well liked within the auto press corps. Bradsher's "jihad" against SUVs, as one veteran Detroit auto writer dubbed it, aimed at ridding the nation's roads of a type of vehicle that was popular with consumers, or at least at winning Bradsher a Pulitzer Prize.[23] But there was no denying that his stories were a leading force in shaping the emerging conventional wisdom in America that SUVs were not only environmentally irresponsible but unsafe as well.[*]

The controversy generated by its corporate citizenship report was a mixed blessing for Ford. It had focused a spotlight on the company's new spirit of transparency that environmentalists found refreshing, especially from an auto giant. Big automakers were notoriously insular and secretive, which gave auto critics plenty of reason to distrust them. But the report's candor also shown a spotlight on societal shortcomings of heavy, fuel-thirsty SUVs. With its iconic Explorer, the mammoth Expedition, and the truly gigantic Excursion, Ford was the leading producer of SUVs – and the SUVs were the most profitable vehicles in the Ford lineup. As the voices criticizing SUVs for a variety of reasons grew louder, the company began to look to make improvements in the vehicles to address criticism and, ultimately, to remove objections from potential customers' decision-making process. Ford would move beyond merely acknowledging the existence of issues raised by SUVs to making firm commitments to make its SUVs more socially acceptable. And there was an obvious place to focus: fuel economy.

Improving fuel efficiency would address SUV customers' Number One complaint (high fueling costs), while simultaneously addressing global warming concerns, the number one issue of the NGO environmental action groups. The main questions became: How large of a fuel economy improvement could be achieved across the Ford's fleet of SUVs? At what expense? How quickly?

The regulatory planners from the company's Environmental and Safety Engineering department studied Ford's SUV cycle plan along with market forecasts and anticipated competitive product actions. They looked at available and emerging technologies that could be applied to upcoming SUV models, being careful not to count on a new technology until it had been thoroughly proven to be safe,

---

[*] *Indeed, Bradsher would be a finalist for a Pulitzer in 2001 (and did win the George Polk Award) for his extensive body of work in the* New York Times *questioning the safety and environmental responsibility of SUVs. He would chronicle his SUV reporting in a book,* High and Mighty: SUVs – The World's Most Dangerous Vehicles and How They Got That Way, *that would subsequently receive a glowing review in the* New York Times.[24]

reliable and durable so that it could be deemed "implementation-ready."

The analysts developed an aggressive six-year plan to increase the company's SUV fleet fuel economy by 25 percent over 2000 model year levels. Ford executives reviewing the plan grew nervous not wanting to be boxed into a commitment that might not be achieved if some of the assumptions proved incorrect or the business climate soured – making it difficult to find the investment dollars to develop and apply the necessary vehicle technology. A 25 percent improvement might not seem overly difficult to people outside the auto industry, but it truly did represent a mammoth under-taking for a company engineering, building and selling seven different SUV models through its Ford, Mercury and Lincoln brands. The company could get a 25 percent gain by converting the entire SUV fleet to run on hybrid electric power at enormous expense (if it could crank up the global supply base for the necessary power electronic components and high-capacity batteries). But there wasn't a business planner at Ford or any other automaker who believed that there would be the demand anytime soon for a million SUVs a year with an unproven powertrain that would cost at least $3,000 more than the engines customers were used to. The only feasible way to get a 25 percent improvement over the whole SUV fleet was through a concerted, broad strategy of selling more of the smallest SUVs, fewer of the largest ones, plus at least 20,000 hybrid SUVs a year, while rolling out many other technologies that each would contribute a small gain in fuel efficiency – 2 percent here, ¾ of one percent there.

A meeting including several vice presidents had been set to agree on the scale and timing of the commitment. I would represent Public Affairs. I had been working with the regulatory planners in developing an achievable plan that would get maximum positive exposure for the company. The plan would deliver the 25 percent improvement by the end of 2005. (The plan actually delivered nearly 28 percent improvement, providing some extra margin in case some of the technologies slipped in development readiness.) We would clearly state that the 25 percent improvement would be measured against a base of the 2000 model year. We would announce a "25 percent by '05" commitment. The media almost surely would shorthand this to "25 percent in 5 (years)." But because 2006 model year products

13

would be introduced by the end of '05, we would actually have six model years to get the job done. Even still, Martin Inglis, executive vice president in charge of North America who came up the ranks from Finance, declared at the meeting that he wanted a seven-model-year plan to provide even more contingency against delays. The fuel economy planners were silent, waiting to gauge the level of resistance of the VPs before giving in and weakening the commitment. Then I spoke up. Seated directly across from Inglis, I argued against the extra year as it would dilute the news impact of our commitment. We shouldn't expect much in the way of favorable news coverage if we stretched out the improvement over seven years, I said. Gurminder Bedi, the vice president in charge of all trucks, jumped in to support me. Gurminder favored bold action and was continually frustrated by the in-bred cautiousness at Ford that had held the company back so many times in the past. Eventually, our "25 by '05" plan prevailed. Those at that meeting recognized that we were witnessing a seminal moment for the company; the old, conservative and deliberative Ford management style was finally fading away. In the "Cleaner, Safer, Sooner" era, policies were being made at Ford in a new way: responding to Bill Ford and Jac Nasser imperatives to lead the industry in a variety of ways, Public Affairs would advocate for a big, news-worthy commitment, which invariably would be awfully expensive in the disapproving eyes of the Finance people who would have to find a way to budget for it. And unsettling to the engineers who would have to find a way to get it done on time.

Nasser announced the SUV fuel economy improvement com-mitment at a speech at the National Press Club in Washington, D.C., July 27. A flood of print and broadcast stories followed, pointing to Ford's continued environmental leadership under Bill Ford and Jac Nasser. "'We are taking this very significant action with some of our most popular products because it is the right thing to do for our customers and for our stockholders,'" said Nasser in a *Ward's Auto World* story. "'It is the next logical step in our 'Cleaner, Safer, Sooner' campaign, which we began with the announcement two-and-a-half years ago that all Ford Motor Company SUVs would be low emission vehicles...'" The 25 percent SUV fuel economy commitment "strengthens Ford Motor Company's environmental leadership role," Nasser added.[25]

This was the last straw for Harry Pearce. He stewed for a couple of days and then called the hastily arranged "I'm annoyed at Ford" news conference. GM had (slightly) better truck and SUV fuel economy, he said; Ford was just playing catch up. But it didn't matter. Ford had made a bold commitment, the mark of a leader. Ford was on top of the world, the most profitable auto company in the world and the most widely admired. In fact, Nasser wanted company managers at all levels to begin thinking of leadership beyond the auto industry, setting the goal to become not just the world's "leading auto company" but the "leading consumer company."[26]

Nasser and Bill Ford were creating a new company culture of empowered leaders at all levels striving to deliver what customers wanted while acting as a good corporate citizen. A key tenant of this new corporate culture was the commitment to be "open and transparent" – forthright in addressing concerns and criticisms legitimately raised by stakeholders and critics alike.

Meanwhile, trouble was brewing with tires. Trouble that would severely test the company's commitment to open and transparent public discourse. In fact, just six days after Pearce's petulant news conference and only 13 days after Nasser's well-publicized promise in Washington to increase SUV fuel economy, Ford executives would be back at the National Press Club to join Firestone in announcing a massive tire recall. Trouble was indeed brewing, soon to erupt into what would become the most intense media feeding frenzy ever seen in the automotive industry.

CHAPTER TWO

RUMBLINGS AROUND THE WORLD

"Stories like this distinguish you. Every station is trying to break away from the pack. Some do it by contesting; we do it by content."
- *Mike Devlin, KHOU news director[1]*

* * *

Like so many local television stations fighting for every ratings point in the continuing hunt for advertising revenue, Houston's KHOU had created an investigative team in 1998 to pursue stories their viewers would find compelling. "The Defenders" specialized in stories about local residents being victimized by uncaring institutions or shady businesses. These were the kind of features that drew viewers to a local newscast, especially if there was compelling video footage and an emotional angle. Often these stories focused on some aspect of human tragedy. The old TV news rule "If it bleeds, it leads" had become cliché, but it was still a guiding principle of many a news director in Houston and a hundred other local markets.

A television station's advertising rates are determined by its viewership during three week-long ratings periods dubbed "sweeps weeks." Success or failure during these three weeks literally makes or breaks a station's financial performance for the year. The Defenders' work would be especially important to KHOU during sweeps weeks. The team was determined to deliver.

Feeding Frenzy

In December 1999, KHOU investigative reporter Anna Werner set out to conduct the routine, often tedious work of an enterprising journalist: calling on potential sources for promising leads to pursue. Like other investigative reporters, Werner knew that trial attorneys often were the best source for a "David being victimized by Goliath" story that was the Defenders' specialty. A firm of plaintiff attorneys might have any number of cases that might interest TV viewers. And, of course, the firm wouldn't mind helping the station tell a story portraying one of its clients as victim to the brazenly callous company being sued. To the law firm, a well-produced investigative piece was pure gold, several minutes of free air time that could break the will of a company resisting an expensive settlement. It would also help draw future clients who would be attracted to the successful, crusading attorney as they were nearly always portrayed in such investigative stories.

One of the Houston attorneys Werner contacted told her of a case he had that involved a fatal accident caused by a tire failure. Not a blowout, but something called a "tread separation." In a tread separation, the attorney explained to Werner, a steel-belted radial tire could suddenly rip apart as the vehicle sped down a freeway, coming apart between the steel belts so that the tread peeled off the rest of the tire like a large rubber pelt and sending the vehicle out of control. The attorney was suing the tire maker, Firestone, for making a defective tire and was pretty sure there were other similar cases. Werner was interested.[2]

Over the next several weeks, Werner and the other members of the Defenders began calling law firms, in Texas and then in other states as well, in search of other instances of crashes caused by tire tread separations. They uncovered 20 accidents that had killed nearly 30 people. Every accident involved Ford Explorers with Firestone Wilderness or ATX tires.

With the help of trial attorneys in Texas and Florida, Werner began contacting accident victims and their families. She knew what she was looking for – a uniquely sympathetic victim who could humanize the story, make it about something compellingly personal. The piece was already taking on scale, but it needed personality. The story wouldn't just be about tires; it would focus on human tragedy.

Werner found the humanizing face for her story in an African-American choir director in Houston named Cynthia Jackson who had lost her husband in a 1997 tread separation accident soon after the two had married. Although Jackson survived the accident, she sustained numerous serious injuries that required surgery to amputate both her legs below the knees. A woman of faith who sang gospel music in a church choir, she spoke eloquently and emotionally on camera about all that she had so suddenly lost. And while there was, of course, no video footage of the accident as it had happened so suddenly, photos of the mangled vehicle from the accident scene and a shredded tire could help tell the story of the tragic crash.

In mid-January, Werner called Joan Claybrook, who had been no friend of the auto industry when she headed the National Highway Traffic Safety Administration (NHTSA) during Jimmy Carter's term as President. It was Claybrook who had ordered a most unwilling Firestone to recall millions of Firestone 500 tires in 1978 in what was still the largest tire recall in history. Later, as head of corporate-watchdog Public Citizen, Claybrook had become even more shrill in her criticism of the automakers. As Werner detailed the number of tire tread separation accidents that the Defenders had documented, Claybrook became enthused, telling the reporter she was on to something big. Werner recalled later in an interview published in *The American Journalism Review* that Claybrook had said, "The problem is enormous. If you have found this many cases, the real number is probably 20 times as many out there." As soon as she hung up the phone, Werner rushed into the office of KHOU News Director Mike Devlin and quickly convinced him to green-light further development of what was shaping up to be a major investigative story.[3]

*　*　*

The KHOU investigative team flew to Washington February 2 to interview Claybrook, who declared on camera that she believed a massive tire recall was needed. The Defenders then traveled to North Carolina to interview a former Firestone factory employee, Alan Hogan, who could certainly be described as "disgruntled." Hogan talked of the intense pressure workers were under to meet quotas that sometimes meant using inferior too-old rubber stock instead of

19

discarding it. Hogan apologized on camera to the family of Daniel Van Etten, a 22-year-old Floridian who had been killed in a tread separation crash. "I'm sorry you lost your son," Hogan said. "Sorry people like me were building the rags your son was driving on."[4]

The KHOU reporting team also talked to a number of expert witnesses retained by the plaintiff attorneys who provided their thoughts and theories about potential causes of the tire failures. Werner and producer David Razig began editing the raw footage and piecing together the elements for a two-part investigative series that would air during February sweeps weeks. All the elements were there for a ratings hit.

No one from KHOU had yet contacted Firestone.

When Werner finally called Firestone and then Ford – because the vehicles in both the Jackson and Van Etten crashes had been Ford Explorers – it was to seek comment to be included in a piece that was nearly complete, rather than to ask for perspective to help Werner and her editors shape the direction of a developing piece. While hardly a fair and impartial methodology if the object of the reporting was to piece together the objective truth, this was (and remains today) standard practice for investigative reporting, particularly in broadcast journalism, for several reasons. First, a news station doesn't want to tip its hand too early for fear another station will get wind of the investigation and rush a story of its own that might air first. Second, the news media expect a company caught with a problem to stonewall unless confronted with the imminent reality of an investigative piece nearing final production. And finally, TV stations feared legal repercussions if they confronted a major corporation with unfounded accusations. Station lawyers insisted that the Defenders thoroughly complete their homework before contacting Firestone or Ford. As Devlin told the Poynter Institute for an online story, "Breaking the Big One: How KHOU Did It:"

> *We are like a Mom and Pop operation compared to Bridgestone/Firestone and Ford. We knew we had to be right and that we were going to need great legal help from our station attorneys. I am not going to lie to you and tell you I wasn't concerned (about the legal impact of the stories.) These corporations can tie you up and cost you millions of*

dollars by filing suit. Our team persevered. This was a high level of reporting.[5]

Both Firestone and Ford declined on-camera interviews, providing short statements stressing the safety record of their respective products. Firestone's statement read in part: "The Radial ATX has proved to be a reliable workhorse for U.S. consumers. Our experience … indicates high consumer satisfaction with the quality and reliability of these tires. No court or jury has ever found any deficiency in these tires."[6]

Ford let Firestone speak to the tire issues. The focus of the auto company's statement was to put to rest any questions about the safety of the Explorer. The world's best-selling SUV remained stable and controllable even after a tread separation, the company said. Rollover accidents following a tread separation were "isolated" incidents that "clearly resulted from driver error." Ford also provided video that had been produced as part of the company's defense in a lawsuit alleging defects both in the Explorer and in Firestone's tires.[*] The video had been produced at one of Ford's test tracks and depicted an Explorer traveling down a straightaway at highway speed when one of the rear tires separated (the tire's tread had been pre-cut by test engineers so that its tread would peel off in the test). The driver continued to maintain control until the vehicle came to a complete stop. As the video continued, a split screen added another camera's view of the driver repeating the test, this time taking his hands completely off the steering wheel and again, the Explorer continued straight down the track until coming to a complete stop.[7]

The Defenders took Ford's statement and videotape to Rex Grogan, a tire expert who had been a paid witness for one of the lawyers KHOU had contacted. Grogan dismissed the significance of Ford's Explorer demonstration video, saying, "The driver is an

---

[*] *Automakers are routinely sued after serious crashes with an assortment of allegations of product defects. Many, if not most, of these thousands of lawsuits are completely spurious. The lawsuit that led Ford's defense team to create the video did not spark an understanding among the automaker's management that there might be a problem with the Explorer or its tires. As the video demonstrated, the Explorer could easily be brought safely to a stop after a tire failure.*

experienced driver and he knows something's about to happen and what he's supposed to do. This isn't the same as Joe Public, driving along not anticipating danger." As to Ford's contention that the rollovers were "isolated incidents," Grogan posed a rhetorical question: "What you are saying is that it's okay to kill a few people, so long as you don't kill too many. Well, is that moral?"[8] Grogan looked up and smiled smugly as he finished the soundbite, obviously quite pleased with himself. Grogan's Cheshire cat grin was incongruous to the somber mood of the point he had made, but Werner did not ask him to reshoot the bite.

*   *   *

KHOU began promoting the investigative series, teasing viewers with hints of an investigation into a major safety hazard that might put them – or their loved ones – in danger. The first segment aired Monday February 7, running more than nine minutes, an extraordinary length for a news piece. The station continued to refer to and promote its tire story and, three days later, a second segment aired with more interviews from victims and tire experts. The series was a ratings hit. In fact, it became evident that the Defenders might have the opportunity to continue the saga of deadly tires: the station was getting inundated with calls, letters and emails from viewers who told of their experience in similar accidents.

Firestone's immediate reaction was to attack the reporting, insisting that the tire failures cited had been caused by customers' poor maintenance and under-inflation. In one of the cases mentioned in the KHOU report, Firestone protested, there was evidence that a puncture in the tire had been improperly repaired, which plausibly might have led to a slow leak leaving the tire severely under-inflated and susceptible to failure when the owner unwittingly continued to drive on it. On February 10, Firestone's public relations vice president, Christine Karbowiak, wrote a scathing letter to the CEO of KHOU's parent company:

> *This series ...contains falsehoods and misrepresentations that improperly disparage Firestone and its product, the Radial ATX model tire. The program and related activities*

22

*give the unfortunate appearance that KHOU is more con-
cerned with sensationalism and ratings during the February
sweeps period than its commitment to the presentation of
truthful and objective reporting.*

*As responsible executives and managers of a major
media company and one of its leading TV outlets, you should
be concerned with the obvious fact that your reporter, Anna
Werner, and/or her producers have been co-opted by
plaintiffs' personal-injury lawyers and their purported
"expert" witnesses to present a one-sided view of Firestone's
product. This series has unmistakably delivered the false
messages that Radial ATX tires are dangerous, that they
threaten the safety of anyone using them, and that they should
be removed from every vehicle on which they are installed.
Each of these messages is simply untrue.* [9]

Karbowiak's letter betrayed her fundamental misunderstanding of
TV news, especially local investigative reporting. The continuing
episodes of the Defenders were never about objective fact-finding;
there really was no pretense of balance or a sense of fairness to the
companies involved. The Defenders were acting on behalf of the
viewers in the tradition popularized by CBS' *60 Minutes*, intentionally
putting big companies off-balance in a way that the "little guy" never
could. Like other investigative news teams, the Defenders was a proud
member of the "Fourth Estate" pursuing the higher calling of putting
those who would abuse power on notice that someone was watching.

Karbowiak was right, of course, that the series had been
developed and promoted with a keen awareness of the February
sweeps period. And she was right in calling out the story's sources as
plaintiff attorneys with obvious financial motives, as well as the
"expert" witnesses' ties to these same attorneys. Unfortunately, she
was dead wrong in protesting that the Firestone ATX tires were not
defective and dangerous.

Lesson Learned: Understand the Rules of Engagement. *Fight for
fairness and balance but don't be surprised when you don't receive it,
especially on local television. Don't expect a fair fight. Think of other*

ways to get your message out. But first do your due diligence on the accusations being made. They just might be onto something.

* * *

Meanwhile, in a number of countries with extremely hot climates, notably Saudi Arabia and other Gulf Coast Countries (GCC), as well as Malaysia and Venezuela, Ford was becoming aware of a troubling number of accidents resulting from the failure of Firestone Wilderness AT tires. In January 1998, Glenn R. Drake, regional marketing manager in the United Arab Emirates for Ford, expressed concern about Firestone's response to tire problems (that tread separations had been caused because of chronic under-inflation and improper repair and maintenance) in an email to other Ford managers: "If this was a single case, I would accept Firestone's response as they are the experts in the tire business, case closed. However, we now have three cases and it is possible that Firestone is not telling us the whole story to protect them from a recall or a lawsuit."[10] Still, with only a few occurrences in the region, it was understandable that Ford GCC management did not at this point alert operating management back at the company's Dearborn, Michigan, headquarters.

But in subsequent months, reports of serious, and often fatal, accidents resulting from Firestone tread separations continued to come to the attention of Ford's GCC sales operations. In February 1999, John Garthwalte, Ford's national service director in the region, questioned Bridgestone/Firestone about problems with Firestone 16" AT tires, expressing his conviction that there was "a distinct problem with all or at least a certain production run of this particular tyre." And in a subsequent letter to another Firestone manager Garthwalte wrote, "These incidents involving Firestone P255/70/R16 tyres is [sic] beginning to become an epidemic...Nothing in your reply has done anything to re-assure me that there may not exist a defect in a particular batch of your product."[11]

In August 1999, Ford initiated an Owner Notification Program in Saudi Arabia (and subsequently in a total of 10 GCC countries) to replace Firestone tires equipped on Explorers with new Goodyear Wrangler tires. "Unique GCC usage patterns [sustained high-speed driving], environmental conditions [extreme heat and pavement temperature] and maintenance practices [customers would often let air out of their tires before off-roading through the desert sand on soft, compliant tires but then fail to restore proper air pressure when they returned to the highway] may result in tire degradation and potentially, tread separation. Nineteen rollovers, fourteen fatalities and ten injuries are alleged to have been attributed to this condition."[12] Firestone strongly objected to Ford replacing its tires with Goodyears, but Ford GCC dealers said that their customers had lost confidence in Firestone tires.

Reports of crashes resulting from Firestone tire failures were also being noted in Venezuela. In August 1999, Firestone sent letters to owners of light trucks equipped with its tires, offering free tire inspection and free rotation. Over the next several months, Ford would continue to ask Firestone to replace tires that were involved in an increasing number of deadly rollover accidents. Again, factors unique to the market, including an extremely hot climate, rough roads and the habit of many customers of driving for long, sustained periods at extremely high speeds, contributed to the failure of the tires. Firestone insisted that its tires were not defective and refused to replace them. Reports of accidents continued to mount. Finally, in May 2000, Ford acted on its own to replace tires for its customers in Colombia, Ecuador and Venezuela, using Goodyear tires as replacements and setting off a major confrontation with Firestone.

It would be in Venezuela that Firestone first would suggest that the stability of the Ford Explorer was the real safety issue, not its tires. Allegations that Ford had known about problems with the Explorer for years were supported by an undated memo (believed to have been written in 1997) from a lower-level Ford engineer in Venezuela describing a meeting with lawyers representing four Explorer customers whose vehicles "would turn over unexpectedly as a consequence of tire explosion." The memo also stated that the Explorers swayed at high speeds when driven on uneven payment.[13] The memo writer had carelessly restated allegations without qualification, leaving the impression that he, and Ford Motor Company by extension, accepted the statements as factual and, therefore, "knew" the Explorer could be prone to instability at high speeds.

Lesson Learned: Things are not always as they appear. Continue to push for answers and persistently question assurances, particularly on issues related to safety. But insist that anyone representing your company consistently and diligently articulate concerns in proper context whether in reports, emails or spoken conversations. Hearsay should not be represented as fact. Words like "allegedly" or "reportedly" should be used when drawing attention to accusations that haven't yet been verified by trustworthy experts. Getting the truth is paramount – but it's also important to not create a trail of hastily worded documents that can later be taken out of context by your company's adversaries as an admission of your company's guilt.

* * *

The reports of tire failures abroad and, of course, the KHOU series prompted Ford management to question the performance of Firestone tires in the United States. Again and again, Firestone reassured Ford that the Wilderness and ATX tires in question had an exemplary record of performance in the U.S. Each assurance assuaged Ford a little bit less than the last one, so Ford began asking Firestone to allow it to review Firestone's customer claims data. Firestone politely refused each request, citing competitive reasons that it needed to keep the information secret. (Among the hundreds of components on a motor vehicle, only the tires were warranted by a company other than the automaker. The tire maker maintained records of customer claims of premature tire failure that resulted in replacement or partial credit under warranty. The tire maker also maintained records of property damage claims, such as vehicle damage, resulting from accidents allegedly caused by a tire failure, and, of course, statistics on injuries and fatalities resulting from those accidents. Automakers had no access to any of that information.)

Increasingly worried that the tire failures seen in so many hot weather climates might be occurring in the southern regions of the U.S., Ford began pressing Firestone for more solid information. Again, Firestone reassured Ford that the tires were performing well in the U.S. Finally, Firestone agreed in December 1999 to participate with Ford in a study to examine tires in service in Texas, Nevada and Arizona, which would have seen severe hot-weather duty. The tires were harvested from customers bringing in their Explorers for routine service and who would be pleasantly surprised to be offered a free set of tires in exchange for their old tires with 30,000 to 40,000 miles of wear. Dubbed the "Southwest Study," it entailed x-raying the used tires, then cutting out cross-sections and examining the dissected pieces in search of any evidence of early signs of the treads peeling or the belts separating. The five-month study was concluded in April 2000 with none of the nearly 250 tires showing any signs of failure, seemingly proving Firestone's continuing contention that there was no issue with the tires in service in the U.S.[14]

Four months later, when Ford and Firestone would announce a massive recall of the Firestone Wilderness tires, it became evident, sadly, that the "Southwest Study" had been grossly inadequate. Firestone had been truthful in saying that the overall claims rate of the Wilderness tires was well within acceptable ranges. But the more important data would be found in the much smaller numbers indicating the frequency of accident claims resulting from tread separations. It would later be evident that Wilderness tires had a relatively higher rate of these accident claims, albeit still in quite low numbers. The tread separation failure rates of the Firestone tires that would be recalled could be stated in terms of double- and triple-digit numbers of defects *per million tires*. In retrospect, not finding a defect among a sample of only 250 tires should not have been reassuring. The 15 million Wilderness tires installed on Explorer since 1990 represented "the largest single-vehicle application in Firestone's history and perhaps the largest in automotive history."[15] The overwhelming majority of these Firestone tires would perform well. But when a tire did suddenly and violently rip apart – almost always during highway cruising and often at speeds far exceeding posted limits – all too often the driver lost control resulting in a deadly rollover crash.

* * *

Looking back at the events of the late '90s and the first half of the year 2000, one might wonder why neither Ford nor NHTSA, the federal government's top automotive safety agency, could piece together enough of this tragic story to put more pressure on Firestone to recall the population of tires most likely to fail in a dangerous tread separation. (As we will see in the following chapters, it later became clear that members of Firestone management were aware of troubling numbers of accident claims from tires produced at one U.S. plant long before they agreed to the recall.) It is true that Ford had already been served a number of lawsuits for injuries and deaths sustained in crashes involving the Explorer and Firestone tires. So how could the automaker insist it did not know about the wave of terrible accidents that were occurring long before Anna Werner began the KHOU investigation? And how could NHTSA not know what was going on?

It is important to remember that more than 40,000 people are killed each year in U.S. automobile crashes of all kinds during nearly 3 trillion miles of driving.[16] That includes fatalities from drunk and drowsy drivers; inattentive, distracted and inexperienced drivers; speeding drivers; those who happened upon icy conditions, dangerous intersections or poorly marked road construction; as well as drivers who lost control over their vehicles because of some malfunction in their vehicles' steering, brakes or tires. A crash was often "caused" by a number of occurrences happening together. NHTSA and local authorities studied accident data constantly looking for patterns that may indicate a safety issue that might need to be addressed. For example, if an inordinate number of fatal crashes happened along a particular curve in a highway, it might indicate that the section of the roadway was to "blame" and should be studied to see if it could be improved to be made safer.

The same analysis can be (and is) applied to accident statistics for particular types of vehicles. But simply comparing the gross rate of fatal vehicle accidents for various vehicle types can be quite deceptive because driver behavior is such an integral part of any vehicle's safety performance. For example, minivans are the vehicles that perennially have the best safety record of any type of vehicle. Minivans manufactured by each of the automakers have good performance in crash tests and are often loaded with impressive safety technologies. But their "real-world performance" is also enhanced by the safe driving of their owners who typically are mothers who are far less likely to speed or to drink-and-drive than are the general population of drivers. Similarly, sport utility vehicles (SUVs) are often described by trial lawyers as especially prone to rollover accidents because of their relatively high center of gravity. Yet, year in and year out, a vehicle

28

with an extremely low center of gravity, the Chevrolet Corvette sports car, is among the worst in terms of rollover fatalities. The Corvette is an exceptionally well-engineered, stable vehicle and its poor rollover record is clearly the product of the aggressive driving behavior of its predominantly male drivers. (And which vehicle has the highest center of gravity and also the lowest rollover fatality rate year in and year out? The answer is: the school bus.)[17]

From its very first year, 1990, the Ford Explorer was the most popular SUV in America. In some years, sales exceeded 400,000. Inevitably, large numbers of such a popular vehicle are involved in fatal accidents – some involving drunk or drowsy drivers, speeders, icy roads and so forth. Yet the reality is that in litigation-prevalent America, nearly every fatal or serious injury auto accident results in a lawsuit alleging a vehicle product defect. Most of these are purely spurious claims, filed by plaintiff attorneys hoping to coerce some modest settlement from the automaker. A much smaller number are legitimate grievances filed on behalf of victims hurt or killed because of a defective vehicle or component. The fact that some number of lawsuits had been filed against Ford and Firestone for accidents involving one of the most popular vehicles of all time – and its tires – did not provide a clear signal to either company. In fact, only a handful of cases against the Explorer had proceeded to trial, and Ford had been successful in its defense each time.

Similarly, with 40,000 highway fatalities a year with a myriad of causal factors, NHTSA needed to document a significant number of accidents involving a particular product before launching a time-consuming and expensive investigation. With so many accidents, so many potential causes, who could connect the dots to say there was a pattern here and another pattern there that needed to be studied to try to get to what was truly relevant and what was just coincidental randomness? How many hundreds of thousands of unremarkable tire failures were there a year, blowouts, slow leaks as well as tread separations? Such a small percentage of all tire failures get reported – only those that lead to an accident causing property damage or injury – and in how many of those did the person completing the report know to use the words "tread separation" when one had occurred? In July 1998, a State Farm administrator, Samuel Boyden, had sent an email to William Duckwitz at NHTSA to alert him to 21 Firestone ATX tire failures causing injury accidents. Fourteen cases involved 1991-1995 Ford Explorers. The problem was dismissed as "unremarkable" by NHTSA.[18]

CHAPTER 3

SHOWDOWN IN DEARBORN

"Because tires are the only component of a vehicle that are separately warranted, Ford did not know – I'll repeat that – Ford did not know that there was a defect with the recalled tires until we virtually pried the data from Firestone's hands and analyzed it ourselves."

- *Jac Nasser, Ford President and CEO, testifying before the U.S. House Commerce Committee, Sept. 6, 2000*

* * *

After KHOU aired its series on the tire failures, NHTSA received a flood of new complaints of tire separation accidents. The agency opened a preliminary inquiry into the issue on March 6, 2000. One of the first actions NHTSA undertook was to contact Samuel Boyden, the State Farm administrator it had rebuffed in 1998, for updated records on Firestone tread separation accidents he had chronicled. In response, Boyden in April emailed an analysis of 70 accidents involving Firestone ATX, ATX II and Wilderness tires.[1]

Meanwhile, Ford pressed Firestone for more and better information, and Firestone continued to resist, citing competitive concerns.

On May 2, 2000, NHTSA opened a formal investigation of 47 million Firestone ATX, ATX II and Wilderness tires blamed for 33 crashes including four fatal accidents and 17 injury accidents.[2] Just three days prior to the opening of NHTSA's investigation, Firestone's

31

Vice President of Quality Assurance Bob Martin retired, closing the door on a distinguished 42-year career with the tire maker.[3]

* * *

Unknown to NHTSA, plaintiff attorneys throughout the country collectively knew of far more Firestone tire accidents than the agency did – lawsuits and notices of intent to file already accounted for at least 35 fatalities and 130 injuries. In dozens of other cases, plaintiff attorneys were patiently waiting to bring the cases forward until the statues of limitations for filing the suits nearly ran out. The delaying tactic was often employed in lawsuits in which other causal factors, like drunk driving or dangerous road conditions, muddied the case for claims against the tire maker and auto company. It was harder for the companies to mount an aggressive defense when the remains of a crashed vehicle no longer were available and witness' memories had grown dim.

Although Ford and Firestone would come under much criticism from Congress and others for not alerting NHTSA earlier of accidents and tire recalls in other countries, plaintiff attorneys and their research centers (such as "Strategic Safety") also failed to notify NHTSA of injury accident lawsuits. As would be documented by Keith Bradsher in the lead story on the front page of the June 24, 2001 Sunday *New York Times*, trial lawyers kept quiet to protect their own interests. The lawyers feared that NHTSA might take notice of the complaints but find them insufficient to open an investigation, or worse yet, conduct an investigation that might ultimately exonerate the tires or the vehicle, significantly hurting the lawyers' chances for a quick settlement or a jury victory. Bradsher's assessment of the actions of the trial lawyers and their "safety consultants" stood in stark opposition to their public posturing as selfless advocates for the safety of the driving public.

"A group of personal-injury lawyers and one of the nation's top traffic-safety consultants identified a pattern of failures of Firestone ATX tires on Ford Explorer sport utility vehicles in 1996," Bradsher's story began. "But they did not disclose the pattern to government safety regulators for four years, out of concern that private lawsuits would be compromised."[4]

Sean Kane, a partner heading tire issues at Strategic Safety, identified 30 cases of tire tread separation failures in 1996, including some fatal crashes, the *Times* story said, after he was retained by plaintiff lawyers in Texas preparing suits against Firestone. "But Mr. Kane and the lawyers, lacking confidence in federal regulators, repeatedly decided not to tell the National Highway Traffic Safety Administration about the problem," wrote Bradsher. "As Strategic Safety began working on Explorer crashes with lawyers across the country, the consultants and lawyers chose not to submit the safety complaint forms that might lead to government investigations."[5]

Why wouldn't these "safety advocates" turn over information that could help federal safety investigators and regulators recognize and act on a serious automotive safety hazard? Shouldn't public safety trump all other concerns – so that additional tragic accidents might be avoided? Bradsher's reporting made clear that for many of the lawyers and their resource groups, another concern, namely a concern for profits, often did trump their regard for the public welfare.

Kane himself admitted to Bradsher the reason for the trial lawyers' reluctance to turn over information to NHTSA: "'Everyone was very leery of the agency getting involved with this, because a number of plaintiff lawyers have been burned when an investigation has been opened and closed without a finding of a defect,' Mr. Kane said."

Undoubtedly letting down his guard in talking to a reporter from the generally liberal *New York Times*, Kane freely stated that winning a large settlement or damage award was a plaintiff attorney's highest priority. "Mr. Kane said that the lawyers' first duty was to win as much money as possible for the crash victims whom they represented. The lawyers typically work on contingency and collect up to a third of any settlement or court verdict..."[6]

Bradsher asked Dr. Ricardo Martinez, who had led NHTSA from 1994 to 1999, what he thought of Kane's admissions. Ricardo "was appalled to learn that information had been kept from his staff for years. He said he would have ordered an immediate investigation if anyone had told him of the tire problems. 'It's outrageous – I can't say that enough.'"[7]

Finally, Bradsher showed how the trial lawyers' reluctance to file suits in a timely fashion or to report known concerns to NHTSA threw

Ford's safety analysts off the scent when they went looking for tire problems in the U.S. in the wake of accidents in Saudi Arabia and Venezuela. "Ford engineers were falsely reassured in 1999 when they checked the federal complaint database and found it virtually empty — because lawyers had not filed complaints," Bradsher wrote.[8]

* * *

Six days after opening its formal investigation into the tire accidents, NHTSA sent Firestone a list of interrogatories it wanted answers to by June 19. On May 10, NHTSA sent Ford its own set of questions and requested Ford to respond by June 23. Both Firestone and Ford would ask NHTSA for more time to complete the interrogatories.[9]

Ford continued to press Firestone for a detailed analysis of its claims data to look for patterns that might help make sense of the tire mess. Firestone continued to decline. Meanwhile, media were turning up the pressure. By the end of July, tire stories were becoming front-page news, and also were getting prominent airtime on TV and radio. On July 25, Los Angles CBS-affiliate KCBS aired a hard-hitting story raising further questions about Firestone tires. (Ironically, that same day, a tire blow-out was blamed for a horrible crash of a Concorde jet taking off from Paris, killing 113. The burst tire apparently sent debris hurling into the jet's engines, leading to a fiery crash that would devastate the supersonic airliner's safety reputation.)[10] The next day, July 26, CNN gave extensive play to a suit filed by two Florida families against Firestone and Ford that claimed negligence in regard to a fatal rollover accident of an Explorer. On July 31, Strategic Safety released a statement to the news media detailing Ford's recall of Firestone tires in Venezuela. In response to a deluge of media inquiries, Ford confirmed the actions it had taken in Venezuela, the Gulf Coast Countries, as well as Malaysia and Thailand, emphasizing the extreme conditions tires were routinely subjected to in those countries. Firestone continued to emphasize its confidence in its tires around the world; on close inspection, tire failures invariably were seen to have been caused by improper repair and maintenance, the tire maker said.[11]

On August 2, *USA Today* ran a front-page story by Jim Healey that began: "Millions of people in the USA are riding on tires that are the focus of a federal safety probe, and that have been recalled and replaced in six other countries, according to government files." The newspaper cited updated numbers from NHTSA – 193 reports of crashes involving Firestone ATX and Wilderness tires, including reports of 21 deaths – up from just four it knew of earlier that week. "Reports of the incidents say the treads inexplicably peeled off the tire casings, causing skids," Healey wrote.[12]

On August 3, Firestone announced through a statement attributed to Christine Karbowiak, Firestone's vice president – Public Affairs, that it was offering its customers a free inspection of their tires (to look for unusual signs of wear and to check that they were properly inflated). "We understand that many of our customers are concerned by recent news reports regarding the safety of the Firestone ATX and Wilderness tires," her statement read. "Although these tires are safe and are not the subject of any recall, customer confidence in these tires is our top priority."[13]

On August 4, Sears, Roebuck and Co., the nation's top tire retailer, announced it would stop selling certain Firestone tires. Again, this news played prominently across the nation. The thumping drumbeat of tire stories had become a steady roar.[14]

* * *

Again and again, Ford asked Firestone for its claims data but was repeatedly rebuffed without any real explanation. Eventually, Firestone officials told Ernie Grush, Ford's safety manager, that the tire company did not have the computing power it would require to properly analyze the reams of claims data they had gathered. Grush immediately offered the services of several analysts and the use of Ford's vast computing resources to crunch Firestone's data. Finally, Firestone agreed to accept the help. In late July, Grush and some of his safety team drove down to Ohio in a Ford Excursion mega-SUV to copy the data and bring it back to Michigan for a rapid analysis.

When the Ford safety engineers returned to Dearborn on July 28 with the Firestone claims data, they took up residence in an executive conference room on the 11th floor of Ford's 12-story World Headquarters, known inside the company as "the Glass House." The top two floors of the Glass House were reserved for executive offices and plush conference rooms named after company products. The large conference room Grush and his team took over was the "Mustang Room." (There wasn't a precedent in anyone's memory for a team of middle managers and analysts occupying a coveted executive office but the space had been assigned to them by CEO Jac Nasser, who wanted them to be close at hand until the tire crisis had subsided.) Inevitably, the conference room became known to the growing tire team as the "War Room" – although Public Affairs quietly interceded to change its nickname to the "Tire Room" as we did not want any connotation implying that Ford was at war with Firestone. (In fact, the tire team quickly outgrew the confines of the Tire Room and soon no fewer than seven executive conference rooms and a number of other rooms on non-executive floors had been taken over by a cadre of engineers, logistics experts, customer service managers, safety analysts, lawyers and public relations people. But for the next year or more, WHQ's Mustang conference room would continue to be known as *the* Tire Room.)

It didn't take Grush's team long to make a preliminary analysis of the data Firestone had provided. By the end of the week, they had briefed Ford management on their findings, which raised far more questions than answers. Now they needed to share what they had learned with Firestone and press the tire maker for explanations.

On Friday, August 4, Ken Zino asked me to attend a meeting that had been called with little notice; it would begin at 4 o'clock. Of course, the last thing anyone wanted to do late on a Friday afternoon was go to another meeting, but this one promised to be interesting. Driving over to the Glass House from my office in the Product Development Center, I recalled the first time I had been briefed on the developing trouble with the Firestone tires. It was two months earlier, in June. I had just flown into Reno, Nevada, where we would conduct a fairly simple on- and off-road drive program of a freshened Ranger pickup truck for two waves of auto writers. The Public Affairs launch manager for the new Ranger, Becky Bach, had just briefed me on the state of readiness for the program, which was excellent. Everything was in order. Just as I was thinking about how best to use the next 60 minutes of rare unstressed time before my next scheduled telephone meeting, Tom Baughman caught me by the arm in the lobby of the hotel where we were staying and asked if he could talk to me for a few minutes. Baughman was the executive director in charge of truck engineering and was our senior operations executive for the Ranger media launch. He was the consummate engineer: extremely knowledgeable, precise in his answer to any question, steady and unflappable, a big bear of a man in his fifties who had spent his entire career in Ford Truck. His large head was naturally ruddy but it turned beet red when he was angry or stressed. Baughman immersed himself in the hard facts, with an engineer's faith in the quantifiable. He could be tough and intimidating to underlings who needed to step up their performance or to peers who made the mistake of taking him on without a full grounding in the facts and the data. He also had a warm and caring, softer side. Several months earlier, Baughman and I had participated with the other senior leaders in Ford Truck in a three-day management retreat aimed at building on our positive qualities and affirming the strengths of the Truck team's culture. Three days of working on soft skills was sheer torture for a results-oriented and extremely busy executive like Baughman but he warmed to it, participated enthusiastically and, in the end, had only praise for our instructor and for the program.

Baughman led me to a quiet corner of the spacious hotel lobby and brought me up to speed on the tire issue. I had seen the KHOU stories in February but had heard nothing more about it. I knew that Firestone had insisted that grossly under-inflated tires – slow leaks from shoddy repairs, improper maintenance and so forth – had been the causal factors in the tire failures named in the series. But now Baughman was telling me that other events had led him to question this explanation. The accident database NHTSA maintained had swelled after the KHOU series, and in May NHTSA had opened a formal investigation. That same month in Venezuela, Ford's South American management team had lost its patience with Firestone and was replacing customers' Firestone tires with new Goodyear tires. Continuing to insist that the tire failures were being caused by under-inflation and excessive speeding on notoriously rough roads, Firestone's South American management had reacted angrily to Ford's unilateral recall. The disagreement in South America was causing tension between Ford and Firestone in the United States, which was a

37

problem in itself. The two companies needed to cooperate to fully respond to the NHTSA investigation, and even more importantly, to get to the bottom of the tire failure mystery.

Baughman's demeanor changed somewhat as he described with exasperation a deadlock that had risen and was impeding his investigation: despite repeated requests from Ford, Firestone had not provided the data analysis needed to isolate the population of tires that were failing. It was not clear whether Firestone lacked the ability or the will to analyze the data that could yield the source of the problems. Giving Firestone's integrity the benefit of the doubt, Baughman offered to crunch the data for the tire company, making use of Ford's extensive computer resources and expertise. But weeks had gone by and Firestone had not delivered the claims data. Baughman had clearly come to the end of his patience. Ford lawyers and Firestone lawyers had drawn up a "joint defense agreement" and still no data was forthcoming. Finally, Nasser had told the Ford lawyers to give Firestone an ultimatum, Baughman whispered. If the tire company wanted to continue to do business with its largest customer, they would turn over their claims data so the two companies could determine if there was a pattern of failure that could lead to a recall aimed at protecting their mutual customers.

I don't remember if Baughman told me there in Reno, but it would soon become clear that heat was an important contributing factor in the tire failures. As we discussed these things in the air-conditioned lobby of a hotel in the hot Nevada desert, a summer was already upon us that would bring with it a rash of deadly rollover crashes.

* * *

One of the famously speedy elevators inside the WHQ Glass House rocketed me up to the 11th floor. I walked toward the "Motorsports" executive conference room, passing the closed door of the Mustang conference room where the tire team had quietly been working for the last few days. Just inside Motorsports, the chairs around a huge oval-shaped polished wood table were being filled with lawyers, customer service people and engineers from Ford Truck. I sat down next to Baughman.

38

Just one week earlier, on Friday, July 28, Firestone had finally relented and agreed to turn over the claims data. The Ford Excursion carrying Grush and several of his analysts from Ford's Automotive Safety Office drove from Dearborn to Akron, Ohio, to collect the claims data that might unlock the mystery behind the growing string of tread separation accidents. The Ford team had asked for the claims records for all 15" Firestone ATX and Wilderness AT tires including records that could link each separated tire to a specific Firestone plant and the date it was produced. What they were given by Firestone was a mish-mash of records – some on computer discs but much of it printed on paper. The Ford analysts spent the rest of the day discussing the collection of data with their Firestone peers to fully understand what they had been given. On Saturday they drove back to Michigan and began the painstaking task of keying into a Ford computer each claims record and coding it to a Firestone plant and two dates: when the tire was built and when it had failed. For some claims the information was incomplete or not legible; the team indicated this so they would not distort the analysis.

Nasser had taken a personal interest in the Firestone investigation as was made clear by his authorizing the executive conference room to be taken over by Grush and his team of number crunchers. Ford's CEO wanted the team to be nearby. By the following Thursday, the team presented preliminary findings to Nasser and his executive team. As I would soon learn, the data was clearly pointing to a preponderance of tread separation failures from a Firestone plant in Decatur, Illinois. There was no way to know what had gone wrong at Decatur but it was time for Firestone to answer some hard questions. Nasser asked the team to double-check their analysis and when the team reported that the review had only increased their confidence in a Decatur-centered problem, a 4:00 pm Friday conference call was arranged with Firestone executives and quality control people.

Soon after I settled in to my chair next to Baughman, Ford Truck Vice President Gurminder Bedi strode into the room and sat down at the center of the table, on Baughman's other side. The side conversations throughout the room quickly subsided. Bedi asked us all if we were ready to begin and was answered by a roomful of nodding heads. Baughman reached toward the center of the table for a black, flying-saucer-shaped Polycom speakerphone command module and keyed in the number for Firestone's Akron office where a roomful of executives were waiting. Microphones at either end of the table connected to the flying saucer so anyone speaking in our conference room could be heard by the others on the call, but they really weren't needed. Baughman, Bedi and Grush would likely do all the talking for the Ford team.

Baughman welcomed the Firestone group to the call. Then he quickly mentioned the names and positions of the Ford people in the room around him. The voice on the speakerphone responded by rattling off the names of the Firestone participants, including Robert Wyant, who had succeeded Bob Martin as vice president of Quality Assurance.

Bedi leaned forward and spoke into the microphone in front of him. No one had to be reminded, he said, of the seriousness of this meeting and the importance of finding a quick resolution. Wyant responded that Firestone shared the sense of urgency. Bedi smiled, pleased with the tone he had established. "Now we are going to fax you a summary of our analysis of the claims data you have provided us and we will take you through what we're finding. I think this will help us isolate the source of the problem so we can move forward with taking care of it."

"No," came a voice over the speakerphone. "Don't send the fax."

A confused look came over Bedi's face, mirrored by the expressions of those in the room around him. "What's the matter?" Baughman asked, "Is your fax machine not in a secure location? Are you worried about confidentiality?"

For an agonizing several seconds, a muffled tone of hushed voices was all that we could hear from Akron. Then, Wyant said haltingly, "I've been advised by my legal counsel that we cannot accept that fax, that receiving that information might be inadvisable at this time."

Bedi, Baughman and the others sat dumbfounded. Finally, Bedi broke the stunned silence. "Listen," he said, "I want you and your team to get up here to Dearborn right away. Tomorrow morning at 8:00 we are going to review this in person. We are not going to ignore this."

With that, the call with Firestone was terminated. So the Ford team alone reviewed the data. Grush methodically went through a series of simple black-and-white overheads that detailed the analysis his team had conducted since obtaining the Firestone claims data seven days earlier. Although Grush was a superb number crusher who made steady use of computers in his daily work, he was strictly old-school about his presentations; no fancy PowerPoint and no color graphics. In his mind, the data should speak for itself and didn't need to be dressed up for executive review.

Grush's voice showed no inflection, revealing no emotion. Everyone else in the room, except for me, apparently had already heard Grush run through this information and they nodded knowingly as we progressed quickly through each flimsy on the overhead projector. Still, they listened carefully, intent on ensuring the soundness of the analysis and of Grush's conclusions.

The series of charts showed the rate of claims and lawsuits against Firestone for tread separations. The claims rate grossly understated the actual rate of tread separations, Grush explained, because it included only claims for property damage and personal injury. It did not include warranty adjustments to pay for tires that had failed in the form of a tread separation but had not caused an accident. If a driver experienced a tread separation but safely navigated the vehicle onto the shoulder without incident, he likely would bring the damaged tire back to the Firestone store and receive a pro-rata warranty adjustment to help pay for a replacement tire. The amount of adjustment would be proportional to the amount of tread wear remaining on the tire (likely determined by measuring the depth of tread left on one of the vehicle's other tires, as the damaged tire would have shed its entire tread like a long, black animal pelt littering the shoulder of the highway).

Since the amount refunded was often quite small, the tire retailer might be less than diligent in recording the specifics of the tire failure, not bothering to distinguish between a tread separation and the much more common puncture or blowout. The smaller but much more reliable accident claims data base counted only tread separations that had led to an accident (and resulted in a lawsuit or claim for reimbursement for personal injury or property damage), as well as claims in which there was no crash but there was significant damage to the paint and metal around the wheel well as it was struck by the separating tread. Since these claims were for much larger sums of money than a partial reimbursement for a single tire, the record keeping was much more precise and accurate than the warranty claims totals. Firestone continued to refuse to provide Ford with its warranty claims data, Grush said, but it was unnecessary now that Ford was making progress in analyzing the claims for property damage and personal injury. The analysis of that data was yielding an unsettling picture, he said, that would demand a response.

The first charts looked at the number of claims against Firestone for ATX, ATX II and Wilderness AT tire failures plotted by the year the claim was filed, beginning with 1990, the first year of production of the Ford Explorer. The numbers were tiny – 0, 1, 3, 0, 7, 1 – with no evidence of any trend until 1999 when they jumped to double digits and then 2000 which had already seen more than 100 property damage and personal injury claims filed against Firestone. It wasn't clear what had caused this recent spike in claims, Grush said.

Next, the charts looked at the claims plotted by year in which the tire was manufactured. This showed claims scattered throughout the earlier '90s, peaking in 1994, 1995 and 1996, then steadily decreasing in the most recent years leading up to 2000. Age or wear apparently was key to this trend, Grush explained, which meant that one would expect more tread separations and more accidents to occur on the recently produced tires as they aged in the field.

Lesson Learned: Don't shy away from numbers. *How many times have you heard a PR person say, "Hey, I never was good at numbers. That's why I went into PR." That cop-out is an insult to those of us in the PR profession who expect to be taken seriously by the company's operations management. Our ability as communications professionals to effectively broker fair media coverage of complex issues in the tire crisis so often came down to an understanding of the numbers. And it surely will not be the last corporate crisis requiring communicators with analytical skills. If you can't make sense of the financial tables in your company's Annual Report, or basic statistics in a quality report, quietly ask someone to teach you. Just don't let anyone hear you whine: "I don't do numbers."*

The next few charts looked at the rate of failures per million tires for each year of production. Again, the 1994 through 1996 tires had the largest rates. Then Grush showed the rate of tread separations broken out for each of Firestone's manufacturing plants. At this point, the inflection of Grush's voice changed and eyes all around him widened. This evidently was new material for others in the room besides me.

Tires produced at Firestone's Decatur plant had a much higher rate of failure than those produced at its other three tire manufacturing plants in North America. There was little difference in this analysis between tires built in Firestone plants at Wilson, North Carolina or Joliet, Quebec. But the rate of failure for the Decatur tires was much, much higher. And it didn't matter which year of production you looked at – Decatur tires were failing far more often than other Firestone Wilderness and ATX tires. While tread separation failures for even the worst populations of Decatur tires were relatively uncommon – just over 100 claims per million tires in this first analysis – they were much more likely than tread separations for tires built elsewhere. There was no good explanation why the Decatur tires were more prone to failure – if you accepted Firestone's assessment that improper customer maintenance was to blame. It wasn't plausible that Explorer customers whose Firestone tires had come from the Decatur plant were much more likely to abuse their tires than Explorer customers whose tires happened to come from another plant. And it wasn't the case that a predominance of Decatur-built tires ended up in hot climates. Tires from each of Firestone's tire plants that had made Wilderness and ATX tires supplied the two Ford plants that built Explorers. And Explorers from each Ford plant were delivered to dealers in every state (and numerous countries). Something was wrong with the Decatur tires that left them susceptible to tread shedding during hot weather highway driving. More accidents were sure to follow until the defective tires were replaced.

* * *

The next morning a little before 8:00, more than 20 people from Ford and Firestone took turns filling their mugs with coffee in the executive conference area's anteroom. Most wore jeans and golf shirts; casual dress was the only good thing about a Saturday morning meeting. I spotted John Behr, Firestone's Ford sales rep and the only one from Firestone who hadn't had to fly or drive up to Michigan the night before. I walked over to shake his hand and say "good morning."

43

Behr and I knew each other outside of work – we both were lectors at our Catholic church in Canton and we often played pickup basketball together in a neighboring elementary school gym. I knew him to be a good and honorable man. Months later when things turned ugly between Firestone and Ford, and especially as I was continually quoted in the papers defending the Explorer and blaming the tires, our relationship grew tense. In fact, he purposely avoided me, and the truth is, I didn't seek him out either. He started going to an earlier Mass on Sundays and neither of us played much basketball. It was probably three years later that we ran into each other again, at the little gym for pickup basketball. He and I ended up on the same team the first game. We shook hands and started playing. I made a point of passing to him often and complimenting him when he made a shot. He did the same for me and then we were pretty much back to the way we were before that August 2000 weekend. Sometimes that's the best way for two guys to work things out. We never talked about the tire recall and still haven't to this day.

When Behr saw me that Saturday, he smiled and accepted my handshake. Laughing, he said, "What's a PR guy doing here? This is a business meeting, you know."

I didn't say anything in response; just smiled. But his remark spoke volumes about the differences between Ford and Firestone. At Ford, public relations most definitely had a "seat at the table," a voice in business decision-making *before* the decisions were made. At Firestone, like so many companies, PR handled the announcement *after* the decisions were made. It was clear to me that a PR professional who had earned a seat at the table by understanding the business should be thinking ahead to the reputational consequences of proposed actions. PR pros could envision how a proposed action might play out on the front page of the *New York Times* or *USA Today* and could help shape decisions and plans to maximize the possibilities for positive coverage or minimize risks of negative coverage. Sometimes it might require the PR person to say, "No, we shouldn't do that" to a more senior executive.

Firestone PR had no such seat at the table, so it was not surprising that no one from Firestone PR had made the trip to Dearborn. It's absurd, really, that two companies would decide to take an action of historic scale to address an issue with profound and devastating implications on each company's reputation and yet with only one company's PR staff represented at the critical moment. Sure we were inside doing work on a beautiful Saturday in August, but as a PR guy, there was nowhere on Earth that I would have rather been than in my front-row seat as the biggest business story of the year reached a critical juncture.

Lesson Learned: Reputation management is our job. *Public relations must earn a "seat at the table" by providing strong and relevant counsel and by understanding the fundamentals of the business. Business leaders, in turn, should pay attention to the advice from their PR counsel who acts as the "conscience" or the "voice of reputation." Companies in which even the senior PR people are nothing but mouthpieces and mop-up crews should not be surprised to find themselves in messes they might have avoided.*

* * *

After greetings and introduction, Baughman asked Grush to begin his presentation. Using the same slides we had reviewed the previous afternoon, Grush slowly went through his presentation, explaining his methodology and analysis. He stopped frequently to ask his Firestone counterparts if they understood and agreed with what he was saying. Often they would have questions or ask for more detail, and Grush or one of the people on his team would offer an explanation until there was agreement on each point and we could proceed to the next flimsy. It was a tedious process, taking nearly two hours to get to the final slides; the day before Grush had covered the entire presentation in about 15 minutes.

Finally, Grush came to the analysis of the failures specific to each plant and each year of manufacture. Grush pointed out the painfully obvious: tires produced at the Decatur plant were failing at a much higher rate than any others. By far, the worst rates of failures were on tires branded "ATX" and "ATX II" that had been built at Decatur from 1991 to 1996. These were the problem tires, the ones we would expect Firestone to recall, although Ernie didn't say that yet. Throughout these last slides, there were no questions. Finally, Wyant leaned in to talk to a member of Firestone's legal team, then said, "How about we take a 10-minute break?"

During the break, each side adjourned to separate areas – the Ford team mostly congregated in the "Tire Room" and much of the Firestone team appeared to be caucusing in another conference room down the hall. Ernie huddled with Baughman, preparing to answer whatever objections Firestone would raise when we reconvened.

As we all gathered up again in the conference room, Ernie alone remained standing, waiting patiently to continue his presentation. But before he could start, Wyant informed the room that we should begin planning immediately for a recall of *all* Decatur-built 15" ATX, ATX II and Wilderness AT tires – a larger population of tires than we had planned to ask Firestone to recall. Clearly expecting to hear more questions or challenges to his findings, Ernie sat down, knowing that only a fool continues to make a pitch after the other party has agreed to the sale. I began to draft the beginnings of a joint press release.

The meeting continued for several hours with discussion about all that needed to be done in the next few days before representatives of the two companies could meet with NHTSA to request the agency's agreement to Firestone's voluntary tire recall. It became obvious that it was too early to work on the press release, so I began making a list of the things the two companies' PR teams would need to do to prepare for the press conference that would make headlines all over the world. Then I spent the next several hours listening and learning about tires, and especially about tire procurement and logistics. Perhaps the biggest challenge ahead was to secure enough replacement tires and to get them to Ford and Firestone dealers and other retail tire stores, so that when millions of owners of Explorers and other affected vehicles with Firestone tires heard the news there would be replacement tires waiting for them. From what I was hearing, it would take many months to obtain the tires and replace them for customers.

Evening twilight painted the windows orange in the southwest corner conference room on the 11th floor of the Glass House as the Ford and Firestone people filed out to go home or to their hotel rooms, with another full day of work ahead of them Sunday. As I gathered up my notebook, I walked over to two of my colleagues from Ford's tire team. They were talking in hushed tones, and they repeated the thought for my benefit as I drew near.

"They folded too quickly, Jon. There's no way they had time to fully process Ernie's presentation, understand its implications and get

approval from Japan in the ten or fifteen minutes they had for a break."
(An iconic American manufacturer founded in 1900, Firestone had
been taken over by Japanese tire maker Bridgestone in 1988.)

"You mean, they already knew Decatur was the problem before
they got here?" I asked.

"Exactly right. They've known for who-knows-how-long that one
plant, Decatur, was producing the lion's share of the separations. And
they knew that if one plant's production was behaving way worse than
the others', there must be a manufacturing problem. And that means
they can't keep blaming this all on customer under-inflation."

"And they must have gamed this all out with Japan ahead of time,"
the other one said. "They were prepared to fold if we showed them that
we had found out their problem plant. They even went further than what
we were going to insist be recalled. Wyant doesn't have the
firepower to agree to such a massive recall. Bridgestone must have
given him pre-approval for the recall if our analysis pointed to Decatur."

When Grush had shown them that we had the damning evidence
of consistent over-representation of claims from Decatur, the Firestone
team had called a time-out, made a quick call back to the parent
company Bridgestone's senior execs in Japan who were waiting for
just such a call.

One other detail about our showdown with Firestone troubled
Baughman, he told me quietly. "After Ernie presented the data
pointing to problems at Decatur, just before the break, a peculiar look
came over the face of one of their senior engineers. Not apprehension
or stress, but relief. Unmistakably relief." Could it be that the Firestone
tire engineering executive had known of the problems for quite some
time, brought them to the attention of his bosses but then saw them
swept under the rug? And that he knew that once we identified the
problem plant a recall was inevitable that would begin to put an end to
the deadly accidents?

This was all just our speculation at this point, of course. But I
began to wonder as I drove home that evening: How long had
Firestone management known they had a real problem, even as they
continued to deny it? And how many people were still driving around
on Decatur-built tires with a small but not insignificant chance of
becoming the next fatal accident statistic?

47

CHAPTER 4

DAY OF RECKONING

"We spent the past 10 years trying to rebuild the image of Firestone. Then this happened."

- *Kenichi Kitawaki, Bridgestone's PR manager, in* TIME *magazine, Aug. 21, 2000. (Bridgestone purchased Firestone in 1988, a decade after the American tire maker nearly sank in the aftermath of the Firestone 500 recall in 1978.)*

* * *

That Saturday night, I arrived home just as my wife Mary was finishing cleaning up from what had been our first pool party. Construction was newly completed on our large in-ground pool and even with the landscaping unfinished we had made plans to have several families over for a barbecue on the afternoon of the first Saturday of August. Before I left the house early that morning with everyone still in bed, I had whispered in my sleepy wife's ear that I'd be home in plenty of time to help host the party, if she could just get things started.

Lesson Learned: Don't make promises you might not be able to keep, especially to your spouse. If you're in the midst of a crisis and you have communications responsibility, you aren't going to be home in time for dinner.

I made several phone calls home throughout the day, apologizing each time as it became apparent that I would not be coming home when I said I would. As I walked around back to the patio, I apologized to Mary. Then I told her I would likely be spending Sunday at work as well. We could go to church together as a family, if we went to the early Mass, but then I'd have to spend the rest of the day at Ford. The kicker was that I couldn't tell her much that was going on. She knew this was about "the tires" and those "awful rollover accidents" that were getting so much attention in the news lately. But I couldn't yet tell her that a recall was imminent and that I likely would be traveling somewhere in the next few days for the recall news conference. Maybe to Nashville, home to Firestone's corporate headquarters in the U.S. No way did we want to hold the press conference in Dearborn; this was primarily Firestone's announcement.

* * *

Long before I arrived at WHQ Sunday morning, Baughman and Grush were already poring over tire claims data together. Five simple words gnawed at Baughman. And he needed Ernie's help to figure out what, if anything, they meant.

The day before, when Firestone had agreed to recall more tires from Decatur than we had thought needed to be replaced, Baughman had asked them why they would replace tires outside of the band of poor performers Ernie had identified. The mysterious five-word answer from one of Firestone's senior tire engineers, "We have to protect Decatur," hung in the conference room air pregnant with unspoken meaning. The engineering executive didn't elaborate. Perhaps there had been brief and subtle eye contact with one of Firestone's lawyers, or perhaps his own intuition told him that he had already said too much. Those words – "We have to protect Decatur" – had kept Baughman awake Saturday night. He needed to dig into the data with Ernie to see if they meant what he thought they meant.

Baughman suspected that the tire engineer had meant that Firestone needed to "draw a fence around" the Decatur tire problems to ward off calls for a devastatingly expensive recall of Firestone tires from all plants. He called Grush and asked him to come in early Sunday to take another run at the data, cutting it different ways to see if there was a pattern of other problem tires beyond those built at Decatur. The other plants' production looked good overall. But when they isolated the different tire models for each plant and each year of production, a different picture emerged. The Wilderness AT tire had very low claim rates at every plant outside Decatur consistently for every year. But the failure rates for 15" ATX and ATXII models for each plant had spikes of relatively high failure rates for many of the years in the mid-90s. Tires produced in the late '90s were either much less prone to failure or were simply too recently built to have enough usage and wear to fail in significant numbers.

Baughman and Grush presented this further analysis to Firestone later in the day. The tire maker agreed to expand the recall beyond Decatur; all 15" ATX and ATXII tires from all plants and all years of production would be included as well.

* * *

I spent most of Sunday with the Ford lawyers, safety analysts, truck engineers and tire experts, learning as quickly as I could about tires and everything related to the tread separation accidents. I already had a pretty fair, if basic, understanding of vehicle dynamics, having organized and executed a series of driving dynamics programs at Ford proving grounds on both sides of the Atlantic for American and European motoring press. But as I would find out over the next several months, there was so much more to learn.

In one of our joint meetings Sunday, the Firestone team raised the issue of tire pressure. It was standard industry practice for the vehicle manufacturer, working with its tire suppliers, to determine the tire pressure recommendation for the vehicle's optimal performance – including steering responsiveness, ride quality and fuel economy. These were competing objectives – a tire inflated to a high pressure was stiffer and more rigid, so it had less rolling resistance and thus better fuel economy, but it also would contribute to a harsh ride so that vehicle occupants might feel every bump in the road. There was also was an optimal tire pressure for each vehicle for steering responsiveness, so that the vehicle could be relatively agile, allowing drivers to avoid potential accidents. Before the Explorer had gone into production in 1990, Ford's product development engineers had conducted numerous driving tests with prototype Explorers and concluded that 26 pounds per square inch (psi) would be the optimal tire pressure for the new SUV's front and rear tires. Compared with other similar vehicles, this pressure recommendation was on the low side but it was by no means unheard of. Firestone signed off on 26 psi as the recommended pressure for the Explorer.

But on Sunday, August 6, the Firestone team asked Ford to raise the recommended pressure to 30 psi. Firestone was convinced that extended driving at high speeds on severely under-inflated tires was the culprit in nearly all of the tread separations. Heat would build up in under-inflated tire under stress, and excessive heat could lead to the treads becoming "de-laminated" – the tread and outer steel belt peeling off the rest of the still-inflated tire as it sped down the freeway, the spinning tire's centrifugal force ripping the tread off in a long pelt of hot rubber and steel fiber. Firestone believed the tires that had failed were running with far less air pressure than recommended – perhaps on less than 10 psi in many cases. Raising the recommendation to 30 psi would provide an extra margin of error, figuring that many customers would run well under whatever level was recommended.

The Firestone team was worried, they said, that tread separation accidents would continue through the hot months of August and September – and into the following summer. It would take many months, perhaps as long as 18 months to get enough replacement tires to customers to complete the recall. In the meantime, raising the recommended tire pressure and raising customer awareness of the importance of maintaining proper inflation were two things that could be done to help reduce the risk of additional accidents.

The Ford team huddled to discuss Firestone's request. Explorer customers riding on tires with 30 psi would experience a harsher ride – and ride harshness already was one of the few complaints Explorer customers had with their vehicles. But 30 psi was in the range of tire pressures in which the Explorer had safely completed a stringent set of severe driving maneuvers, so perhaps it would be best to acquiesce to Firestone's request to provide an additional cushion for those customers who drove on chronically under-inflated tires. Explorer customers who did maintain their tires at 30 psi would experience an even-more truck-like ride than they already did, but the extra tire pressure would not impair the vehicle's ability to respond safely to a variety of extreme steering inputs.

But many on Ford's tire team did not like the idea of raising the tire pressure in the midst of a crisis. They worried that it would send a signal that Ford agreed that the relatively low tire pressure recommendation of 26 psi was somehow the cause of the tragic accidents. That's when I weighed in, agreeing that it certainly would be confusing to the public for Ford to change the tire pressure recommendation in the middle of a recall, but – I said – the overwhelming consideration should be what would be best to prevent future loss of life. I will never forget the reaction of the rest of the group in our Ford team huddle: each of them looked at me and nodded, some saying things like, "Yes, of course." Some looks carried with them an unspoken chastisement to the PR person who was interjecting in a crucial engineering discussion with a statement of the obvious, but no one disagreed.

The solution that the Ford team proposed, and that was accepted by Firestone was this: when Firestone announced the recall, the tire maker would stress the importance of customers maintaining proper air pressure in their tires. Further, they would say that Firestone recommended a tire pressure of 30 psi to best enhance the tire's durability, and that Ford agreed that 30 psi was a safe pressure to maintain the Explorer's tires. Ford would raise its recommendation to a "range of 26 to 30 psi."[1] These convoluted messages were by no means ideal to communicate during a crisis. Although it seemed to be the best compromise, it led to customer confusion and it underscored the crack that was developing between the two companies. The tire pressure controversy would be one of the main continuing story lines in the deluge of media coverage that had just begun.

Lesson Learned: Customer safety has to come first. Contradictory messages breed confusion and weaken your effectiveness. But sometimes you have no choice. Protect your customers and strive to communicate the rationale for the change as simply as possible.

* * *

I had apprised Jason Vines and Ken Zino late Saturday afternoon of Firestone's stated willingness to recall the suspect tires, and we agreed that the three of us would meet Sunday late afternoon. I also sent word through the Firestone team that we would want to talk to Christine Karbowiak, Firestone's vice president – Public Affairs, to begin coordinating our communications plans.

At six o'clock Sunday evening, Vines, Zino and I sat in Jason's executive corner office at the opposite end of the hall from the Tire Room on the 11th floor of the Glass House. As we waited for Karbowiak's phone call, Vines entertained us with his legendary sense of humor, running through a riff of impressions: President Clinton, Elvis, Clinton doing Elvis and finally, Elvis doing Clinton. During the harried times of the next weeks and months, Jason's joking would keep us loose even when the tension was at its greatest.

When Karbowiak's call came through to the Polycom speaker-phone in the center of the table, it immediately became clear that she didn't have anyone to keep *her* loose. In a tense voice, she said she had been briefed by the Firestone management team on what had progressed in Dearborn, including their agreement to recall some of the tires. She clearly did not understand what had compelled her management to agree to recall tires whose performance she had been adamantly defending for months. The idea that Firestone had apparently produced a sizable number of defective tires had not yet fully registered with her – she, of course, had not seen Grush's slide presentation Saturday or taken part in the many discussions over the rest of the weekend in the Glass House.

I asked Karbowiak what her thoughts were on the location of the news conference to announce the recall (Nashville or Washington, D.C., were the logical choices). Her reply, in a halting, barely audible voice, caused the three of us sitting at Vines' meeting table to stare at each other in disbelief. Firestone wasn't going to have a press conference, she said. The tire company would issue a press release and would provide comment to media in a "one-way satellite feed."

I broke the silence. "Christine, that won't work," I said, stating what was perfectly obvious to the three of us in Jason's office. "Media are all over this story. Anything less than an open press conference will just infuriate them and give them every reason to believe you have something to hide. You'll just prolong the story." Zino and Vines, of course, were in complete agreement. "Why don't you want to do a press conference?" Vines asked her.

"We just think it will get ugly," she said.

"It will *really* get ugly – for Ford as well as Firestone, if we try to duck legitimate questions," I said. I didn't need to tell her that *USA Today* and other prominent publications had been running front-page stories about the tire crisis nearly every day for the past 10 days or so.

Then Karbowiak told us her real issue – none of Firestone's executives would agree to stand in front of the cameras and endure the heat of what clearly would be a difficult news conference.

Again, I took the lead in responding to Karbowiak – Zino and Vines were deferring to me because I had spent my whole weekend in the Glass House meetings and was the one most immersed in the issues at play. But there was no doubt what our position would be and I felt no need to ask for their thoughts before addressing her: "Christine, it's your job to find a senior leader who can stand up in front of a room full of media and answer tough questions," I said firmly. "No one wants to be that person, but it's absolutely necessary. We can help you media train your executive and, of course, our people will be there to answer questions that are our responsibility."

Karbowiak agreed to go back to her leadership team with the objective of selecting and preparing a lead spokesperson for the news conference.

Lesson Learned: Stand up and face the music. There aren't that many hard-and-fast rules in PR, but this is one of them: When accusations linking your product to an ongoing string of bloody accidents have been front-page national news for several days and you finally relent to the pressure and agree to a recall of historic proportions, you hold a press conference. You can't hide in your office and issue a statement and a "one-way feed." Unless this is the Soviet Union and you're the Kremlin (but it isn't and you aren't).

* * *

Baughman and Helen Petrauskas, Ford vice president – Environmental and Safety Engineering, along with a number of Ford lawyers and Government Affairs people left Monday afternoon on a company jet to D.C. There they joined a Firestone contingent in a Tuesday morning meeting with NHTSA to review the proposed recall plan. With an active investigation underway, the federal safety agency was entitled to a full review of the methodology used to determine the population of tires to be recalled, as well as the plan to replace millions of customers' tires. But the recall could properly be described as "voluntary" and "precautionary" since Firestone was acting before any request – or order – from NHTSA to recall tires.

Vines, Zino and I would each pack an overnight bag and bring it to work on Tuesday. As soon as we received word that NHTSA had signed off on the recall, we would take another company jet to Washington.

The call came through shortly after noon; we were a "go" for a Wednesday morning press conference. Jason and Ken scurried down the hall to Vines' executive office. I gathered up my suit bag and my laptop computer case, which I had stashed under my customary spot at one of the long tables in the Tire Room. I took special care to pack the computer disc on which I had been backing up the long, detailed Q&A that would serve as the principle briefing document for our spokespeople. Before closing down my computer, I emailed my comments on Firestone's draft press release to our Washington Public Affairs office, along with Ford's draft press release which would be titled "Ford Motor Company Statement in Response to Firestone's Recall," so our people in D.C. could continue working with the Firestone team on language agreeable to both companies.

I scurried down the hall toting my suit bag and computer case; Vines and Zino hurried toward me from the opposite corner of the Glass House executive floor, bags on the end of their arms just like me. Just before we met at the elevator bank in the middle of the corridor, Vines captured the surreal moment perfectly, making a snide reference to that slang term for PR people we liked only slightly better than "spin doctors." "Don't miss the latest action-hero TV series," he said in television announcer baritone. "Flacks!"

* * *

As our small Ford jet sprinted down the runway and made its steep ascent into the skies, we continued to discuss the big day ahead of us Wednesday. With the help of our experienced PR team in Washington, we had high confidence in the proper handling of many small details that were essential to a smooth-running news conference, allowing us to concentrate on the messages the two companies' spokespeople would deliver and, even more importantly, how they would answer the many questions from the media throng.

This was to be Firestone's news conference with Ford in a supportive role. But it had been made abundantly clear from our initial conversation with Karbowiak that Firestone was woefully ill equipped for modern crisis communications. It would be incumbent on the Ford team to lead the overall communications strategy development to protect the mutual interests of the two companies.

One critical issue still needing to be resolved was whether or not to provide media with the analysis of the claims data. Our position was that we needed to release a summary of the data to explain, as Firestone and Ford had in their closed-door meeting with NHTSA, why the recall included certain tires but excluded many similar tires. In the absence of the finding of a specific defect in the manufacturing process at the Decatur plant or a design defect in the Wilderness tires, the claims analysis was driving the decision to recall certain Firestone tires. Firestone needed to share that data with the news media, we argued, or there would be no rebuttal to the critics' inevitable calls for an even wider tire recall. Firestone was dead set against releasing the data. No explanation was given but clearly their actions were being driven by their lawyers and the desire to limit their liability. Language would be carefully chosen to state that the recall was precautionary in nature and to emphasize their continuing contention that improper maintenance by customers was a principle causal factor. Any inclusion of data would center attention on Firestone's tire design and manufacturing processes, particularly at the Decatur plant. This appeared to be a classic case of clear communications losing out to legal concerns aimed at limiting liability by limiting information the company would provide. But it was a strategy sure to fail from the point of view of media relations and reputation management. Legitimate questions left unanswered always fester until they no longer can be ignored, like a kinked rubber hose backing up unstoppable water pressure until the hose bursts in an uncontrollable mess. Firestone would continue to ignore our requests for the release of the claims analysis and the pressure would swell up just as we had predicted.

Lesson Learned: Don't stonewall. There are some pieces of information that, sooner or later, you are going to have to make public. As soon as you are sure enough about the quality of the information that you're ready to base a multi-hundred-million-dollar recall on it, and disclose it to the Federal government, it's time to release the information to the public, on your terms. That way you get to interpret what the information means and have at least an even chance that most people believe you. If you wait until your adversaries demand the information so loudly that you finally have to sheepishly release it, don't expect to have anyone believe your side of the story.

* * *

As our jet made a sharp turn over the Potomac and then the steep descent toward Reagan National Airport, I noticed that Jason had grown quiet and was fidgeting nervously. Our fearless leader had a fear of flying, I thought. I had traveled with Vines before on commercial air flights and hadn't noticed him tense up. Evidently the sharper movements of our small, agile jet were harder for him to stomach. Armed with this information, I decided to mess with him, all in good fun, as he most certainly would have messed with me.

Looking out the window at our wing tip, I motioned to Zino, a pilot who owned his own small airplane. "Hey, Ken," I said in mock terror. "The wing's not supposed to be doing *that*, is it?" Then I turned to look for Jason's reaction.

He glared back at me and raised his right hand at me with the middle finger pointed up. The three of us burst out laughing. This was certainly the first time I had been flipped off by a Ford vice president. Oddly, I took it as an expression of endearment and respect. I had noticed a weakness in my boss and had called him on it, using silly, sophomoric humor. I was speaking Jason's language.

We landed at Reagan, turned our cell phones back on and began retrieving our messages.

"I can't believe it," Vines muttered.

"What?" Zino and I asked at the same time.

"Healey left me a voice mail," Vines said, referring to Jim Healey, the *USA Today*'s auto editor. "He got word leaked through NHTSA that Firestone is going to announce a recall tomorrow, and when he asked Karbowiak, she flat out denied it. Healey knows she's lying and he wants our comment."

We all knew that we couldn't confirm the recall yet. The lawyers from both companies had agreed that no mention could be made of the news conference planned for the next morning until after 4:00 p.m., when trading ended on the New York Stock Exchange. (Bridgestone traded on the Tokyo exchange where it would at that time be 6:00 am and also closed.) It was nearly 3:00. In just over an hour the two companies would get the word out that a major news conference would be held the next morning at 9:30, and given the huge amount of interest, no one had any doubt that, despite the short notice, the National Press Club would be packed with media. The only correct course of action for a PR person caught in such a bind was to defer comment until 4:00 – certainly not to deny plans for a recall only to announce those plans hours later. Lying was not only wrong; it was flat out stupid.

"It's not going to be easy working with these pikers," Zino said.

Lesson Learned: Don't lie. Ever. *If you are in a blackout period and aren't able to provide any comment, wait to return the call. Or say, "I can't tell you anything about that right now." This is so fundamental I'm embarrassed to include it as a Lesson Learned.*

* * *

We went right to Ford's Washington office, a few blocks from the White House on "I" Street. We took over the main conference room and spread out on the huge mahogany table. Baughman, Petrauskas and a bunch of lawyers already were camped out there, ignoring the motley arrangement of half-empty bottles of water and juice, now-cold coffee and what appeared to be the remains of a pizza strewn in the middle of the table.

I sat next to Helen and booted up my computer to continue working on the Q&A. Occasionally, I would read a question and its proposed answer aloud, waiting for a comment from the appropriate expert. If it was a question related to safety, Helen would give me her thoughts. Questions about the development of the Explorer would elicit a response from Baughman. Often, no one would bite, and I'd get on the phone to the Tire Room to try to track down some fact or figure.

* * *

The story of the Explorer's development had inspired a myriad of conspiracy theories. Lawyers hunting huge settlements insisted that the Explorer had been rushed to market. Ford's senior management had brushed aside concerns from the engineering team about the vehicle's ability to safely negotiate a sequence of sharp turns, the trial lawyers said. The Explorer was too heavy for its tires, its suspension springs too harsh. Furthermore, engineering memos written during the Explorer's development "proved," the lawyers declared, that Ford knew the vehicle was flawed; yet the company had callously refused to delay the program.

But that's not really what had happened.

The Explorer would debut in 1990 as a replacement for the fairly successful Bronco II small SUV, which Ford had built from 1984 to 1990. The Bronco II had been a derivative of Ford's popular compact pickup truck, the Ranger. Like Ranger, Bronco II appealed to young buyers as a small, affordable alternative to the boring, econo-box compact cars of the day. To understand the Explorer development story, you had to start with Ranger and Bronco II.

Chevrolet had introduced its S-10 small pickup in 1982, a year before the Ranger. Both trucks were already late to the party. Nearly a decade earlier, Toyota, Datsun (later renamed Nissan) and Mazda had created a new segment in the American market, the compact pickup. The Japanese automakers couldn't yet compete credibly in the lucrative full-size pickup truck market, so they had imported slightly modified versions of the small trucks they sold in Asia. The little pickups were reliable, affordable, and most important, fuel efficient. Rising gasoline prices in the 1970s helped these mini-trucks take off in the American marketplace. The Big Three domestic automakers began the four-to-five-year process to develop their own small trucks. In the meantime, Ford arranged to sell a twin of the Mazda B-series truck, badged the Ford Courier, until its own small pickup was ready. Introduced in 1983, the Ford Ranger was far superior to the Courier and soon proved quite popular in the marketplace. In fact, Ranger would become the best-selling compact pickup in the U.S. in 1987 and hold that distinction until 2004.[2] Affordability was crucial to Ranger's success, which was good for its mostly entry-level buyers but meant razor-thin profit margins for Ford.

As Japanese and American automakers found a ready market for their small pickups, they began to design derivatives to expand their trucks' appeal and to help cover product development costs. The American companies had a head-start in that they already had developed large utility vehicles built off their best-selling full-size pickups. Ford Bronco, Chevrolet Blazer and Jeep Cherokee provided a rear bench seat for passengers and an enclosed cargo area in place of a pickup bed. The rugged utility vehicles were offered in two-wheel-drive and four-wheel-drive models, both with plenty of ground clearance to allow them to travel far off the beaten path. Although they became known as "hunting and camping vehicles" – the term "sport utility vehicle" had not yet been popularized – their enclosed storage area more often carried tools and work gear, and they offered little in creature comforts beyond optional air conditioning and automatic transmissions. The market niche was pretty limited, but these derivative utility vehicles didn't cost much to develop and could be built in the automakers' existing truck plants alongside the pickups, so they were fairly profitable, albeit in small numbers. The American automakers naturally looked to these big, rough and tumble utility vehicles as the design templates when they made plans for the smaller derivative vehicles to be developed using their new compact pickup platforms. The Japanese automakers had similar plans. But each of the auto companies soon realized that the customer appeal of the new small utilities would be quite different from their workman-like, full-size cousins. Each company drew inspiration from the little Jeep CJ – the direct descendant of the jeeps that had helped win World War II for the Allies. Jeep CJ had become associated with fun and adventure as opposed to rugged utility. That spirit was bred into each auto-maker's entry into this new category of small sporty utilities. Isuzu introduced its Trooper in 1981, followed in short order by the Chevy S-10 Blazer in 1983, the Toyota 4Runner and the Ford Bronco II in

1984, and the Suzuki Samurai in '85. These small jeep-knockoffs were relatively tall given their short wheelbases. They had sufficient ground clearance to be driven through woodlands or over rocky terrain, but their go-anywhere image was clearly more about fun than work. They were relatively inexpensive and fairly fuel-efficient. And they became a hit with young customers.

Unfortunately, this demographic of young, predominantly male drivers tended to get in a disproportionately high number of accidents. They often drove recklessly. In the hands of an inexperienced driver steering too aggressively and then over-correcting, driving too fast into a sharp curve in the road, losing control and sliding sideways into a curb or careening down an embankment, the small SUVs might roll over. Rollovers were violent crashes. Unbelted occupants often were thrown to their deaths or to serious injury. Even those wearing safety belts could be horribly injured or killed as the vehicle tumbled on its side, over and over again. Most small SUV drivers, of course, would operate their vehicles safely through the life of the vehicle. But it was obvious that the tall, new SUVs had a higher center of gravity than cars and were, therefore, comparatively tippy. Driven too aggressively, they had less of a safety margin against a rollover than a shorter, squatter vehicle. They simply had to be driven differently than other types of cars. Just as one shouldn't attempt to drive a sports car through a forest, one shouldn't try to drive a small SUV like a sports car. On the other hand, customers had every reason to expect any vehicle sold for highway driving to remain safe and stable except in the most extraordinary circumstances.

Automakers conducted tight handling maneuvers to test vehicles being developed to ensure that they would not tip up on one side. Any two-wheel lift would fail the test as a dangerous condition that could lead to a rollover. These tests were quite severe. But no automaker could design a vehicle that would remain stable no matter how hard or recklessly it was driven. And when a vehicle did crash, a trial lawyer was sure to file a suit claiming the automaker had been negligent in not designing it to better protect its occupants for exactly that type of accident. Every one of the new, small SUVs were involved in fatal accidents, including rollovers. And each automaker began to face lawsuits with allegations that its small SUV was dangerously unstable.

The news media had already demonstrated their interest in the issue. In 1980, when the market segment was limited to one entry, CBS' *60 Minutes* had demonstrated how that vehicle, the Jeep CJ, could be dangerously unstable. Viewers of the program saw a CJ repeatedly rise up on two wheels as it was driven through a series of maneuvers by a robot driver. The test vehicles were fitted with "outriggers" – a set of two small wheels, one extended off each side of the vehicle on a metal arm, like a set of giant training wheels. The outriggers were high enough off the ground to allow the vehicle to rise up on two wheels but not high enough to allow it to roll over. Viewers of the program saw the Jeep CJs ride up on their sides, time after time, as they were driven through a course with some hard turns but nothing that seemed too crazy. Viewers were *not* told, however, that testers had put the Jeeps through 435 runs to get the eight rollovers featured in the piece, including a single CJ that endured 201 hell-raising runs on the same set of tires, resulting in four rollovers. Neither were viewers informed that the robot driver was able to spin the Jeep's steering wheel "at rates almost doubling that used in emergency driving while gunning the accelerator," as *Accuracy in Media* would later report.[3]

Other small utility vehicles would also come under fire. Toward the end of its production run, Ford's Bronco II came under particularly intense criticism by trial lawyers and safety advocates who petitioned NHTSA in 1989 to order a recall. They cited federal crash statistics showing Bronco II having the third-highest fatality rate among SUVs and an "avoid" rating by *Consumer Reports*, as well as being singled out by the Insurance Institute for Highway Safety as particularly worrisome. In 1990, NHTSA refused the petition, finding that the Bronco II did not have a safety defect in that it performed comparably to other vehicles in its class.[4]

Production of the Bronco II ended in early 1990 after a run of less than six years. Its replacement, developed under the code-name UN46, would be named Explorer. Early on in the UN46 program, the decision had been made to scrap the Bronco II name for the next-generation vehicle, which would have a longer wheelbase, more spacious interior, numerous refinements and a whole new marketing approach. Explorer was designed to be a family adventure vehicle, an alternative to minivans that were already losing its appeal with many buyers. The Explorer would be able to comfortably seat five people and all their gear. It would be designed for the great outdoors but be equally at home running errands in suburbia.

Was the Bronco II name dropped to distance the new SUV from a history associated with rollovers? Yes and no. While Ford never conceded that the Bronco II was rollover prone, it was clear that the company wanted a new name for the UN46 that would help position it as a new vehicle with a different mission than its predecessor. Explorer's marketing would target young professionals with families, a larger and more affluent customer base than the entry-level customers who had bought the Bronco II. The marketing staff understood that more and more family buyers would turn away from minivans if they were given a more desirable alternative. Minivans were the kind of vehicles parents with several children drove because they had to; the Explorer would be a vehicle its buyers truly desired. In marketing lingo, Explorer would be "aspirational," which to an automaker meant "lucrative." As it turned out, there would be an added benefit to the new marketing strategy – young professionals with families would tend to be more experienced and conservative drivers who would get into fewer serious accidents, leading to a better safety record for the Explorer and fewer lawsuits for Ford.

Explorer was an immediate hit, doubling internal sales projections. Ford had sold 130,000 or so Bronco IIs a year; Explorer was soon selling better than 400,000 a year. Unlike the Ranger and Bronco II that followed other competitive vehicles into their segments, Explorer was clearly out in front of anything on the market, as a mid-sized SUV and as a family vehicle that families could get excited about. Ford Explorer quickly became the best-selling SUV in the world and has held that title ever since. It also far exceeded its profit goals. The marketing strategy proved spot-on; Explorer demonstrated that an SUV could be an aspirational vehicle. Customers piled on the option content. A powerful optional V-8 model easily outsold the base V-6. The 4x4 model outsold the standard two-wheel-drive version. Over the years, top-end Explorer models were added – first the Eddie Bauer trim level and then the Limited edition as well. Explorer was Ford's cash cow, and likely the most profitable vehicle in the world.

The secret of Explorer's success was how well it used toughness to convey its aspirational appeal. It was muscular and capable both in its engineering and in its presentation. Every visible component on the

Explorer was designed to evoke a spirit of adventure. Not a rugged and rustic sort of adventure in a crude "hunting vehicle" like the big Ford Bronco, but a modern, comfortable sort of adventure in a vehicle that was tough and capable but could come with leather bucket seats and a sweet-sounding stereo. Even Explorer's tires had to fit that image. Ford's marketing team insisted on an aggressive tread pattern to look like an off-road mud-and-snow tire yet deliver the ride and handling properties of an all-season, on-highway tire. Firestone designed the ATX (and subsequently, ATX II) tire to feature a deep undercut on the tire's "shoulder" to provide strong visual emphasis to the mud-and-snow type tread pattern. The tires would look mean and aggressive, but at the 26 psi recommended pressure level, they would help soften the Explorer's ride. The young professional families buying Explorers wanted a spirit of adventure, but they didn't want to sacrifice comfort along the way.

Lesson Learned: A well-executed, authentic brand adds real value to the base product. Customers were willing to pay a premium for a high-end Explorer compared with more utilitarian alternatives. Although they seldom would drive Explorer off-road, they placed a high value on its spirit of adventure. Customers weren't "tricked" into paying more for Explorer's brand promise with fancy marketing. They bought into that promise and found it to have lasting appeal – Explorer owners were among Ford's most loyal customers.

* * *

Six hours after we had arrived in the D.C. office, most of us were still sitting in the conference room. Even more antsy than the rest of us, Jason declared we needed to break for dinner. It was nearly 11 o'clock and we were indeed hungry. Helen and Tom opted to head back to the hotel. Vines, Zino, a couple of lawyers and I, headed over to a Thai restaurant. Soon after we received our entrees and made quick work of them, I excused myself from the group to go over to the hotel where I worked on the Q&A on my laptop until 1:30 a.m.

When I walked into the Washington office five hours later, Helen and Tom already were seated at the conference table nearly finished with what I assumed was their first cups of coffee.

65

"Hey, Jon, this Q&A is well done, very thorough," Baughman said to me as I slipped my computer bag's strap off my shoulder.

"Thanks, Tom, but let me give you an even better draft," I said, telling him of the revisions I had made in my hotel room while my stomach had attempted to digest the Thai food.

Then I discovered three problems. My computer refused to open the disc with the latest changes. "Warning: Corrupted Disc," read the words on the screen like some bad dream. The second problem was that I had made the rookie mistake of not saving the last version to the hard drive as well as the disc. And the third problem was that no one had informed either of the secretaries in the Washington office that we needed them to report extra early. As a matter of fact, one office assistant would be on vacation that day and the other wouldn't arrive until nine o'clock, just thirty minutes before the beginning of the most highly anticipated business news conference of the year.

Lesson Learned: Back important documents up! *This also is so fundamental, I'm embarrassed to include it. But Murphy's Law is real, so be prepared for the computer freeze and the corrupted disc (or lost memory stick). Oh, and the jammed copier. And, for gosh sakes, make sure everyone on the team knows when you need them to report.*

I tried to pull through some of the more important changes I could remember, but time was running out. I printed out a final draft and enlisted help from whomever I could find to print out 20 copies of the lengthy document. Naturally, because we were operating without an office manager, the copier jammed. Then it ran out of paper and none of us knew where the paper was. We settled for three-hole-punch paper and resumed copying. After this incredibly painful comedy of errors, we passed out the Q&A for final review.

Just a few minutes later, it seemed, it was time to head over to the National Press Club. Three limos carried the Ford team off. Except for me. I was still trying to track down one more piece of information and told them not to wait for me. The National Press Club was only two and a half blocks away and I preferred a brisk walk to clear my head. I was disappointed when I bounded out of the building onto the "I" Street sidewalk and was not at all refreshed by the air outside. It wasn't even 8:30 but the air was already growing heavy with humidity.

It was going to be one of those unbearably sticky hot Washington days.

The Ford teams and the Firestone teams huddled in separate sides of the massive green room at the Press Club, like two football teams in their respective locker rooms before the big game. Periodically, one or another of us would go over and talk to the Firestone group, or one of tire maker's people would mingle with us. But by and large we stayed apart. Then as show time drew near, the executive participants from both companies met together for a final pre-conference discussion. Vines, Zino and I sought out our counterparts from Firestone's Public Affairs, and I suppose the lawyers and government relations people from both companies met together as well. The only thing missing was a coin flip.

In the public relations huddle, we began to discuss final logistics, particularly how we would handle the inevitable "scrum" – the free-for-all of media questions that immediately follows the end of a formal press conference. The Firestone PR people didn't understand what we were asking and seemed unable to provide any information in the absence of direction from their leader, Christine Karbowiak, who had her back to us as she applied her lipstick.

I slipped into the main room of the press club where an over-flow crowd of media jostled each other for the best sightlines to the podium at the front of the room. On the riser in the back of room, at least 40 television camera crews prepared for the start of the press conference. At least that many still photographers sat or kneeled in front of the rows and rows of chairs filled with hundreds of journalists. Others stood in the back and on both sides of the room. They were getting restless for things to start. And they smelled blood.

Shortly before the news conference started, the journalists were given the press releases from the two companies. Firestone's release announced the recall and included several quotes from Gary Crigger, Firestone's executive vice president - Business Planning, taken directly from the comments Gary Crigger would soon read to the gathered media. Crigger was a curious choice to lead the news conference; he was neither the most senior Firestone executive in North America nor the best communicator. And he had a distressing, almost sinister, habit of frowning under his long, black moustache and scrunching his thick eyebrows as he listened to a difficult question.

67

(When we returned to Dearborn, Jason would refer to Crigger as "Snidely Whiplash," after the arch-villain in the old Dudley Do-right cartoon series.) From what Christine had told us on the conference call, we were sure she hadn't had a lot of willing volunteers to choose from.

Ford's news release emphasized the company's support for Firestone's actions and its solidarity with its largest tire supplier. There was no hint of the cracks in the two companies' relationship that would widen to a gaping fissure in subsequent weeks. "Ford Motor Company has worked closely with Firestone to thoroughly investigate tire tread separation concerns," the statement began. "As we have repeatedly stated, we are absolutely committed to doing the right thing to protect our customers and to maintain their trust."

Next the statement provided assurance that the population of tires being recalled would be adequate to protect customers' safety, though we couldn't say that it would capture every single Firestone tire prone to separation. An analysis of claims data "indicates that tires being recalled today account for the overwhelming majority of tread separation failures reported on Firestone tires ... we are satisfied that Firestone has isolated the affected population of tires that should be recalled..." Unfortunately, Firestone had not agreed to release any of the data on number of claims or failure rates per million tires, so these assertions were left to stand on their own.

The statement noted that NHTSA had not yet finished its investigation, and as such could not order the recall. So technically Firestone was initiating a "voluntary tire replacement program." We went out of our way to compliment Firestone for acting in the interest of its customers' safety: "We strongly support Firestone in its voluntary recall and customer satisfaction actions. Firestone has long been, and continues to be, a valued supplier to Ford."[5]

Karbowiak walked up to the lectern and five executives took seats at a dais to her left. Crigger would be supported by John Lampe, another Firestone executive vice president (who would later become the company's most visible executive leading the recall); and Bob Martin, the former quality assurance executive who had retired in April, shortly before NHTSA opened its formal investigation of the tires, and remained on the payroll as a "special consultant."

The three Firestone execs were joined on the dais by Ford's Baughman and Petrauskas. Karbowiak welcomed the media and explained how questions would be answered after Crigger's opening statement. "I would thank you very much for your attendance and for your attention, and now I'd like to introduce Mr. Gary Crigger," she said.

Then Crigger announced what would eventually become the largest tire recall in history:

> First, let me say that at Bridgestone/Firestone nothing is more important to us than the safety of our customers. That's why the reports of vehicle accidents involving our tires are very disturbing.

> Today, in the interest of safety and to help strengthen customer confidence, Bridgestone/Firestone is taking the extraordinary step of announcing a voluntary recall of all P235/75/R15 Firestone radial ATX and ATXII tires produced in North America, including Mexico. To ensure that we are completely addressing our customers' concerns, we are taking the additional step of voluntarily recalling all of Firestone Wilderness AT tires in the P235/75/R15 size produced specifically at our Decatur plant in Illinois.[6]

As soon as Crigger finished, a female reporter standing next to a camera crew shouted out the first question, interrupted haltingly by Karbowiak who hadn't yet announced that questions would be entertained. But the TV reporter persisted, reading her lengthy question from a notepad because, as the *American Journalism Review* would later note, "she was so full of adrenaline she had to write her question down."[7] She was Anna Werner, the investigative reporter from Houston's KHOU who could deservingly take credit for breaking the tire separation story back in February. "To both companies," she stammered, "You've been quoted in reports saying you began investigating the problem in May. Prior to our February 7 report, when we called you with about two dozen lawsuits, did you not investigate then?"[8]

Crigger ignored Karbowiak's continued protestations to Werner and attempted to answer the question. But he got all tangled up. Lawsuits weren't always indications of problems, he said. They could be sometimes. But sometimes they were, uh, often ill-founded; there were many causes of tire failures, he said. Firestone was acting now to restore "customer confidence." His meandering answer did not bode well for the rest of the news conference for two companies on trial in an unruly court of public opinion. Werner had regained her composure and interrupted Crigger to finish her question, which was as much about playing to one of the KHOU cameras as well as grandstanding to the room of other reporters as it was about getting an answer. "...after we documented more than two dozen death claims and lawsuits nationwide, did you not start investigating then?" she asked. "Even if you had not noticed the list of lawsuits, certainly that was notification of at least two dozen accidents across the country?"[9]

Crigger answered: "We investigate every accident, and every incident, and in the preponderance of those accidents we find that damage coming to the tire from outside is the cause of a failure. So, yes, we investigate every incident."[10]

Then Helen Petrauskas stood up and walked to the podium, following her instinct to help a wounded colleague. Helen was in many ways the ideal spokesperson for a crisis: soft-spoken, yet tough as nails; both a lawyer and an engineer, she was intelligent and credible; a frail grand-motherly woman with a gentle demeanor, she was empathetic of the accident victims and a sympathetic character herself.[*]

Petrauskas would be described in a glowing feature in *American Woman Motorscene* later that year as a "brilliant scientist turned

---

[*] *The author's bias is evident here; a gushing description of the Ford spokeswoman undeniably at odds with the harsh assessment of Firestone's Crigger, but clearly she was the more convincing and likable spokesperson. We were blessed with a one-of-a-kind spokesperson in Helen Petrauskas, or so we thought. When she retired in December 2000, Ford hired Sue Cischke away from Daimler-Chrysler and found another gem cut from the very same cloth. Ford's new vice president – Environmental and Safety Engineering, Cischke was a bright and charming lawyer-engineer executive who like Petrauskas before her could speak empathetically about the accident victims in one moment and sharply rebut a false accusation in the next. Helen Petrauskas died March 8, 2006 of heart disease. She was 61.*

lawyer (who) has succeeded in the emotionally charged arena of environmental and safety debate, regulation and litigation with a fundamental belief that clear reasoning can overcome confrontation." Petrauskas, the story continued, had built "unprecedented cooperation with calm words, and always with consideration for the interpersonal side of even the most technically complex issues." [11]

When she reached the microphone, Petrauskas looked at Werner directly, ignoring for the time being the sea of other reporters and camera crews:

> *Let me answer your question. Actually, we first became involved in an investigation of tire tread allegations probably in the summer of 1999. And it actually happened outside the United States, and what we were getting were anecdotal reports of people taking sport utility vehicles, loading them up very heavily, deflating the tires, and taking them out for riding around in the desert, and then getting back on the highway, and then reporting tread separation. We also had anecdotal evidence of some maintenance concerns.*
>
> *In any case, we started the investigation, I believe in Saudi Arabia... then decided to look at other countries with very hot climates. Right about the time you ran your program, what we were doing together with Firestone was an investigation in the Southwest of this country, and what we actually did is we had vehicle owners come in, and those that had very high tread usage, we exchanged tires with them, so we could take those high-use tires back to the laboratory and investigate them.*
>
> *When we looked at those tires, what we did not find was evidence of the kind of tread separations we were seeing outside of the United States. So really, from about last summer on, continuing on until today, we have had a very, very vigorous investigation under way.[12]*

Media questions continued, most directed at Firestone. Crigger answered for the tire company, occasionally deferring to Lampe.

Petrauskas and Baughman responded to questions directed to Ford, or when Crigger asked for their additional comment on a question he had answered. The tone of the questioning was fiercely skeptical and there seemed no end to the journalists' appetite for answers, or at least for quotes.

After perhaps 45 minutes, Karbowiak announced that the next question would be the last. Moderating a major news conference is a fine art, and perhaps the most difficult decision is when to end it. Ending it too abruptly can give the impression that the moderator is afraid things aren't going well and may deteriorate further, or that the company has something to hide; let it go on too long and things indeed *will* deteriorate. With the executives beginning to whither under the unrelenting questioning yet with many journalists' hands still raised, Karbowiak made the call to end it. Predictably, this cued the journalists to rush forward around the executives as they attempted to exit the room. Many journalists save their best questions for these "scrums" – wanting as few of their competitors as possible to over-hear their questions and possibly guess what brilliant story lines they're developing. Lacking opportunities for one-on-one interviews, a scrum offers the next best opportunity for a journalist's semi-exclusive access to information or a quote. And it has the added bonus of occurring after a draining news conference when executives will often let down their guard. The trick to managing a scrum is to have the executive briefly and confidently answer a few questions before excusing himself or herself and leaving the room. The PR person must not only listen to the questions and the executive's responses, making note of any questions that require a follow-up call (for example, if a fact or figure is requested that the executive cannot readily recall), but also ensure that the executive's exit path is not sealed off. The Firestone and Ford PR people did the best we could sheparding our executives away from the room, then returned to talk to some journalists still remaining, again taking requests for information that the reporters needed to complete their stories. This was also an opportunity to gauge how well things had gone, whether our key messages were resonating or not, and whether our adversaries' continuing accusations were gaining or losing traction.

When I returned to the pressroom, I saw a clean-cut young man being interviewed by the KHOU television crew, with two other TV crews cued up to be next. I stepped closer to listen in. He was Sean Kane, the co-founder of Strategic Safety, a plaintiff attorney resource center in Washington – the "safety consultant" to plaintiff attorneys who months later would be quoted in Keith Bradsher's scathing *New York Times* story admitting to withholding information from NHTSA. I was familiar with the acid flavor of Kane's accusations against automakers but had never seen him in person, and I was struck by how young he was – probably in his late 20s but looking more like a high school upperclassman. He was berating Firestone and Ford for not providing any detailed information on how the population of tires to be recalled had been determined. Without this information, how did the public know that dangerously defective tires would not still be on the road after the recall? Specifically, he asked, why hadn't Firestone included the 16" Wilderness tires that had also been fitted to Explorers and were the same size tires that Ford had replaced in Saudi Arablia?[13]

I walked away from Kane's impromptu news conference and headed toward the back of the room where Jason was talking to three young female reporters. He introduced me to the women, all of whom as it turned out I had spoken to by phone but never met. Dina El Boghdady was a Washington-based correspondent for the *Detroit News*. Cindy Skrzycki wrote for the *Washington Post*. And Nedra Pickler was a Washington reporter for the *Associated Press*. Three unique and memorable names for three bright and ambitious reporters who would write some of the most thoughtful and balanced stories during the long ordeal ahead. I would establish a good working relationship with each of them, frequently speaking to them early in the development of a story, something I always appreciated. I believed I earned their respect as well. Each of them would gain confidence in me as someone who could be relied on to provide truthful and helpful information to weigh along with whatever they were hearing from the plaintiff attorneys and their "safety advocate" shills.

Lesson Learned – Establish a solid professional rapport with the journalists who will shape the coverage of your crisis and set the tone other journalists will follow. *Provide insight that will be genuinely useful to the journalist as early as you can to help shape the story. Some of that direction may necessarily have to be offered "off-line" as "background" – that is, the reporter cannot attribute the in-*

formation to you or even to an unnamed person from your company or organization, depending on the ground rules you strike with that reporter for that particular story. The point is you can't establish these ground rules if you don't have a mutually trustworthy relationship with the journalist. And you simply cannot be effective in managing crisis communications if you are afraid or unwilling to work stories on background. There are too many situations requiring delicate handling beyond what you can say with your name attached to it. (Remember in media training, how you tell your executives never to go on "background?" That's for them. You're the professional communicator; different rules apply.) Nobody said crisis communications was for the faint of heart.

CHAPTER FIVE

MEDIA FEEDING FRENZY

"It is a very frenzied situation out there."
- *Chuck Sinclair, Goodyear's director - public relations, Aug. 10, 2000, on demand for replacement tires to help Firestone complete its recall. Orders for 15" Goodyear tires were up 2,500 percent since Firestone announced the recall the previous day, he said.*[1]

* * *

A cacophony of sounds filled the executive office in Ford's Washington Office Wednesday evening. The Public Affairs team was in its element. Coverage of the recall on every network and cable news station played on a bank of many small televisions. We scribbled on notepads and talked on our cell phones, answering some of the same questions over and over, and some new ones as well. As editors read over the stories the reporters had filed, they invariably identified a missing piece of information or raised a question that couldn't be answered in the newsroom. We had to be accessible by cell phone well into the night. By this point we had a very good command of the many related historical facts and figures or had them close at hand.

The next morning's papers all carried Page One "above the fold" stories with similar banner headlines: "Massive Tire Recall," "Recall Targets 6.5 Million Tires," and the like. Some were more original, such as the *Wall Street Journal*'s "Firestone Tire Recall Wears Out Retailers." Most of the coverage used the 6.5 million number that Firestone and Ford had highlighted in releases and statements – referring to the estimated number of tires that were still in use out of the 14 million-plus tires that were actually subject to Firestone's recall. Most of the tires from the early- and mid-'90s, of course, had worn out through normal driving and had long since been replaced. But 6.5 million was still a huge number of tires that needed replacing and much of the coverage talked about overwhelmed dealers and tire retailers soon to be over-run by customers demanding replacements.

Completing the recall would take more than a year, perhaps 18 months, Firestone had conceded in the press conference Q&A. The recall would be completed in phases, beginning with four hot climate states – Florida, Texas, Arizona and California – where the majority of the tread separations had occurred. Then a second tier of states with the next-most separation accidents would get replacement tires. Finally, in a year or so customers in the rest of the nation would get their tires replaced.[2] Though logical and necessary, the phased nature of the recall caused an immediate uproar among customers in states that would not get replacement tires immediately, and the issue would become a major bone of contention at Congressional hearings the following month.

There was another problem, which amazingly, no one from Firestone or Ford had identified before the news conference. The recall included all Firestone 15" (the measurement of the inside diameter of the tire) ATX and ATX II – the tread separation claims rate for these tires had been relatively high for every year they were manufactured and regardless of manufacturing location. ATX and ATX II were brand names clearly identified on the tires, as was the tire size – P235/75/R15 – denoting the 15" tires in question. But the recall also included 15" Wilderness tires that were manufactured at the Decatur plant, but not 15" Wilderness tires made at any other Firestone plant. The Decatur-built Wilderness tires, in fact, had the highest claims rate in the Firestone data that Ernie Grush's team had analyzed. But here was the question that none of us had thought to ask – how were customers supposed to know where their tires had been manufactured?

It turned out the each tire plant stamped its unique two-letter designation on every tire it built. But for reasons no one could explain, this plant code was stamped on the opposite side of the tire as the rest of the lettering. So with the tire mounted on a vehicle, a customer would have to crawl under the vehicle, probably needing a flashlight, to read the embossed black letters on the black tire wall facing in.

Some customers undoubtedly would jack up their vehicles to get a better look – but the two companies certainly didn't want to encourage customers to raise their vehicles on a teetering jack and then crawl under the vehicle to get a better look at the hard-to-read lettering. Asking millions of customers to crawl under their vehicles was not a good idea. But asking them to bring their vehicles in for a free inspection was problematic – Ford dealers and Firestone retailers already were besieged with customers demanding replacement tires.

And then, we learned of a nasty little ironic twist that under other circumstances might have been funny: the two-letter code for tires built at Decatur was "VD." (Naturally, it *was* funny to Jason. He began referring to the Decatur plant as "Syphilis.") As if the workers at Firestone's Decatur plant weren't already feeling the butt of a horrible joke, the plant's VD designation had become the new scarlet letters of the tire industry.

No one knew why the Decatur-built tires were especially bad actors, but questions were being asked about a long, rancorous strike there in the mid-'90s. "The low, sprawling Bridgestone/Firestone Inc. tire factory (in Decatur) has become the epicenter of one of America's worst controversies involving a product recall," began a story in the *St. Louis Post-Dispatch*. "The theory making the rounds is that either angry union members or incompetent replacement workers in a bitter 1994-'95 strike are to blame for some of the highway tragedies." Workers at the Decatur plant rejected those "theories" and felt betrayed that their company hadn't come to their defense. Those quoted in the story said they suspected that the plant's hourly workforce was being made, in the reporter's words, "scapegoats for global corporate bosses facing a public relations nightmare. If the cause isn't the workmanship, after all, then it may be the tire's design. That would strike at the core of the [tire] company's existence."[3]

In the *Los Angeles Times*, Myron Levin described the tension at the Decatur plant:

> *Embarrassed plant workers and union representatives say they have been unjustly stigmatized. They say they follow the same designs and specifications as other Bridgestone plants. And they say the company hasn't shared the data on which the conclusion is based....*

> *It has also kindled hushed speculation about possible links between the tire problem and a bitter strike in 1994. Inexperienced replacement workers filled many jobs at the plant, and the dispute wasn't fully resolved until a new contract was signed in 1996 – about the time the Decatur plant began making some of the tires that are being recalled....*

> *But some workers speculate that if there were quality problems, they may have been linked to massive turnover and inexperience in the aftermath of the strike.[4]*

Some newspapers had whole teams of reporters covering the tire mess – including both Detroit papers, the *New York Times*, the *Wall Street Journal*, the *Washington Post* and *USA Today*. Each of these newspapers had prepared a package of stories ready to be finalized when the recall inevitably came. *USA Today*'s coverage was particularly voluminous. Its August 10 package featured no less than eight stories, including "Bridgestone to take $350M charge for recall," "Slow reaction may haunt Firestone" and "Ford dealers worry about tarnished image." Another story in the newspaper's Firestone recall package was different from any other story in the hundreds of articles we had comes across, and it immediately set off red flags among the Public Affairs contingent in our Washington office that morning. The story, "In Tokyo, fingers point at Ford," had been filed by a *USA Today* reporter in Japan:

> *...several analysts in Tokyo questioned whether Bridgestone and Firestone bear responsibility for alleged safety problems with the tires. They said that Ford may be using its supplier as a scapegoat and that the problem-plagued tires may not be compatible with Ford's popular Explorer SUV.*

> *"Something is probably wrong in the match between the vehicle and tires. But it was Ford Motor that OK'd the combination. It is a carmaker's responsibility to determine what kind of tires should be fitted on which vehicles," said Noriaki Hirakata, auto analyst at Morgan Stanley in Tokyo.*

The problem "may not be in the tires," says Hiromasa Irie, analyst at Nomura Securities. "Failures have occurred only in tires applied to Ford. The failure may be due to a bad match, severe environmental factors such as unusually warm weather, and high-speed driving."[5]

The analysts obviously were repeating explanations they had heard from Bridgestone people in Japan, who had declined to comment to the newspaper on the record. That Bridgestone was blaming the Explorer in conversations with analysts in Japan was a very bad omen and we did not miss its significance.

Tensions would flare between the two companies' U.S.-based teams two days after the historic recall announcement. Just as the Ford PR team had warned, journalists began pressing to see the claims data that was the basis for the decision to recall 6.5 million tires but not to recall many millions more. The trial lawyer research group, Safety Forum, said it knew of numerous reports of 16" Firestone tires that had failed and caused accidents – so why weren't they being recalled? The employees at the Decatur plant wanted to see the claims data, too; they suspected they were getting rail-roaded by Firestone management covering up a design defect. Journalists trying to make sense of all this – and looking for the next big story – pressed for the claims data, too.

As the media requests for the claims analysis piled up, we leaned harder on Firestone to agree to release the information. Firestone stubbornly refused. The only way to show that the non-recalled tires were safe was to show how much more likely the recalled tires were to be subject to a property damage or injury claim, we argued. No, Firestone repeated without explanation. Up to this point we had made all major media-relations decisions collaboratively with the Firestone PR team, but this disagreement was testing our resolve to play nice.

Failing to deliver the data the journalists wanted, we tried to placate them with "color" for feature stories. We told the media how Ernie Grush and a small team of safety analysts had driven down to Ohio to help Firestone make sense of the mountains of data, how they had brought the reams of information back to Dearborn in their Ford Excursion and painstakingly analyzed the data using Ford's vast computer resources until they "cracked the code" and identified the bad tires. With three giant Cray super-computers in its engineering complex, Ford had more computing power than any other industrial corporation in the world except Boeing, far more than Firestone had. The Cray computers were used for complex calculations needed in product development, math models that could simulate full vehicles in motion enabling engineers and designers to fine tune development even before expensive prototypes were built for testing. "Ernie brought all that seemingly disconnected data that Firestone could make no sense of," Jason would say, "and he put it through our Cray computer and in a few days, he and his team had cracked the code."

A week or so later, we were all in the Tire Room. Ernie called Jason and me over to where one of the safety analysts was working. "See that laptop, he's using?" Ernie asked us, pointing at the dull silver-colored notebook computer on the table in front of us. "That's the so-called Cray supercomputer we've all been reading about in the papers. That's really all we used to 'crack the code.'"

Jason didn't miss a beat. "Cray computer? I never said, 'Cray computer.' I said, 'Gray computer!'"

(Ernie Grush and his team had, in fact, returned to Dearborn with reams of data. It was an enormous undertaking to manually go through the paper files and floppy discs and enter it in an orderly fashion into a series of spreadsheets. It was a big job, but separating and analyzing it didn't take much computer power.)

By the afternoon of Friday August 11, Jason couldn't stand it any longer. He called me down to his office. "Those stupid Firestone people!" he fumed. "They still won't release the claims data and now no one will believe anything they say – or we say. It's in their own best interest, and ours, if that data gets published. I've made a decision. Wait until 4 o'clock. Then I want you to fax the data summary out to the top 10 or 12 media. When you're all done, we'll tell Firestone so they aren't surprised when the stories come out."

I didn't know what to say. Firestone was going to be seriously pissed, but Jason was right, it *was* in their best interest to publish the data. So I quickly wrote out a list of those I thought were the top 12 media to send the information and showed it to Jason. He crossed out the *New York Times* off my list and added another publication. "How can we not include Bradsher at the *Times*?" I asked.

Jason grinned slyly. "No need to. I already sent it to him."

It was nearly 5 o'clock when I called Karbowiak. She hit the roof, but it was too late; the claims data was out. She told me she was angry and needed to think what should be done next. Don't go home, she said, until I call you back.

As soon as we had hung up, she must have called Jason to complain about my apparently unethical behavior. I have no doubt that Jason took the heat as the one who had made the decision. In any event, the two of them decided we would conduct a joint conference call for media the next morning, Saturday, to go through the claims data analysis. It was always a good idea to guide media through any data dump to help them understand what conclusions could be reasonably drawn. Otherwise, adversary groups would fill the vacuum with their own interpretations. I didn't mention to Karbowiak that the reason it had taken me an hour to fax a few pages to 12 journalists was that I had taken the time to walk each one through the data so they wouldn't misinterpret what I had sent them.

Then Karbowiak called me back with another request. I needed to try to undo the harm I had caused, she said. If the data had to be released, it should come from both companies jointly. Otherwise, it would look like Firestone had something to hide, she said. ("No, your refusing to release the data all this time has made it abundantly clear that you do have something to hide," was my unspoken thought.) She insisted that I call back every journalist who I'd sent the data and explain that it had been jointly released by Ford and Firestone. And so that's just what I did. But every one of the journalists I spoke to laughed when I told them Firestone had agreed jointly with us to release the data. Maybe it was in the tone of my voice as I explained that Firestone *really did* want them to have the data.

Firestone PR wasn't the only organization unhappy with our surprise Friday afternoon data drop; newspapers that didn't carry a weekend edition were more than annoyed. *USA Today* and the *Wall Street Journal* wouldn't be able to cover the story in print until Monday; the weekly *Automotive News* was even more put out because it had put to bed its next week's issue (to be published Monday) by noon Friday, so it was out in the cold for a whole week. (Of course, each of these publications had a website that would quickly reflect the news of the data analysis, but back in 2000 news websites were

81

considered poor cousins to the real deal, the print edition. The timing of our release would have been far less of an issue today.)

Thus the unbroken string of days I had worked continued that weekend, as it would the next weekend and the next, and on and on. Little did I know in the days immediately following the recall announcement, but the media feeding frenzy had just begun. My life over the next few months would consist of working on my laptop in the tire room, updating the massive Q&A with answers to the latest questions, waiting to talk to a vehicle dynamics engineer or a safety analyst to firm up another answer, waiting for my conference call with the Ford team in Venezuela, meeting with a lawyer to review the answers I had drafted, ignoring for the moment the vibration of my pager with the latest journalist's request that I would attend to once I had cleared the voicemail on my cell phone and finished up the conversation on the land line in front of me.

Every day was like that. It was draining and daunting, but it also was exhilarating. We were fighting for the company's reputation and we knew we were conducting crisis communications on a scale few ever had, and with new rules for the 21st century that we were learning in real time. And although "crisis experts" were always ready with a quote for the media criticizing our effort, we knew we were competing in a struggle in which they had no real experience. We were battling adversary groups in an instant news media dynamic, while in an uneasy relationship with a clumsy dance partner and with Congress looking over everything we did, in a crisis that kept us on the front page nearly every day for 14 straight weeks. We were rewriting the textbook on crisis management and, by and large, we were succeeding in achieving balance as we emphasized straightforward messages and vigorously disputed misleading allegations. And all the while, we knew we had the direct and constant support of our CEO, Jac Nasser.

From the beginning of the tire crisis, Nasser stayed personally involved. The leaders of every aspect of the tire effort began participating in daily reviews at 5 o'clock – meetings that were initiated two days before the recall announcement and continued literally every day, weekends included, for the next several months. (At some point in December, the meetings became weekly and would have fewer participants. But they would continue in some form well into the following summer.) Nasser presided over most of the tire meetings in the early days. He and other senior leaders would go through the same agenda each meeting, for the latest update on every facet of the recall – how many tires Firestone and Ford had replaced, how many more replacement tires we had located, how many customers had called the toll-free information line, what questions media were asking that day and what stories might we expect in the morning, and so forth.

Vines wanted the outside world to see the extraordinary steps Ford was taking every day to secure replacement tires, and to get those tires to customers, while also conducting a massive investigation into what was causing the tire failures and the rollover accidents. So he invited *Wall Street Journal* Detroit Bureau Chief Robert Simison to spend three remarkable days with us. His inside account ran on Page One Sept. 11, 2000 (the last time, as it would turn out, that September 11 would seem like any other day on the calendar):

DEARBORN, Mich. – Late every afternoon, Ford Motor Co. executives gather to review the efforts of a 500-person team they have marshaled to cope with the Firestone tire crisis. The team now occupies eight conference rooms spread across the 11th and 12th floors of Ford headquarters here. ...

Individual groups are working on logistics, data analysis, technical issues, communications, legal and governmental affairs, and customer and dealer issues.

For Ford President and Chief Executive Jacques Nasser, the damage-control effort has become nearly a full-time job that promises to make or break his career. He participates in each daily crisis meeting, even when he's out of town. He arrives armed with information gleaned from outside his usual reporting channels. He has taken to calling dealers, suppliers and even owners of Ford vehicles who have written or emailed him. He has called Ford's own customer hotlines, and those of Bridgestone/Firestone, posing as a customer. He goes online to see what people are saying about Ford in Internet chat rooms.[6]

In the daily tire meetings, Nasser pushed the team to speed up the execution of the recall. At first, Firestone had insisted that all replacement tires would be Firestones, which had led to estimates of 18 months or more to complete the recall. In the days before the recall was announced, Nasser had convinced Firestone executives to allow other tire companies to supply replacements. Our truck engineers dropped everything to evaluate dozens of potential replacement tires through Ford's rigorous protocol of testing to ensure they were fully compatible with the Explorer, evaluating limit handling (how well the vehicle could complete an extreme slalom maneuver), handling on slick surfaces, ride comfort and rolling resistance (for fuel economy). But even as additional tire brands and models were approved for use as replacements, tire shortages were causing long waits for customers who understandably worried for their safety. Nasser authorized the expenditure of pricey new tire molds for a number of competitive tire companies, an expense that an automaker wouldn't ordinarily incur, to expedite production of new tires. He also authorized a three-week shutdown of three assembly plants producing Explorers and Ranger pickup trucks, so that the tires that would have outfitted the vehicles in the foregone production run could be sent to Ford dealers for use as replacement tires in the recall.

BusinessWeek's Joann Muller summed up the extraordinary efforts Ford was making to support Firestone's recall. "The auto maker analyzed reams of data to identify the suspect tires when Firestone's own engineers couldn't," she wrote. "Then, it pushed Firestone to speed up the recall by allowing competitors' tires to be used as replacements. Ford even shut down three of its truck assembly plants, sacrificing $100 million in profits in order to free up new tires." Her story ended with a question and her own answer. "Is it enough? No matter what Ford does now, one criticism abides: It should have acted when tire problems on its vehicles first appeared overseas three years ago."[7]

* * *

The history of problems in other countries continued to haunt Ford and Firestone. And Venezuela, in particular, remained very much a hot spot. The rate of fatal accidents involving tread separations of

Firestone tires on Explorers was apparently much, much greater than in the U.S. There were about 39,000 Explorers on the road in Venezuela, just over 1/100th of the more than 3 million Explorers on U.S. roads. Yet at a time when NHTSA had counted 62 deaths in the U.S. attributed to Firestone tread separations on Explorers, the Venezuelan federal safety agency INDECU believed that more than 100 people had died in Explorer tire accidents in that country.[8]

INDECU had been investigating the roles of both the tires and the Explorer itself in the all-too-common rollover accidents in Venezuela. Ford had been meeting with INDECU, led by an investigator named Samuel Ruh, and had been frustrated with the lack of anything close to scientific precision in Ruh's investigative techniques. INDECU was a severely under-funded agency lacking testing equipment, and with accident records notoriously unreliable in Venezuela, had no ability to analyze tire failure rates in any meaningful way. Anecdotal evidence carried the day in absence of data. There were persistent rumors of bribes being paid by other interests that wanted INDECU to implicate the Explorer. It was all very tawdry, but INDECU's influence could not be ignored. The agency seemed to be headed to recommending criminal charges be filed against officials from both Firestone and Ford. And INDECU's influence reached far beyond South America. To our continual frustration, U.S. media often reported statements from the Venezuelan agency as if it was equal in credibility to NHTSA. But comparing INDECU to NHTSA was on par with comparing the "Bad News Bears" Little League team to the N.Y. Yankees – they might both play the same game but one was infinitely more sophisticated and capable than the other.

On August 29, Ford Venezuela officials met with INDECU to call again for a recall of the Firestone tires that Ford was already in the process of replacing, and to defend the design and performance of the Explorer. That same day, Ford conducted a media conference call on the situation in Venezuela, with information Zino and I had stitched together from the lawyers in the Tire Room and countless calls we had made to bilingual executives, lawyers and Public Affairs people from Ford of Venezuela. Jason Vines spoke for the company. In his opening statement, Vines noted that Ford's tire replacement program in Venezuela was about 70 percent completed, and that as the company had replaced Firestone tires, Ford engineers had cut them open to inspect for signs of tread separations. There were two startling results of these inspections, Vines said. First, an alarming number of the tires showed at least early signs of the belts coming apart – 500 times greater than the rate of failure among the Firestone tires being recalled in the U.S. And secondly, more than half of the tires cut open in Venezuela did not have the "nylon cap" that Ford had contracted Firestone to include. The nylon cap was intended to serve as extra protection against the unique rigors of the Venezuelan environment (hot temperatures for most of the year, rough road surfaces and the common practice of drivers maintaining speeds of more than 100 miles an hour for highway driving stretches of an hour or more). All the tires had been marked to indicate they included the extra ply of nylon, but fewer than half actually did.[9] Later, in individual conversations with media on background, we would point out that this "mislabeling" (as Firestone called it[10]) was either a clear indication of deceit on the part of Firestone or the company's jarring lack of quality control. Either way, we said, it didn't reflect well on the tire company, did it?

* * *

As it became evident that Ford's troubles in Venezuela were only worsening, Vines grew impatient with the flow of information from Ford of Venezuela. And he suspected that the Public Affairs people in Venezuela weren't being as assertive as he would have liked in their defense of the Explorer. But it was impossible for him to tell from such a distance. So Vines sent a trusted and experienced media relations professional, Mike Moran, to Venezuela to help ensure consistency of message and process. Moran had just been appointed director – International Public Affairs. His first assignment in the new role would be a memorable one.

Moran was greeted at the airport in Caracas by the head of Ford of Venezuela Public Affairs, Ricardo Tinoco, and a driver. It was evening. After the long flight including a lay-over in Miami, Moran was looking forward to getting some sleep. But first there was a two-and-a-half hour drive west to Ford of Venezuela's headquarters in Valencia. Tinoco pointed out landmarks passing by as dusk turned to darkness. Moran noticed that the highway had no shoulder, just a steep drop off to the right. A shorter but equally steep drop to the left led to a "V"-shaped concrete channel between the east- and west-bound ribbons of asphalt highway, designed to control water run-off in a heavy rainstorm, Tinoco said. There were no guard rails on either side of the roadway. Despite this, the driver seemed intent at maintaining a higher speed than was surely legal, although Moran didn't spot any signs denoting a speed limit.

Darkness had set in. The road began to wind in increasingly tighter turns as the highway climbed up one side of a mountain and down the other. The rhythm of the switchbacks in the road intensified when the incline grew steeper. Still, the driver maintained a brisk speed. Moran clutched the hand grip above his door as Tinoco continued to chat about the countryside, the weather, some family activities. Discussion about tires would wait until the morning.

Moran would travel this highway many times over the next two months, traveling from the Valencia Ford offices to Caracas, the capital city and media hub, and back again. He would come to learn the colorful, local nickname for the section of intense switchbacks: "La Guillotine."

Two days after he arrived in Venezuela, Moran watched a televised news conference from Caracas held by INDECU's Ruh. It was quite unlike the orderly American press events Moran was so familiar with. There were no neat rows of chairs for journalists to sit patiently during prepared remarks and a one-at-a-time question-and-answer session. Instead, Ruh stood at a lectern filled with microphones and droned on, periodically interrupted by a shouted question from one or more of a throng of hovering journalists. It was more like the "scrum" that inevitably followed a well-attended U.S. press conference. Except that microphones feeding live broadcasts captured a spirited exchange that continued for more than two hours.

It was at this news conference that Samuel Ruh first publicly raised the possibility of criminal charges being filed against Ford. The Explorer had an unsafe suspension, Ruh charged, that made it prone to rollover. No other vehicle was involved in rollover accidents in Venezuela, he said again and again, caught up in the moment and playing to the cameras. Moran had arrived at an interesting time indeed.

The possibility of criminal charges not only hung ominously over Ford's reputation in Venezuela; it represented a real danger to Ford

87

officials there. Under Hugo Chavez, the government of Venezuela was fully capable of imprisoning corporate leaders accused of unseemly behavior. The day after Ruh's news conference, judicial police arrived at the Ford headquarters building in Valencia, creating a near panic in the crisis room. For twenty minutes, visions of shackles and dark prison cells raced through Moran's mind. He wondered why he had ever agreed to come to the country at such a volatile time. Then it became evident that the police were only there to deliver legal documents unrelated to the Firestone crisis.

The Ford of Venezuela crisis team continued to work to gather data to address the accusations Ruh was raising. But there were no computer records to be analyzed, compared and put into meaningful context. Accident data had to be compiled from hand-written logs maintained by local police. Often the information was incomplete or ambiguous. Ford investigators traveled to accident sites and nearby junkyards, identifying the wrecks that had once been shiny, new vehicles. Some of the wrecked SUVs wearing the unmistakable hallmarks of a rollover crash – smashed roofs and busted-out glass – turned out to be Toyota Land Cruisers, Jeep Cherokees and Chevrolet Blazers. The investigators shot photos of each vehicle wreck they inspected. Ford officials presented copies of the photos to Ruh, so he might stop making the ridiculous accusation that the Explorer was the only vehicle involved in deadly rollover crashes. Tinoco made sure journalists had access to the photos as well.

The photos proved that the number of rollover fatalities attributed to Ford Explorers had been inflated. Still, the number of reasonably well-documented Explorer rollover crashes was far higher than one might expect given Venezuela's population of less than 40,000 Explorers. Moran's anecdotal experience from his white-knuckle drive along a treacherous highway on his first night in the country illustrated a most important contributing factor – Venezuela's lack of uniform highway safety standards. Unregulated speeds, winding highways, a lack of guard rails and steep embankments combined for an extremely hazardous environment to endure a tire blow-out or separation – no matter what vehicle one was driving.

Moran helped improve the flow of information between Ford's offices in Dearborn and Valencia. And he tried to bring more structure to Ford of Venezuela's press relations. But he also saw the value in stepping back and allowing Tinoco to respond to media in his own culturally attuned manner. Tinoco clearly had superb relationships with most of the key business writers and his patient work with them was reflected in relatively balanced media coverage.

Firestone stepped up its attacks in Venezuela against the Explorer, first with a whisper campaign to government officials and the media, and then brazenly in full page newspaper ads. Moran directed Ford of Venezuela to respond forcefully, in press backgrounders and in its own "setting-the-record-straight" newspaper ads that stressed the Explorer's safe design and reliable performance. Government officials and key journalists were invited to a rented test track near Valencia to drive Explorers to better appreciate the vehicle's handling capabilities. Company engineers prepared a stripped-down Explorer chassis, so journalists and government officials could be shown the changes Ford had made to the SUV's suspension to provide a firmer ride more appropriate to the rough road surfaces throughout Venezuela. (The company's critics insisted that the suspension changes were "proof" that Ford knew the Explorer was unsafe and was trying desperately to fix the problem.)

The importance of Moran's presence in Venezuela, he would later tell me, was to reduce discordances caused by an "echo effect" of crisis coverage in the two countries. U.S. media were keenly interested in news from Venezuela regarding Ford and Firestone. And Venezuelan media were closely monitoring the U.S. Congressional hearings and other news developments from the States. Inflammatory accusations and misinformation reported in one market would "echo" in the media of the other market unless Ford's communications teams worked diligently to guide balanced coverage and refute inaccuracies.

Lesson Learned: Each crisis "hot spot" can contribute to overall media attention that refuses to die down. *Work diligently to closely coordinate messages and to refute or temper allegations that jump from one crisis location to another. Even relatively remote media today are connected to mass media in major markets; a problem anywhere in the world can quickly become a problem everywhere in the world. Be consistent in how questions are answered in each location; frequently share Q&As and talking points. But be sensitive to cultural differences and rely on the expertise of your local team (or* *agency) to execute media and government relations consistent with the company's overall communications strategy yet in a style and tone appropriate to that location.*

Moran's stint in Venezuela lasted two months, broken twice with quick trips home to his family for three-day weekends. He would return to Valencia in May 2001 for another three weeks when tensions between Ford and Firestone erupted both in the United States and in Venezuela.

* * *

Back in Dearborn, the daily tire meeting usually lasted more than an hour, sometimes nearly two hours. Although time-consuming, it was critically important to go over the latest status of every aspect of all the work being done for the team's collective understanding. On weekends, we generally held the meeting at mid-morning and used a conference room with good acoustics so those not at work could phone in. The extraordinary circumstances called for our almost non-stop effort. We didn't complain. But when weeks turned to months and we were still going at it nearly 24-7, there were times when it did become too much.

I remember one of those times very clearly. I was sitting in my Ford Explorer parked behind a junior high football field talking on my cell phone as a Saturday morning conference call droned on. I could see through my windshield, in the distance, my eighth-grader son, Mike, run out on the field to be part of the opening kickoff coverage team. My cell phone back then didn't have a mute feature, so I had to stay in the quiet inside my Explorer to participate on the call. But my son's football game had begun and I didn't want to miss it. I stepped out of the SUV and started walking toward the grandstand, holding the phone up to my ear with one hand while I tried to cover with the thumb of my other hand the little hole on the phone where the microphone was. I didn't want to have to explain to Nasser and half a dozen VPs why they suddenly were hearing cheering sounds on their conference call. But then I looked up to see that the offensive unit was on the field and my son was in the huddle. For the first time that fall, Mike was in the starting lineup. Suddenly, I no longer cared that much

90

about tires. I knew Vines and Zino were on the call and I wasn't on tap that meeting to report out on anything. So I hung up. Hung up on Nasser and the other VPs and on all the worries and concerns in the Glass House that day. Soon enough I would be back in the fray but for now my whole attention was riveted on the grass field in front of me.

Lesson Learned: If a crisis drags on, provide relief for everyone on the team. Times of crisis call for big sacrifices in work-life balance. But we all need to get away from it periodically.

* * *

Another memory from that blurry patch when time spent working dominated days and nights, weekdays and weekends: A Sunday, I had taken my family to early Mass, so I could participate on the tire call, then we had loaded our four boys up in our minivan for whatever activity we had going on that day, probably a soccer game. But the tire call ran long, as it so often did. Rather than pack everyone up and have my wife Mary drive while I sat in the passenger seat with my right thumb serving as a mute switch, I decided to send her on with three of our kids. My sixth-grader son, Timmy, and I would catch up later in my Explorer.

But the subject of the call turned to our unhappiness with a piece Lisa Stark had reported on for ABC News. I don't remember the particulars except that we had made our case to an executive producer and ABC had agreed to interview a Ford executive for a follow-up piece which would include more of our side of the issue. On the conference call we weighed our options and decided that Tom Baughman and John Rintamaki, an executive vice president and Chief of Staff, would go on camera and I would represent Public Affairs and see that it all ran smoothly. We would have to get to the studio of ABC's Detroit affiliate Channel 7 in an hour and a half. I needed to leave right away for the Glass House to meet up with Rintamaki and Baughman before heading up to the studio in Southfield, 20 minutes or so to the north of Dearborn. I called my wife and told her there had been a change of plans. Timmy and I jumped in my Explorer and headed to Dearborn. We met up with the others in Rintamaki's executive office, talked a bit about what they would say; then we took the

91

executive elevator to the WHQ basement garage and jumped in Rintamaki's Lincoln Town Car. Rintamaki drove, with Baughman riding shotgun and General Counsel John Mellen, Timmy and me in the spacious back seat. Rintamaki joked with my son and seemed pleased to have him join in our impromptu mission. Timmy was quiet and well-behaved and a little bit curious about what a TV station would be like. But he discovered that mostly there was a lot of waiting around. Whatever we were intent on telling ABC's national audience seemed rather boring to him so he tuned us out and read a football magazine.

* * *

Mike Vaughn, the Public Affairs manager in charge of Ford Customer Service Division, handled more media calls than any of us during the Firestone recall, more than 100 nearly every day. At the beginning, it was completely his responsibility. If the tire recall had been more like the other recalls Mike handled, the senior leaders in Public Affairs would have been only passively involved. As a member of the FCSD operating committee, Mike was constantly involved in the routine work of gathering information about customer problems and accidents, looking over reports of investigations and evaluations – and after a fix to a problem had been identified, the supply of replacement parts located and a recall approved by NHTSA – notifying the media of the specific details of the recall and answering journalists' questions.

But the Firestone tire mess would be no ordinary recall. When NHTSA opened a formal investigation in May 2000, Vaughn began handling the media communications, assisted by Susan Krusel, the Public Affairs manager for legal matters, who had worked with Werner on the KHOU story back in February. Vaughn and Krusel periodically took calls from television and print media working on stories about tread separation accidents throughout the spring and summer. When Ernie Grush briefed senior management of his team's preliminary findings from the Firestone data dump in late July, it became clear that senior Public Affairs leaders needed to work closely with Ford Truck management, the lawyers, FCSD leaders and all the others who would be needed to guide what was shaping up to be a major effort.

Later, Vaughn would confide to me that he and Krusel had at first bristled when Vines, Zino and I began taking an active role in managing the crisis. "Now that this is getting interesting," he had grumbled, "the super-heroes have parachuted in. They'll be there for the TV cameras and then drop it all back in our laps when they get bored with it." He mentioned this to me several months later after we had spent countless days and nights in continual crisis mode, working well together and somehow keeping up with each new day's onslaught of media inquiries. By then he could share the story with a laugh as it became evident that the "super-heroes" were working at least as hard as anyone and had no intention of leaving the project until our job was done.[*]

We divided the media inquires in this fashion: I would handle the bulk of questions that were technical in nature – concerning the engineering decisions made during the development of the Explorer, about the vehicle's driving dynamics, about tire construction and other questions related to product development and current product performance. Zino, an engineer by training who had come to Ford from *Road & Track* magazine where he'd been editor, gave me considerable direction and also handled many of these technical questions. Once we understood an issue thoroughly and had handled the immediate inquires about it, I added it to the Q&A so others could answer further questions on that issue in a consistent manner. Periodically, Zino or I would huddle with Mike and Susan to explain the intricacies of an issue and how the question should be answered again and again in the days after it first surfaced. So much of the media was playing catch-up to the few major players who were breaking most of the new angles to the continuing crisis. (As soon became evident, most of these enterprising new stories were spawned by the nearly daily appearance of a new, enticing document leaked by plaintiff attorneys and their resource groups like Strategic Safety.)

---

[*] *Mike would later serve as the Ford Public Affairs manager for Technology. He died suddenly in August 2004 of heart failure, too young, with so much living still to be done. Those of us who worked (and played golf) with Mike miss his friendship, his professionalism and his biting sense of humor.*

Vines was deeply involved as well, staying abreast of every development and giving us overall direction in handling the media feeding frenzy. He also made a point of talking to the most prominent media every day, answering their questions as well as taking their pulse. Vines loved the interaction with media and would feel disconnected if he went too many hours without speaking to a journalist.

Lesson Learned: The best media-relations people are those who love it. There is considerable art to media relations, both in brokering a positive story placement and arguing persuasively for a corporate viewpoint to be included in a negative story. Media-relations junkies love the thrill of the interaction. They develop strong rapport with a large number of journalists important to their company or cause. Rapport is built on mutual respect, honesty and a keen insight into what makes each journalist tick.

* * *

The blanket coverage, featuring so much criticism and second-guessing, was confusing our customers, our employees and our dealers. So we knew it was critical to communicate directly to each of these groups. We authored emails for Nasser to send to employees and dealers. Fact sheets with simple illustrations and graphs explaining Ford's thinking on contentious issues around the tire crisis and the Explorer proved such a hit with dealers that we reprinted many thousands more for our employees and for dealers to give to customers who wanted more information. Marketing and Public Affairs worked together to produce newspaper ads that helped explain to customers how to tell whether the tires on their vehicles were subject to the recall. Firestone followed with newspaper ads of its own.

In addition to explaining which tires were subject to the recall, both companies' ads were intended to reassure those customers with tires not subject to the recall that their vehicles were safe. But sometimes events conspired against the companies, undermined the messages. Ford ran full-page ads in major newspapers around the country Sunday, August 13, stressing the safety of Firestone tires not subject to the recall. That same day in Florida, two different Explorers, each equipped with Firestone Wilderness AT tires that were not part of the recall, suffered tread separation accidents that resulted in significant damage to the vehicles but no injuries. Despite the fact that no one was hurt in either accident, CNN *Headline News* featured the wrecks in national broadcasts repeated every half hour throughout the day. The news reports included a sound bite from "safety expert" Ralph Hoar (founder of the trial lawyer resource group *Safetyforum*): "They're still handling it as though it's just the Decatur plant, and it's just the 15-inch tires," Hoar said. "They should recall 16-inch tires."[11]

Nasser also was featured in television commercials the company made to get its messages out to customers. The idea was to use the high-impact medium to underscore how seriously Ford's senior management was taking its responsibility to safeguard its customers. In a spot that ran repeatedly on the networks the last week of August, Nasser noted that more than one million tires had been replaced and he assured viewers that Ford was going to extraordinary lengths to speed the completion of the recall: "That's good progress, but it's not good enough," Nasser said in this thick Australian accent. "We now have commitments from other tire manufacturers, including Goodyear, Michelin and Continental, to double their capacity and help make replacement tires available sooner."[12]

The message was well-scripted, but the TV spots did not live up to their promise. The hastily filmed commercials seemed designed more to please Nasser's considerable ego than to communicate to customers a sincere sense of empathy and compassion. The rather diminutive executive was filmed in an exquisitely tailored Saville Row suit standing on the steps of the staircase that connected the two executive floors at the top of the Glass House. Nasser's regal presence and his Aussie accent did not connect well with the majority of Ford's American customers.

"I admire Jac as a leader but his Australian accent and the fact he did these TV spots in his building aren't as effective as they could have been if the company chairman, named Ford, had done them at a Ford dealership," one anonymous dealer told *Ward's Auto Dealer*. Other dealers agreed that the well-liked Bill Ford would have been a better choice to feature in the ads, but according to an unnamed Ford spokesman quoted in the article, Bill Ford believed that Nasser "would be more credible doing the commercials and appearing at Congressional hearings because of his expertise in technical matters and his operational role."[13] Left unsaid was the clear implication that Bill Ford was glad to keep some distance from the increasingly nasty tire mess.

* * *

Not surprisingly, the tire crisis became frequent fodder for the late night television comedians. Jay Leno joked about the "Tombstone" tire brand. Another night he said Firestone was running a huge new tire promotion, "a blow-out sale." Then he showed a home video of a boy happily swinging back and forth on a tire hanging from a rope. When the tire suddenly exploded, the "Tonight Show" studio audience erupted in raucous laughter. Leno kept hammering away night after night, going for easy laughs at Firestone's expense. "This Firestone recall is huge," he said. "It's hitting everyone. Cubans are now switching to Michelin tires to float with. Police are saying that if you do have Firestone tires, it's OK if you go through red lights. It's like driving a hearse."[14]

David Letterman's Aug. 31 broadcast of CBS "Late Night" featured his list of "Top 10 Worst Jobs." Number 2 on the list was "Public relations spokesperson, Firestone tires." (Number one was "David Letterman's barber.")[15]

The Firestone tire crisis had become part of American culture. You couldn't get away from it, even the sport pages referred to it when going for a quick laugh. In October, the winless San Diego Chargers announced they would try a unique, if desperate, strategy in the first half of their next game: they would play two quarterbacks, Jim Harbaugh and Moses Moreno, on alternating series. Quipped Alex Kaseberg to the *San Francisco Chronicle*: "That should be about as effective as rotating Firestone tires on an Explorer."[16]

Although we couldn't help finding the humor in all this ourselves, we knew how destructive it would be in further eroding trust in the Firestone and Ford brands. "While Firestone's parent is vowing to stand behind the brand, the Firestone name has become monolog material for virtually every U.S. comedian, from Jay Leno to Chris Rock," noted an editorial in *Ward's Auto World*. "And this type of ridicule often is most damaging, because Ford's and Firestone's success or failure in the crisis ultimately will depend more on public impressions than facts."[17]

CHAPTER SIX

TRIAL LAWYERS SEIZE CONTROL OF THE NEWS CYCLE

"If you put Charles Manson, John Wayne Gacy and Attila the Hun in a room and ask everybody sitting in this room right now, 'Let's compare these three guys and let's decide who's the best and who's the worst,' somebody's going to be number one and some-body's going to be number two and somebody's going to be number three.

"The question you have to ask yourself with regard to the sport utility market is if you put the Explorer and the Suzuki Samurai and the Bronco II and the Isuzu Trooper and the Toyota 4Runner – if you put all those vehicles in a room, somebody's going to be the worst and somebody's going to be the best out of that group."

- Tab Turner, trial lawyer, in a PBS interview responding to a question about Ford assertions that the Explorer was among the safest SUVs on the road.[1]

* * *

Our adversaries had grown quite skilled in manipulating the media. One plaintiff attorney in particular, Tab Turner of Little Rock, Arkansas, had developed a very profitable business specializing in rollover cases and he did not hesitate to use the media to fatten his cash cow. Years earlier, Turner had taken on a number of clients who had been injured, or family members of those who had been killed in rollover accidents involving SUVs throughout the 1980s and '90s, including the Suzuki Samurai, the Isuzu Trooper and Rodeo, Jeep

99

Wrangler, Toyota 4Runner and the Ford Bronco II. In each of these cases, he alleged that the vehicle's automaker had been negligent in developing a vehicle with an unreasonable propensity to tip over in hard steering on public roads.[2]

I first encountered Turner's work when I handled Ford's media relations for legal matters. He had won a large judgment in a wrongful death case involving a 1992 rollover crash of an '87 Bronco II small SUV, the predecessor to the Ford Explorer. The accident had begun with a sudden tread separation on one of the Bronco II's rear tires; the crash killed 21-year-old Jennifer Cammack. On behalf of the girl's parents, Turner reached an out-of-court settlement with General Tire and then proceeded to play hardball with Ford. The automaker would not agree to his settlement terms and decided to take the case to trial, despite its venue in notoriously plaintiff-friendly Harris County, Texas. The jury found that Ford was negligent in the design of the vehicle, the first time the Bronco II had been found to be defective, but decided that the company had not intentionally harmed its customers. Even so, the jury awarded the plaintiffs $25 million, including actual damages of $2.5 million and $22.5 million in punitive damages (meant to punish the automaker and to discourage future malfeasance). Ford appealed; in 1995 a state appellate court judge reduced the verdict to $5.8 million (including $4 million in punitive damages),[3] and in 1998 the Texas Court of Appeals disallowed all punitive damages in the case and reduced the total award to $621,000.[4] But these appellate victories for the defense did not generate nearly the media attention as the original $25 million award, and did little to dent Turner's reputation as a formidable adversary of Ford Motor Company.

Turner cemented his credentials in auto industry litigation when he defended Consumers Union, publisher of *Consumer Reports*, in a high-profile case against Isuzu in 1996. The Japanese automaker had sued the publisher for defamation in depicting the Isuzu Trooper as dangerously unstable. In a press conference at the time of the article's publication, Consumers Union had called on Isuzu to stop selling the Trooper and to recall all of the units it had sold. Although the jury found that some of the statements by the publisher had shown a "reckless disregard for the truth," it dismissed most of Isuzu's other major allegations (including negative statements, test doctoring and stunt driving).[5] Trooper sales never recovered and the vehicle was discontinued in 2002.

Turner had developed an impressive inventory of Bronco II cases and with his success in the Cammack trial demonstrated that he had the potential to convince juries of the plausibility of his theories that Ford had knowingly produced a dangerous vehicle. Even in cases where there were major extenuating circumstances, he could hold out for large settlements from Ford. After all, in Cammack, the woman who had been killed had not been wearing a seat belt; her fatal injuries had been sustained after she was ejected in the crash. Furthermore, the vehicle contained a total of seven occupants – three more than it had been designed for.[6]

* * *

Ford introduced the Explorer in 1990, replacing the Bronco II. The larger and more stylish Explorer was an immediate hit and quickly became the most popular SUV sold by any automaker. As Turner had begun to specialize in lucrative SUV rollover cases, he began looking for victims in Explorer accidents. He would argue in legal briefs that the Explorer was simply a modified Bronco II allowing him to recycle theories that had worked so well in his Bronco II cases.

Turner, along with other plaintiff lawyers and their legal assistants, also began combing over hundreds of thousands of notes and records created during the development of the Explorer. They studiously mined this new document trail in search of a "smoking gun." They hoped to demonstrate to a jury the callous way, the lawyers surmised, that Ford engineers had hastily developed the Explorer, rushing it to market, knowing full well that safety compromises had been made in the name of quick profit.[7] This conspiracy theory was not plausible to those inside the auto industry for three reasons. One, it just was not possible to "rush a vehicle to market" and have that vehicle become a runaway hit, the No. 1 seller among SUVs of any size and from any automaker every year for the next 15 years. Two, in an era when information moves so quickly and completely, it was patently stupid to knowingly sacrifice real-world safety for some small cost reduction. And three, it ignored the fact that the Explorer's overall real-world safety record (in terms of fatalities per 100 million miles driven) was better than most of the other SUVs in its class and significantly better than the "average" passenger vehicle of any kind.[8]

But courtroom justice bears little resemblance to the empirical exercises familiar to engineers where the correct answer demonstrably prevails. The members of a jury make decisions based on their evaluation of the facts presented by both sides, for sure, but they also are swayed by emotion and intangibles, by what they feel in their hearts. At the center of every serious-injury or fatal auto accident is human tragedy, and often the victims are sympathetic characters. The jury feels sorry for the awful event that has come into the plaintiffs' lives. Then the jury hears the victim's lawyers make accusations about the large auto company with annual profits in the billions of dollars (not recently, mind you, but throughout most of the '90s Ford was immensely profitable). How else is the destitute family coping with tragic loss going to pay the medical bills? Shouldn't someone – or some company – have to pay for what's happened to them? The plaintiff attorney's objective becomes to present just enough of a plausible case to convince a sympathetic jury to award damages against a giant, impersonal company that might amount to a tiny fraction of its profits that year.

Yet, the real secret behind successful plaintiff attorneys was that they only rarely had to win in the courtroom. A successful verdict came only after a lengthy and difficult battle of wits against sharp corporate defense lawyers with vast resources. No, the secret was to create in the defense team just enough fear and doubt, and just enough uncertainty about the jury's sympathies, that the company would decide to cut its losses with a settlement offer. Accepting a settlement also took away the uncertainty from the plaintiff attorneys, who took cases on a speculative basis, collecting one-third of any verdict or any settlement. The object was to win just enough high-profile verdicts to show the deep-pocketed corporations that they could lose if they went to trial, leading to a steady flow of subsequent settlement checks. (Indeed, in 2007 Turner & Associates claimed on its website to have reached out-of-court settlements in more than 150 rollover cases involving 16 different types of SUVs manufactured by eight different auto companies. As of February 2009, the website no longer featured a running total of tragic SUV cases on its website; perhaps the firm had decided it was better to emphasize personal service, just as McDonald's had several years earlier when it stopped updating the neon signs outside each restaurant proclaiming the number of billion of hamburgers served.[9])

And as Turner came to understand better than perhaps any other plaintiff attorney, there were ways to help turn on the spigot of corporate capitulation resulting in large and frequent settlements. Ways that involved turning the tide of public opinion against the company. Tab Turner knew the best way to influence public opinion was through the mass media. And all it took to generate a juicy, inflammatory story was to leak to an ambitious journalist some of the same documents he'd been gathering for years as he spun his conspiracy stories to juries, on those rare occasions when he actually had to take a case to trial.

Turner became so successful that he had bought his own personal jet to more easily move around the country paying visits to grieving families, all the while maintaining a level of comfortable luxury befitting such a successful lawyer. Of course, the image-conscious Turner went to great lengths to down-play the money he was making and the size of his own personal fortune. He did not want anyone to wonder how an extravagant lifestyle squared with a well-developed reputation as the champion of poor, downtrodden victims of greedy, rich corporations. When Turner collaborated with writer Adam Penenberg for the rather sappy biography *Tragic Indifference: One Man's Battle with the Auto Industry over the Dangers of SUVs*, they addressed the issue of Turner's private jet by declaring that it wasn't a "flashy jet," but more like a humble "Plymouth with wings."[10] A few pages later, Penenberg reveals that the jet was actually a Cessna Citation, a sleek and modern aircraft that few of Turner's clients would be likely to confuse with a Plymouth.

* * *

Was Turner to be applauded for championing justice against the automakers and their unsafe SUVs? Wasn't every rollover accident proof of a dangerous product defect inherent in SUVs? As we have already discussed, many factors contribute to accidents, certainly including driver behavior and the effect of vehicle speed, weather and road conditions. The design and construction of the vehicle is important as well, of course. It is widely known that SUVs, because of their relatively high stance, are more likely to be involved in rollover accidents than are other vehicles. Less well-understood is that SUVs as a class are safer than most other vehicles because they tend to afford their drivers superior visibility enabling them to avoid accidents, and because their bulkiness protects occupants better in frontal and side collisions, which are far more common than rollover accidents. Ted Frank of the American Enterprise Institute for Public Policy Research describes the fallacy of isolating one component of vehicle behavior without looking at the purpose of the vehicle and its overall safety performance, in an article titled "Rollover Economics:"

> *Automakers design SUVs to have high clearance so they can traverse rugged terrain. SUVs are, in many ways, safer than conventional vehicles, in part because their larger mass provides more protection when they collide with another vehicle. (In another era, Ralph Nader complained that automobiles needed to be larger to be safer.) But these features have tradeoffs: the higher clearance raises the center of gravity of the vehicle and affects the handling. The SUV is thus more likely to tip and roll over than a conventional vehicle.*

> *Products liability law permits plaintiffs' lawyers to cherry-pick this drawback and proclaim the entire vehicle "defectively designed" even if, holistically, it is safe.... To date, politicians and regulators have elected to permit consumers to choose whether they wish to have an SUV's off-road features, even though doing so means poorer highway performance... The plaintiffs' bar, however, has turned to the courts and has sought for years to punish automakers for providing what consumers want.[11]*

*   *   *

Like any good student of public relations, Turner refined his method of placing stories in the media as he grew more experienced. He and many of the other trial lawyers hired PR firms to help them place stories in the media, but they did it quietly because they certainly did not want to be seen as corporate. By the time of the Firestone tire recall, Turner had developed excellent relationships with many journalists. A number of reporters from prominent and influential publications, notably Myron Levin of the *Los Angeles Times* and Mylo Geylin of the *Wall Street Journal*, were infamously reliant on plaintiff attorneys to bring them salacious stories of corporate wrong-doing.[12] (Inexperienced corporate PR people from every industry had made the mistake of assuming that the *Wall Street Journal*'s reporters would operate from a starting point sympathetic to Big Business. The opposite was often true. Many of the *Journal*'s reporters had a quite liberal disposition and took it upon themselves to provide balance against the paper's overtly conservative editorial page.) Turner had an almost unlimited supply of Ford and Firestone documents from years of depositions. It didn't matter that neither he nor any plaintiff attorney had ever prevailed against Ford in an Explorer rollover trial. He was making a fine living on settlement money. And it didn't matter if these documents had invariably been presented as evidence in court only to be disputed and often thoroughly discredited by Ford's lawyers. If no one had written a story yet about the document it qualified as news, along with the conspiracy theory it "proved." All he had to do was slip the document to the media hounds and watch them ratchet up the public pressure against the automaker.

An example of media behavior following the leaking of one such document demonstrates a deceptive tactic plaintiff attorneys applied over and over again in the autumn of 2000.* The attorney phones a network television reporter he knows quite well. (Let's call her

---

*Documents often are sealed by court order as mutually agreed terms of the settlement. Defendants prefer to keep documents secret to avoid embarrassment if they should become public, especially without context where their meanings can be distorted, as discussed next in the text. Less well understood is the fact that plaintiff attorneys also often want documents and settlement terms kept secret as this information can be a competitive asset for their business. Since leaking sealed documents to news media is illegal, it is done anonymously. I've no direct knowledge of Turner ever breaking the law in this manner. Therefore, throughout the rest of this section, I refer to whoever leaked the Stornant document as "the plaintiff attorney." It may, in fact, have been leaked by another plaintiff attorney, a legal assistant or a plaintiff-friendly resource group.

Sharyl.) He tells Sharyl that he has obtained new evidence that Ford knew the Explorer was dangerously unstable when the company was preparing for final signoff at the end of the vehicle's development program. But Ford went ahead anyway, he says, because profits meant more than lives to the company.

Here's the proof, he says. He has a document he has obtained from Ford in legal depositions that is full of Ford acronyms but, not to worry, he can talk the reporter through its meaning. It's coming over the fax right now. It's a note from a Ford engineer, Roger Stornant, who wrote that the company's lawyers (or OGC for "Office of General Counsel") was worried that in upcoming tests by Consumer's Union (or "CU," publisher of *Consumer Reports*), the Ford Explorer would fail stability tests with its standard tires showing it to be an unsafe vehicle. Further, the engineer worried that Ford would be the only auto manufacturer (or OEM for "Original Equipment Manufacturer" in auto industry jargon) with a vehicle that would fail this test. And most incredibly, he tells her, the note says that Ford "management is aware of the risk" of the tipping Explorer and "has accepted the risk."

Sharyl the TV journalist is naturally excited by her good fortune of being handed on a silver platter the opportunity to break a major story of such sensational nature. Sure enough, the document reads: "OGC is concerned we will be the only OEM with a vehicle that has a significant chance of failing the CU test. I believe that management is aware of the potential risk w/P235 tires and has accepted risk."[13]

The plaintiff attorney provides a few more details about the compromises the Explorer development team supposedly had to make to meet the aggressive timing and cost objectives in the program. Now the journalist has the makings of a great story. She has some good stock footage of Explorers on a test track (previously supplied by Ford) and some B-roll of mangled Explorers after recent crashes. She gets the story assigned a slot in that evening's news. In fact, the anchor may lead with it. Now she just needs to get a brief comment from Ford to complete her story.

I take Sharyl's call and listen to her describe the document and its implications. I ask her to fax me the document in question. She refuses. I ask her how I might be expected to comment on a document I haven't seen. She relents but warns me that time is running short if I want any Ford comment included in the piece. The fax arrives on one of the machines in the Tire Room. I take it to one of our lawyers who recognizes it immediately. It has been introduced in many Explorer cases, always with the same devious implications. "But ask your journalist friend why she doesn't have the whole document," the Ford lawyer says as he hands me a two-page document that certainly brings new meaning to the fragment the journalist has. "OGC is concerned we will be the only OEM with a vehicle that has a significant chance of failing the CU test. I believe that management is aware of the potential risk w/P235 tires and has accepted risk..." the document reads, exactly what Sharyl had faxed me. But the engineer's message continues onto a second page. "(the) CU test is generally unrepresentative of real world and I see no 'real' risk in failing except what may result in way of spurious litigation."[14]

Okay, now it makes sense, I say, thanking the Ford lawyer. I fax the entire document back to Sharyl the TV journalist and get her on the phone. "Your story premise is all wrong," I say. "The engineer wasn't saying that management had accepted the risk of an unstable vehicle. He was worried that the vehicle wouldn't pass Consumer Reports' unrealistic test. There's too much variability in the way a driver can take a vehicle through that test and it was widely understood to be an inferior way to determine real-world stability. So he said that he believed that management had accepted the risk of failing *this test* and that the only real risk in failing would be that it might be brought up in 'spurious litigation.' Perhaps by an unscrupulous lawyer trying to dupe an otherwise intelligent reporter."

And just as I am silently congratulating myself on having knocked down another misleading story, the TV reporter says "I don't have enough time in my story for all that. Just tell me your comment."

Now I'm losing my patience, "No, Sharyl, you aren't listening. Your story is based on a false premise. You don't have a story. You were sold a bill of goods."

But the reporter doesn't budge. "So, is that your comment?"

That's exactly how it went with TV reporters. Sharyl Attkisson of CBS was a multiple offender. She'd set a story in motion soon after she received a seemingly nefarious document (which she would invariably introduce with great fanfare: "In breaking news tonight, CBS News *has obtained* a Ford document that..." – as if it represented expert sleuthing to pick up a piece of paper off the fax machine). Once

107

the network had slotted a story for its evening news, it didn't matter if we could demonstrate that they'd been misled. My protests were of no avail; the story was going to run with or without Ford's sound bite. (Of course, this was before the embarrassing 2004 dust-up at CBS involving Dan Rather's reporting on President George W. Bush's National Guard service based on what turned out to be a forged memo;[15] network TV reporters may be somewhat more careful to be balanced today, but you shouldn't count on it.)

If the journalist had instead been a print reporter, we'd have a better chance of killing a story that had been based on a false premise. But national print reporters, too, could be seduced by the plaintiff attorney's siren offerings of a delicious conspiracy and might refuse to let go, even after being shown the full context. I had a long debate with *TIME* magazine's John Greenwald on the Stornant document before he conceded that his unnamed source for the faxed document had clearly withheld part of it to skew its meaning. When Greenwald wrote about Stornant in a lengthy *TIME* story, he included some context, but introduced the memo in menacing terms, again misrepresenting the "risk" that management had accepted: "In a chilling aside, Stornant wrote that Ford 'management is aware of the potential risk with P235 tires and has accepted [that] risk. CU test is generally unrepresentative of the real world,' Stornant said, 'and I see no "real" risk in failing [the CU test] except what may result in the way of spurious litigation.'"[16]

For a final word on the Stornant memo[*] and the larger issue of taking old engineering memos out of their context to create whatever meaning the lawyer wants, I quote again from Ted Frank:

> *Every safety measure involves tradeoffs; every engineer-ing decision involves discussions of upsides and downsides. The litigation game is played by subpoenaing records of these discussions, searching the millions of pages of emails and documents that express thousands of ideas floated by en-gineers, and using the advantage of hindsight to characterize as the "smoking gun" the one idea eventually rejected as the*

---

[*]*Unfortunately, Roger Stornant cannot answer for himself what he meant by his memo; he died of heart failure in the early '90s.*

evidence of executive disregard for engineers' concern over safety.

Of course, if no such memo exists, one can always be generated by creative misrepresentation.... Astonishingly, [the Stornant memo] was used to justify punitive damages because it was supposedly evidence that Ford executives decided to "accept the risk" of rollovers in favor of profits. In fact, as the memo demonstrates, the engineers decided there was no real-world risk of rollovers and that the only risk was the one of "spurious litigation." (The engineer was prescient in this regard.)

The final insult: the risk identified in the memo was that of failing the artificial CU test – yet the Explorer passed that test when it was performed by Ford, NHTSA, and CU.

In litigation, however, judges' abstention from interfering in adversarial tactics makes this reality irrelevant; what matters is the game show of whether attorneys can persuade a jury to adopt their preferred reading of memos like these.[17]

Tab Turner was perfecting a new art of taking this "game show" routine from the courtroom to the newsroom.

Lesson Learned: Know your adversaries tactics. *Arguing cases in a courtroom is a ruthless game. When trial attorneys bring a mentality of "win at any cost" to public relations, they aren't going to play by the rules we're used to. Know the technical side of your story inside and out. Call out misleading tactics of your adversaries while countering their accusations with facts.*

* * *

Over the next few weeks, Ford continued to be more responsive to the media than was Firestone, and the media noticed. While we prided ourselves in returning media calls promptly and providing complete answers with intelligent, informed explanations of technical issues, Firestone did little to convince journalists that they were committed to answering their questions at all. To be fair, Firestone was not used to handling a steady volume of media calls the way Ford PR was. Ford had simply been in the news much more often than Firestone had.

Firestone had the additional burden of a Japanese parent, Bridgestone, with ultimate authority. Even the most senior Firestone execs had little power on their own. Nashville's impotence was never more evident than in an embarrassing reversal that led to Firestone's crisis public relations firm resigning in protest just before both Houses of Congress opened hearings on the deadly tire failures. The chain of events was almost stranger than fiction, beginning with an ill-advised act of defiance to NHTSA.

As the nation's top transportation safety agency, NHTSA felt extreme pressure to demonstrate that it had not been asleep at the switch while the tally of tragic accidents was growing. NHTSA sifted through Ford's and Firestone's answers to its interrogatories, and the claims analysis from Ernie Grush's team along with more up-to-date claims data from Firestone. The agency's investigators looked over accident reports sent directly to NHTSA that had begun to flow in from Texas after the airing of the KHOU report and from the rest of the country as the story increasingly found airtime on the national news. Analyzing this more complete set of data in much the same way the Ford team had in July, NHTSA concluded that another 1.4 million tires were suspect, and it asked Firestone to recall them.

Firestone refused.

NHTSA then took the extraordinary step of issuing a consumer advisory on September 1 that not only called out the questionable safety of the additional tires, but the intransigence of Firestone in not being responsive to a safety risk:

> *On August 30, 2000, NHTSA staff met with Firestone representatives in Washington and recommended that Firestone expand the recall to include [several additional Firestone] tire models. On August 31, Firestone advised NHTSA that it would not voluntarily expand the recall at this time. We are continuing our investigation, which may result*

in an order directing Firestone to recall these tires and any other defective tires. However, in view of the potential safety risk, NHTSA believes that it is important to alert the public of its concerns now. ...

Since Firestone has chosen not to expand the recall at this time, you may not be able to obtain free replacement tires from Firestone. However, in light of these concerns, NHTSA recommends that you consider replacing the tires in question and that you retain all documentation.[18]

This was harsh language coming from a government bureaucracy. Not only did NHTSA advise customers to replace the tires in doubt, but to save "all documentation" with the implied expectation that it would prevail ultimately in forcing Firestone to recall the tires and reimburse those who had replaced them ahead of such a recall.

NHTSA's dispute with Firestone over the additional 1.4 million tires put Ford in a difficult position. Since NHTSA was acting on its own analysis, we kept our public comments to a minimum, releasing a simple statement attributed to Helen Petrauskas: "We've said all along that data must drive action. The data we have has determined Ford's position and our actions. If government safety agencies have additional data, clearly that data must be considered. We stand ready to make every effort to work with all involved."[19]

As damaging as NHTSA's reprimand was to the tire maker's sinking reputation, Firestone would proceed to make things far worse for itself. Shortly after NHTSA issued its consumer advisory on Friday, September 1, Firestone issued a statement to the media saying that although most of the 1.4 million tires were old and no longer on the road, Firestone would offer to replace those tires if owners were worried about them. Back in the Glass House we all were scratching our heads. Why endure the sledgehammer blow of a nearly un-precedented comeuppance from NHTSA if you are going to go ahead and replace the tires for customers anyway?

Evidently, Bridgestone execs wondered the same thing, because on the very next day, Saturday, September 2, the Japanese parent rescinded the offer Firestone had just made. Bridgestone issued a statement from Masatoshi Ono, its chairman and CEO, saying, "If the tires are subject to our Bridgestone/Firestone warranty program, the tires will be adjusted and processed accordingly."[20] In other words, Firestone might offer partial refunds on a pro rata basis only. If the tire had only 40 percent of its tread left, the customer would qualify for a 40 percent discount on a replacement tire. That was pretty much what any tire company would do to help placate any unhappy customer. Put in an untenable position of having to explain why her boss' offer had been over-ruled by *his* boss, Karbowiak called Ono's statement a "clarification."[21]

The very next day, Sunday, brought the abrupt resignation of Fleishman-Hillard, the PR agency Firestone had hired to manage the growing crisis just eight weeks earlier. It was unheard of for a PR agency to quit a high-profile account worth a reported $2.5 million per month.[22] The only on-the-record explanation Fleishman-Hillard provided media was, "It became evident that we could no longer be of service."[23] Media could only speculate on what advice Fleishman-Hillard had offered that Firestone hadn't act on, or what other frustrations the well-respected agency had run into in its short run with the tire maker. An in-depth article on the tire crisis in *TIME* magazine included this commentary:

While Ford is expected to come out of the pileup dented by a few hundred million dollars, the 100-year-old Firestone brand could be completely totaled. Thanks to generally dreadful crisis management, marked primarily by silence and denials, the Firestone brand has very little credibility left...

As if that weren't bad enough, even Firestone's spin doctors have apparently lost faith in the company; last week, in the wake of the company's refusal to expand the recall to include an additional 1.4 million tires, its p.r. agency, Fleishman-Hillard, quit, reportedly tired of clashing with corporate lawyers. ...

From the beginning, when Firestone announced a staggered recall that would force some customers to wait months for replacements, the company's damage control has been woeful. "P.R. is a business of subtleties," says a leading crisis manager. "These guys are amateurs."[24]

Later that week, the *Wall Street Journal* featured a lengthy analysis of Fleishman-Hillard's sudden resignation, "The Perils and Potential Rewards of Crisis Managing for Firestone," clearly informed by knowledgeable sources within Fleishman:

> *The nadir of a corporate crisis may be when the crisis-management counselor walks away in frustration. ...*

> *The giant public relations firm grew disturbed with Firestone's refusal to communicate the breadth and seriousness of its problems... As the crisis unfolded, Fleishman executives concluded they were receiving incomplete and questionable information from Firestone... Christine Karbowiak, vice president Firestone public affairs, disputes this assessment, saying, "to the best of our ability, we provided information." She says the "integrity" of the information provided to the Fleishman executives "has never been an issue."*

> *In any case, Firestone did not follow most of Fleishman's advice, relying instead on the cautious counsel of its lawyers, individuals familiar with the matter say. The agency, for example, is said to have urged Firestone to move forward with a proactive plan of action to restore consumer confidence. This included issuing an immediate apology for the faulty tires and quickly recalling and replacing those tires.[25]*

As for the Ford PR team, we declined to speculate on a matter that did not directly concern us, having plenty of other issues to keep us fully occupied. But privately we knew that the resignation of the tire maker's hired counselors did not bode well for where all this was headed. Firestone and Ford were reluctant partners in this ordeal and we knew our fates were interconnected. And the timing couldn't have been worse, as both Houses of Congress had called hearings on the tire fiasco that would begin the following week.

* * *

The *Wall Street Journal*'s team of reporters and editors working on the Ford-Firestone crisis were preparing a massive package of news stories, features and analysis to run September 6 to coincide with hearings on the crisis scheduled for both Houses of Congress. Over several days before the Labor Day weekend, I had spent hours on the phone talking with the *Journal*'s Tim Aeppel and Bob Simison. They would mention one allegation after another and I would give them Ford's perspective – about the Explorer's safety record, the history of the development of the Explorer and the many memos from that time, as well as the many issues related to the tires themselves. Labor Day Weekend brought time off to those *Journal* reporters, if not to the Ford tire team. A new team of writers and editors continued working over the long weekend on the tire story package that would come out the following Wednesday. So it was that I spent 90 minutes Saturday on a single call with the *Journal*'s Claire Ansberry, going over the same allegations and questions. I patiently repeated the same answers I had given Aeppel and Simison, even as my pager accumulated additional media calls to return.

The main story in the package, "Road Signs: How Ford, Firestone Let the Warnings Slide By As Debacle Developed," began on the top of Page One and continued in an enormous spread on pages 16-17. After setting the stage for the Congressional hearings and providing an update on the status of the tire recall, the story zeroes in on the Explorer, stating that Ford's popular SUV was named in 166 of the 194 rollovers NHTSA had compiled in its tire investigation.

> *In response, Ford spokesman Jon Harmon says that since most of the recalled tires went on the Explorer, it is natural for that model to be heavily represented on alleged rollovers and deaths. The car maker wants to look at more information about these incidents, Mr. Harmon adds. But he says the Explorer has the second-best safety record out of eight [midsize] SUVs, with a fatal-accident rate of one death per 100 million miles, according to the federal Fatality Analysis Reporting System*

The story details one allegation after another about the Explorer and Ford, each time including my response. By the end of the article, my name would be cited 18 times (not counting several instances of "he said" and "according to the Ford spokesman"). I doubt this set any kind of record for most mentions by a spokesperson in a single national news article, but it did put a smile on my face when friends and family from out of state saw the article and kidded me about how I had hogged the whole paper that day. More importantly, it was clear to journalists from every news organization covering the tire crisis who would find the *Journal* story to be must reading that day that I had shown that the many accusations against Ford and its Explorer were not as cut-and-dry as they may have been led to believe.

The *Journal* article also highlighted an important piece of analysis comparing the safety performance of the recalled Firestone tires to Goodyear tires that had been fitted on three years of Explorer production. The Goodyear tires were, in effect, a control group proving that the Explorer itself wasn't to blame for the tire accidents; we certainly planned to feature this comparison to Congress.

Goodyear supplied about half of Ford Explorer's tires between 1995 and 1997 but dropped the business after that. The Goodyear interlude has become one of Ford's main arguments in blaming the tire failures solely on Firestone, rather than on the design of the Explorer on Ford tire specifications. Goodyear has said it doesn't know of any incidents in which treads peeled off tires it supplied for Explorers. Goodyear also says it can't explain what the difference might be between its tires and Firestone's.

Ford says that even after it became aware in the late 1990s of tire problems overseas with Firestone tires, it didn't conduct any research or commission outside studies to compare Goodyear to Firestone. Ford's Mr. Harmon says the contrast speaks for itself: "It shows that good tires that are correctly made do not separate. Firestone made some tires that are not good tires. This shows it's a tire problem and not a vehicle problem."[27]

CHAPTER SEVEN

CONGRESSIONAL CIRCUS ACT

"We are going to produce a bill that's going to be signed into law by the president before adjournment. Anybody who gets in the way of this will end up steamrolled. Congress is mad and the American public is demanding action. You don't want to be opposite that tag team."

- *Ken Johnson, spokesman for Rep. Billy Tauzin (R-La.)[1]*

* * *

Days after Fleishman-Hillard resigned from the Firestone account, the embattled tire maker hired Ketchum as its new crisis counselor. A well-regarded, global public relations firm, Ketchum had a history of aggressively defending embattled clients, including tobacco giants Brown & Williamson and R.J. Reynolds in the 1970s and '80s.[2]

Commenting on the selection of Ketchum to be its new PR agency, Firestone's Karbowiak said: "Ketchum matched our personality, our overall business, the best. They also have a very strong presence in Washington which is very important to us."[3]

Ketchum would not comment on persistent speculation that the agency had signed onto the account only after getting contractual assurances that Firestone would share all necessary information. But clearly the agency had asked Firestone some pointed questions, as was made clear in reporting by the Pittsburgh *Post-Gazette*: "It was enough to make anyone think hard about taking over when the tire maker's public relations agency, Fleishman-Hillard, quit... So when Ketchum got the call, the agency's top people asked Bridgestone executives a lot

117

of questions about how the tire company planned to behave and communicate with the public."[4]

Executives at Ketchum expressed confidence that they would be representing a new Firestone. "I really believe Firestone will do what it says it's going to do," said Mark Schannon, a senior partner. "It's determined to be more responsive, to move more quickly, open up the process." But, he cautioned, "it's a very large company; it's not going to happen overnight."[5]

Ketchum would assign a small army to the Firestone account, but none as important as Jill Bratina. The 27-year-old Bratina would soon make her presence felt at Firestone, sharpening the company's story and working to ensure that the fiasco of mixed messages and broken promises that brought Ketchum to the tire maker wouldn't happen again.

* * *

Even before Firestone and Ford announced the recall, a number of Senators and U.S. Congressmen had taken a strong interest in the growing crisis, particularly those representing southern states where most of the tire accidents had occurred. The recall announcement did little to quell their interest in a public investigation. In fact, the recall seemed to leave more questions unanswered than it addressed. Congress wanted to know why it was going to take so long to complete the recall, prolonging the time when Americans were still driving on dangerous tires and undoubtedly leading to more accidents and more deaths. Members of Congress from the other 46 states not included in the first phase of the recall were incensed that their constituents would not get new tires right away. Everyone, it seemed, wanted to know more about the earlier tire failures and replacement programs in other countries – why hadn't either company notified NHTSA so that Americans driving on the same type of tires could have been protected earlier? And both Ford and Firestone executives would surely be asked the questions that always became crucial when investigations looked into prior events leading to tragedy – what did they know and when did they know it?

Congress also had many questions for NHTSA, the Federal government's chief automotive safety agency. "We need to know why

NHTSA, which has officials who are paid to do nothing else but monitor accidents, has been asleep at the wheel when it had information served up to it on a silver platter by State Farm Insurance Company which would suggest grave problems with Firestone tires," said Rep. Fred Upton, (R-MI).[6]

With so many unanswered questions, and so much blame to parse, it soon became evident that Congress would hold hearings and that Ford and Firestone would both be in for a rough time. Both companies struggled with the issue of who to send to Washington. For Firestone, it was clear that someone more convincing than Gary Crigger was needed. For Ford, Tom Baughman and Helen Petrauskas were both knowledgeable and experienced presenters but neither were part of Ford's highest echelon of management. Committee chairmen in both Houses of Congress wasted no time in signaling their desire to hear from the CEOs of both companies, even before dates for the hearings had been set. "Sen. John McCain, combative chair of the Senate Commerce Committee, wants to hear from the CEOs' mouths how the Firestone-Ford tire crisis escalated so far, so fast," noted *ConsumerAffairs.com*. "The Arizona Republican also wants to know why [NHTSA] didn't pick up on the problems until May, when Ford had been replacing tires in other nations for a year or more.... Also sharpening the knives is Rep. Billy Tauzin (R-La.), who chairs the House subcommittee on consumer affairs."[7]

Firestone soon confirmed reports that its CEO Masatoshi Ono would represent the company in both the Senate and House hearings, supported by Bob Wyant, vice president of Quality. Meanwhile, a disagreement at Ford delayed the company response to the two committee chairs, let alone to the media. Bill Ford had stayed out of the fray and clearly did not want to jump in just in time to be skewered by angry members of Congress. Jac Nasser was the obvious choice, both as the CEO of the company and as an executive who had genuinely kept a hands-on, daily involvement in all aspects of the crisis. Ford's Public Affairs clearly wanted Nasser to represent the company. But Janet Mullins Grissom, Ford's vice president for Government Affairs, did not want Nasser anywhere near the hearings. She wanted to use back channels to convince both committees to accept the subject matter experts, Petrauskas and Baughman. They could stand up to the blistering criticism they were sure to face.

119

Grissom did not want to subject Nasser to that treatment. She also was anxious to take charge of some aspect of this high-profile crisis that to date had been managed exclusively from Dearborn. The fact that the Firestone recall announcement had been made in Washington without any significant input from Grissom was particularly galling to her. Company managers below the rank of vice president were used to terse, condescending treatment from Grissom on any issue that originated in Washington. "DC is my town; we'll do it my way," she was often heard to say.

Vines quietly took Nasser aside when the two were alone in the CEO's office and begged him to ignore the advice of Mullins and agree to testify in Washington. There will be incredible pressure on you to appear at those hearings, Vines said, and it is going to look like you are afraid to testify. That would undermine the company's credibility, he said.

But Nasser chose to follow the advice of his lead executive in Washington. Ford's Governmental Affairs people told the two committees that the company would be represented by the two executives who were devoting their energy to resolving all issues related to the tire crisis. On August 30, Ford issued a short statement confirming that Petrauskas and Baughman would represent the company at both Senate and House hearings expected in September. Ironically, the statement was attributed to Jason Vines.[8]

Almost immediately, both McCain and Tauzin let it be known that they were unhappy that Nasser would not be present. Nasser had commitments that had been scheduled for weeks, Mullins' people told staffers from each of the two committees. Vines told media the same. That led to an even more angry response from McCain and Tauzin: What was more important than testifying to the American people about problems with your vehicles that were killing people?

Tauzin made note of Nasser's recent TV airtime, as *USA Today* reported in another prominent story before the hearings:

> *"A lot of people will think it's curious that Mr. Nasser has time to make TV commercials, but doesn't have time to appear before Congress on this matter," says Ken Johnson, spokesman for Rep. Billy Tauzin, R-La. ... Johnson noted that Congress has the power to subpoena witnesses.*

"I think Jac's time is better spent leading the effort for getting replacement tires," says Ford spokesman Jason Vines. "And besides, the people we are sending have been on the front lines of the issues that are likely to come up."[9]

It took exactly one day for the pressure for Nasser's appearance to grow too great to be ignored. Nasser called an impromptu meeting in his office for Vines plus Ford's top sales executive, Bob Rewey, and the company's chief counsel, John Rintamaki. Nasser asked about the mood of the media and of Ford's customers as the hearings drew near. Vines immediately piped up: "The world thinks you are a fucking coward."

Nasser didn't like the sounds of that. "I said I would go [to testify at the hearings] if that was the right thing."

"It's the right thing, Jac," Vines answered. Rewey agreed with Jason.

As Grissom's boss, Rintamaki tried to argue against the idea of the CEO testifying, but Nasser made it clear that he'd made up his mind and would hear no more discussion about it.

On August 31, Ford's Washington office notified the two committees that the company CEO would testify in the hearings after all. Nasser participated in a hurriedly arranged telephone press conference from the Glass House announcing that he indeed would appear at the hearings. Before the day was over, Firestone also had held a media conference call with John Lampe confidently setting the tone for the tire maker's Washington testimony the following week. *USA Today*'s coverage emphasized the rift growing between the two companies:

Ford Motor Chief Executive Jacques Nasser said Thursday that he has changed his mind and will testify before Congress starting Wednesday.... Nasser also said he is closer to penalizing Bridgestone/Firestone with lost business for what he called "an extremely difficult and disappointing period" in the firms' nearly 100-year relationship.

Nasser called a news conference, his first since the Aug. 9 recall of 6.5 million tires, on a day when Venezuelan authorities recommended criminal charges against both companies for misconduct and as Ford's stock was taking a beating from media attention...

Bridgestone/Firestone called a separate press conference Thursday, and it became clear that the relationship between the two companies is becoming more strained.

John Lampe...indicated the company's chief executive in the USA, Masatoshi Ono, may take on Ford when he appears before Congress next week. Ono may try to make an issue of Ford's recommendation over the years that the recalled tires be inflated at a pressure as low as 26 pounds per square inch.[9]

With the start of the hearings just days away, we needed to shake off this poor performance. The waffling over Nasser's appearance had been simply embarrassing, a bush-league mistake that was beneath a company of Ford's stature. Then, to top it off, Firestone had demonstrated it could be nimble in getting out its message in the same news cycle with our messages. Score one for Karbowiak and Ketchum. And Lampe had emerged as a capable, confident spokesperson. We had a lot of work to do to prepare Nasser, Petrauskas and Baughman for Congress. There was no room for error on that stage.

Lesson Learned: When Congress calls your company on the carpet, they want to hear from the CEO. *Don't waste time arguing. You're going to need every minute to prepare.*

* * *

Tauzin sent his closest aide and spokesperson, Ken Johnson, and two other staffers, first to Dearborn and then to Nashville, to probe into some of the most contentious issues before the hearings. On August 25, Ford's Helen Petrauskas and Tom Baughman welcomed the House Committee team and led them to a conference room on the second floor of WHQ. Ford lawyers and Government Affairs people sat in on the all-day meeting, and I represented Public Affairs.

Petrauskas and Baughman answered most of the Congressional staffers' questions in direct, conversational language. When the Washington guests asked for documents that had been referenced, the Ford hosts readily produced them. The meeting appeared to be going well. Conversation was often light. When it was time for lunch, sandwiches were brought in so work could continue. By mid-afternoon, the staff investigators seemed pleased with the answers they had received along with the promises the Ford team had made to forward a number of additional documents that could not be located readily.

Tauzin's investigators would return to Washington for the weekend, then visit Firestone's Nashville headquarters the following Monday. Johnson remarked that Ford was cooperating much more readily than Firestone. He left us with the clear impression that Ford's helpfulness and Firestone's intransigence would be reflected in the tone of questions the two companies' executives would face in the hearings the following week. However, Johnson's demeanor would change when he stepped in front of media hungry for their next story. There was more political gain to be had for himself and for his boss by attacking both companies. Johnson and Tauzin would not hesitate to criticize Ford on any issues where they perceived vulnerability. The fact-finding visits by the investigators were all about finding weaknesses and contradictions in the two companies' stories. Congress would have plenty of hard questions for both companies. All we could do was to try to tip the balance of doubt away from Ford.

A pack of media had gathered outside the Glass House, undoubtedly alerted by Johnson that Congressional investigators were in the building. As the three staffers walked out of the building to the Lincoln Town Car limousine we had arranged to take them to the airport, Johnson talked to the journalists, paying particular attention to the two television cameras. Congress was determined to find out for the sake of the American public, he told them, why Ford and Firestone had waited so long to do anything about the deadly accidents.

As the limousine drove off, Jason and I stepped into the throng. Ford was pleased to have the opportunity to set the record straight, Vines said. We were cooperating fully with Congress and looked forward to the upcoming hearings. We want our customers to know that we are doing everything in our power to assure their safety, he said.

* * *

Ford's Public Affairs team had triple duty in the two weeks leading up to the hearings. In addition to handling the deluge of media calls as well as the various pieces of employee and dealer communications, we now had to help Governmental Affairs and our lawyers prepare the written testimony and the vast amount of backup Nasser, Petrauskas and Baughman would need as they were grilled by Congress. The extensive media Q&A that I had continued to add to each day was used as the starting point for the Q&A in the executive backup books being prepared for the Congressional hearings. Not every question was used and many new ones were added. Some answers were too long and some needed further explanation or added detail. We deferred to Governmental Affairs in matters directly pertaining to the hearings, of course. They conducted several extensive training sessions to prepare the executives for the questioning, similar to the media training that Public Affairs routinely conducted for company executives preparing for interviews. But there were fundamental differences, primarily in tone. In addressing Congress, deference was essential. An executive was not used to maintaining humility and respect for a person asking tough, even rude, questions. But a witness at a Congressional hearing must never forget to maintain composure and mannerly behavior at all times. The last thing you wanted to do was to get into an argument with a Congressman in a hearing, an argument you would not win.

* * *

The *Wall Street Journal*'s massive tire crisis package dominated any discussion of news the morning of the first hearing, September 6. In addition to the lengthy main story addressing so many of the issues and allegations surrounding the tires and the Explorer, there were several sidebars. One of the other stories focused on what the two companies had known long before the August recall. This story alluded heavily to lines of questioning expected in the hearing before the House subcommittee on Consumer Affairs, chaired by Billy Tauzin. Ken Johnson was openly stoking the flame of national interest in his boss' big moment.

The story, headlined "Bridgestone/Firestone Fretted About Replacements," opened with a discussion of a Ford memo which referenced concerns the tire company had that Ford's plans to replace Firestone tires in the Middle East would come to the attention of U.S. regulators.

> *"Firestone Legal has some major reservations about the plan to notify customers and offer them an option," according to the memo, written by Chuck Seilnacht in Ford's worldwide direct market operations to Dave MacKinnon, Ford's regional marketing manager in Dubai... "First they feel that the U.S. (Department of Transportation) will have to be notified of the program, since the same product is sold in the United States.*

> *"Second, they are afraid that the Saudi government will see this as a recall and react dramatically, including prohibiting the import of the current tire. They believe the best course of action for the vehicles already in the market is to handle the tire issues on a case-by-case basis."[10]*

The story then quoted Tauzin explaining in plain English the significance of the memo:

> *"The memo basically says "you guys [Ford officials] made the decision to use these tires in the hot desert of Saudi Arabia without consulting us, so you assume responsibility for replacing them. And besides, we [Firestone] would prefer that DOT not know about this program," Rep. Tauzin said in an interview. "It's the first evidence that Firestone may have intended to keep damaging information away from the eyes and ears of the safety agency – in effect, trying to keep attention away from the problem instead of bringing it to the attention of the authorities."[11]*

The story appeared to have caught Firestone public relations off guard; the tire company was not represented in the piece. Ford's PR team did not make the same mistake. We made sure our company's perspective was included in a story that would prove important in setting a tone for national broadcast coverage that morning just before the opening of the hearings. We would have been more circumspect and remained quiet about plans for Ford testimony at the hearings, in deference to the subcommittee chairman, but we knew from the *Journal*'s Detroit bureau that Tauzin had spoken on the record for the story. After receiving assurances that Tauzin's comments would appear first in the story, we agreed to outline our plans for testimony and to provide an interview with one of the Ford executives scheduled to testify:

> *Helen Petrauskas, the Ford vice president in charge of safety and regulatory affairs, argued that Ford didn't need to report the tire-replacement program in Saudi Arabia because the company didn't believe it was dealing with a safety-related defect...*

> *Ford intends to make the case in its testimony that it began aggressively pursuing reports of the tire problems as early as 1998 and that tread separations in the Middle East and Latin America are fundamentally different from each other and from incidents in the U.S.*

> *Ford also plans to argue that, in the U.S., the company acted responsibly in investigating reports of problems and in getting Firestone to launch its recall last month.*[12]

* * *

Tauzin opened the House hearings by showing the nine-minute KHOU story that had aired the previous February. For the next hour and a half, each committee member read an opening statement, each saying essentially the same thing: We are going to get to the bottom of this, so we can safeguard the American driving public. Next up was a grilling of the Department of Transportation. DOT Secretary Rodney

126

Slater had been requested to attend, but he had declined and sent in his place his underling, NHTSA Administrator Sue Bailey (who had been on the job for only three weeks). Tauzin's scathing comments about Slater's absence left no doubt that there had never been any choice in whether Nasser should represent Ford. "This is a life or death hearing involving safety issues on the highways of America," Tauzin said. "I'm astounded that the Secretary of Transportation, who is in town today, and who was twice requested, twice by the committee, once by me personally in a letter just yesterday and publicly over the airwaves to attend this hearing could not find time to be with us today..."[13]

Among the issues Bailey addressed in her opening statement was the need for legislation requiring a company conducting a safety recall outside the U.S. to notify NHTSA of the action.

We now know that in September, 1999, Ford asked Firestone to replace Wilderness tires mounted on Ford Explorers that had been sold in the states around the Arabian Gulf. Similar actions were taken in other countries as well. Ford would have been required to notify NHTSA in such an action if it had occurred in the United States. But our regulations do not apply to actions taken outside of the United States.

Ford, thus, had no obligation to advise NHTSA when it took these actions. If we find that we need additional legislative authority to require manufacturers to provide, in the future, such information, we will seek to obtain it.[14]

Congress would agree that such authority was needed and would soon pass legislation requiring companies to report to NHTSA any overseas recalls involving products also sold in the U.S.

Bailey was repeatedly asked why the agency hadn't clued-in sooner to the tire problems. She testified that NHTSA had only received 46 complaints over nine years out of a pool of more than 47 million tires.[15]

But that didn't stop legislators from piling on NHTSA. "The government's highway safety watchdog apparently was asleep," said Commerce Committee head Thomas Bliley (R-Va).[16]

*   *   *

At the same time in another building on Capital Hill, McCain had opened the Senate hearings on the tire matter. On this day, McCain's witnesses did not include the two CEOs, so there was less media interest in his hearings than there was in Tauzin's. McCain would not make that mistake again, scheduling subsequent hearings on days when Tauzin was not stealing the limelight. The opening of the Senate hearing did provide opportunity for members of McCain's committee to rebuke witnesses from the two companies even if there was no time to actually listen to what they had to say. At one point, Petrauskas was asked if anyone at Ford had notified NHTSA upon learning of the Middle East tire trouble and having received the memo from the Firestone manager who was worried that Ford's replacement action in the Middle East might come to the attention of NHTSA. She began to answer, "We did not…" but was abruptly cut off by the Senator. "Yes or no?" "No," she replied. "We did not notify NHTSA at the time we sent letters to our dealers announcing we would replace the Firestone tires our customers had with Goodyear tires."[17] Petrauskas asked if she could explain further and was told no, there wasn't time. McCain then interjected with another long, rambling version of essentially the same question, allowing Petrauskas to answer briefly and then elaborate with the answer she had wanted to give earlier:

> *I might add, if I may, Mr. Chairman, by coincidence the day before, the day before the memorandum that you've referred to, we received a letter from Bridgestone-Firestone telling us that in their view there was nothing defective about the tires we had in the MidEast – nothing defective, and that their U.S. performance of those tires was very good. The reason they had sent us the letter is because we asked for it. We … wanted to be sure that there was no application of this issue to the U.S.*[18]

*   *   *

Back at Tauzin's House hearings, a number of "safety advocates" were called on to provide their criticism of NHTSA, Ford and

128

Firestone to further set the stage before the main players would face their inquisitors. NHTSA was "an agency that over the years has lost its will and lost its way," said David Pittle, technical director of Consumer's Union.[19] Predictably, Public Citizen's Joan Claybrook called for a broader recall, saying that an analysis of the 90 lawsuits against Firestone to that point, 37 percent pertained to tires that were not subject to the recall. A veteran player both in Congressional witch-hunts and the media relations game, Claybrook brought a compelling visual aid to ensure her testimony would be included in television news accounts – two ugly tire carcasses with their ragged treads peeled off, one a 15-inch tire that had been recalled and the other a 16-inch tire outside the recall.[20]

Finally, late in the afternoon, it was time for Bridgestone/Firestone's Masatoshi Ono to testify. "I come before you to apologize… to accept full and personal responsibility on behalf of Bridgestone/Firestone for the events that led to this hearing. Whenever people are hurt or fatally injured in automobile accidents, it is tragic." Ono said in halting English, reading a prepared statement. "Unfortunately, I am not able to give you a conclusive cause at this time. However, you have my word that we will continue until we find the cause."[21]

Ono (who Jason inevitably had nick-named "Yoko") relied on Wyant and Crigger to answer most questions. They didn't do much better than Ono. Asked why only four states had been originally scheduled to receive replacement tires in the first several months of the recall, Wyant said, "We didn't have a plan that was all worked out. We changed things as we went along."[22]

More damaging to Firestone was the revelation that the tire company had tracked a sharp rise in property damage and personal injury claims back in the late '90s. Tauzin revealed a document that Firestone had provided in response to inquiries his investigators had made the previous week in Nashville. Crigger acknowledged that Firestone had compiled the safety data, but said that it hadn't customarily relied on such data to assess product quality because the numbers hadn't in the past been high enough to guide a meaningful analysis. "In hindsight," Crigger said, "we wish we had looked at claims the way we now look at claims."[23]

129

But Tauzin didn't think much of Firestone's explanation. "This document confirms our suspicions that Firestone officials knew they had serious problems with these tires long before the recall in the U.S. was announced," Tauzin's spokesperson Ken Johnson told the *Wall Street Journal*. "You'd have to have incredibly inept management for your financial folks not to share this with your safety division."[24]

Ford's Vines, who had somehow left the hearing long enough to return some media calls, was quoted in that same *Journal* story expressing dismay at the news that Firestone had tracked safety data years before sharing it with Ford. "This is exactly what we were asking for and they didn't give it to us," he said.[25]

*   *   *

Before the evening was over, Firestone would take additional heat over the phased recall. Rep. Heather Wilson (R-NM) began her questioning of the Firestone executives benignly enough, asking a series of simple factual questions: how many tires needed to be recalled and how the plan for a multi-phase recall had been devised. Her pleasant, friendly demeanor was disarming. Wyant grew more confident in his responses as she continued to ask easy questions. She asked what the states in the first phase had in common, and Wyant answered that they were southern states with extremely hot summers as well as long stretches of highways where people might drive at high speeds for a sustained period of time. Watching the proceedings on a C-Span feed back in a conference room on the 10th floor of the Glass House, I remember saying out loud to whoever was there to listen: "Watch out. She's playing this like a courtroom prosecutor. She's about to go for the jugular."

And just like that her demeanor did change. She began providing the bloody details of one tragic accident after another. Then she asked the Firestone executives what they thought all the accidents she had mentioned had in common. No one answered, instinctively knowing that no good could come from any response they might make. Every one of the accidents, Wilson said, had occurred in New Mexico, which wasn't included in either the first phase or even the second phase of the recall. She asked if the executives knew where New Mexico was –

did they know that the summers could get hot there, and that the state had rather long stretches of highways?

Her voice full of emotion, she declared that Firestone had left the citizens of her state to continue to drive on tires the executives knew were defective. Then she circled back to some of the earlier testimony the Firestone executives had made, as well as their statements in the media, insisting that they hadn't known about the tire troubles until Ford had analyzed the tire company's claims data. She did not believe them, she said.

> *We've seen claims in the last month that you didn't know until July of this year, and now you're working around the clock to find out what's wrong. That's rubbish. You knew you had a problem a long time ago. You had recalls in 18 countries. This committee's staff has uncovered memos going back to 1997 where you knew you had a problem and you didn't do anything about it.*[26]

And on it went. Every committee member wanted a chance to pile on the beleaguered tire maker. Like a pro athlete in the waning moments of a game already won who is still looking to make a big play so he'll be featured on the ESPN highlight show, each Congressperson was going for that killer sound bite that would make all the local news stations back home.

It was well into the evening and Nasser was still waiting to be called upon. He and the others in the Ford contingent – Petrauskas, Baughman, Grissom, Vines and Richard Parry-Jones, an executive vice president and the company's Chief Technical Officer – had been sitting patiently in the front two rows staring at a contingent of camera people who sat or kneeled just in front of and below the elevated dais where the Congress people sat. Members of Congress who were not seated directly next to whoever was speaking could come and go as they like. Frequently there were more members absent than present. It was much more difficult for the Ford people to leave the room or to shut their eyes momentarily to take a short mental break. Any change in expression indicating boredom or impatience would set off a clicking, chirping sound as camera shutters opened and shut. Seated in the front row with Nasser and Grissom, Vines couldn't even sneak a look at his Blackberry, which must have been driving him crazy. Seated directly behind Nasser, Parry-Jones could occasionally read and send notes from his handheld device. As one of the people back at the Glass House often on the receiving end of his notes, I had the benefit of his perspective, included a biting British sense of the irony of the inquisition he was witnessing. Nasser continued to sit upright and alert, but he clearly had grown restless, not used to being made to wait for even a few minutes, let alone for nine hours.

Finally, it was the Ford CEO's turn to speak. As he started reading his statement, Nasser's edginess was noticeable. There were now eight or nine people with me in the WHQ 10th floor Strategy Room seated in the comfortable chairs around the giant oval-shaped table in the center of the room and watching Nasser's face on one of four TVs (hanging from each corner of the room's ceiling). Someone had thought to order pizza. I had been sitting mostly alone in the room for hours, watching the others testify, making notes on my laptop, and occasionally sending an email to Jason or to Parry-Jones. Now that it was finally Jac's turn, other refugees from the Tire Room had come down to the Strategy Room to watch and cheer him on. We each had our back-up books spread out before us, ready reference in case Jac was asked a question he couldn't answer and we were needed to send an answer lickity-split to Parry-Jones, who could lean forward and whisper some words into Nasser's ears. But there were several flaws with this plan. First, Parry-Jones knew everything we did and more – a brilliant engineer and scientist, Parry-Jones led the company's tire investigation. Second, if a moment did arise when Nasser needed a fact that Parry-Jones couldn't remember, there would likely be no way we could type the answer out fast enough to be useful. Third and most important, Nasser never asked for help on any question. He had the gift and curse of the supremely confident, never failing to sink or swim on his own knowledge and wits.

After the briefest introduction, Nasser cut to the chase: "I know that you and the public have questions about the tire recall and I'm here to answer those questions and I will remain here until you are satisfied," he said. "Now let's get to the heart of the issue. When did Ford know there was a problem with the Firestone tires? What have we done about it and what are we going to do about it in the future?"[27]

Nasser began to answer his own questions. Ford had no way to know of the tire troubles until the company had "virtually pried the data from Firestone's hands and analyzed it ourselves." He said that it was easy to look back in retrospect and say Ford should have known the tires were defective when problems first surfaced in the Middle East. "We immediately asked Firestone to investigate," he continued. "Firestone did so, and they concluded that the tread separations were caused – and you heard that earlier this evening – by improper maintenance and road hazards that are unique to that environment."[28]

When Firestone's assurances hadn't satisfied Ford's Middle Eastern customers, it had replaced the tires with Goodyear tires, he said. "We did it because we put our customers first." Ford had continued to ask Firestone about their tires and the tire maker had continued to provide the same reassurances, he said. And then he detailed the two companies' "Southwest Study" earlier in the year that had concluded that Firestone's U.S. tires were not demonstrating any tendency to separate, even after extensive mileage in hot-weather states.

"Looking back, particularly after listening to the testimony this evening," Nasser said, "if I have one single regret, it's that we did not ask Firestone the right question sooner."[29]

Ford and Firestone had replaced more than 1.7 million tires since the recall had been announced, Nasser said. Further, the two companies would not rest until they had completed the recall, working with other tire companies as well so they could "replace bad tires with good tires as quickly as possible."

He mentioned but didn't dwell on the "nearly three million Goodyear tires on Explorers that have not had – as far as we know – one tread separation problem... So we know that this is a Firestone tire issue, not a vehicle issue."[30]

He then outlined two actions Ford would take to help assure that "this just doesn't happen again." One, was an "early warning system," in cooperation with tire makers globally that would include a "better sharing of comprehensive real-world data that we now know is so critical to spotting defect patterns." And, two, was the commitment to "advise U.S. safety authorities of safety actions that are taken in overseas markets and vice-versa. From now on, when we know it, so will the world."[31]

It was classic Ford communications strategy to proactively imbed news into a speech where the company would otherwise be on the defensive. Of course, the first action was really less a commitment for Ford's action than it was a demand for tire makers to share their data. And the second commitment would very soon be made into U.S law.

Lesson Learned: Include news in speeches. *Just because your executive speaks somewhere doesn't make it news. Take the opportunity to make a significant product or policy announcement and you'll get coverage. Making news at events in which your company is being attacked gives you an excellent chance at controlling at least part of the message.*

When Nasser finished speaking, Tauzin began the questioning. His tone was much less aggressive than it had been when he and the other committee members were grilling the Firestone execs. It was as if he and Jac were having a friendly conversation. They talked about the difficulty Ford had in getting the claims data from Firestone – Nasser recounted four separate requests in June and July before Firestone had finally relented. At one point, as Nasser was about to launch into the "safety record of the Explorer, the quality level of the Explorer…" Tauzin disarmingly interrupted him to say: "Mr. Nasser, I'm an Explorer owner. You don't have to sell me. I've bought already."[32]

This good-natured conversation put Nasser at ease, and more than one of us in the room began to worry that Tauzin was about to go all Heather Wilson on him.

Tauzin asked about tests Ford had run with Explorers running on Firestone tires, leading to this light-hearted exchange:

NASSER: *We will give you the records, and they go back to '89 and also to '94, and the tests are 200 miles an hour at a minimum of a hundred miles per hour. We can...*

TAUZIN: *You meant a hundred miles per hour, not 200, I hope?*

NASSER: *Two-hundred miles at a hundred miles an hour.*

TAUZIN: *All right, more like it. I've got an Explorer, it will not do 200, I promise you.*

NASSER: *We'll put a super charger on it for you, Mr. Chairman.*[33]

"Don't get cocky, Jac!" I shouted at one of the TVs. Tauzin yielded to other members of Congress, who were for the most part less critical of Ford than they had been of Firestone. Heather Wilson even commended Ford for taking charge of the analysis of the tire claims data and for prodding Firestone into recalling the tires. Nasser was almost home free. But then he forgot his place in this morality play – that of a humble and contrite manager testifying at the request of the almighty Congress. At one point Tauzin cut Nasser off before he could even get going in his answer. Nasser tried to continue, but Tauzin interrupted again, letting the Ford CEO know who was in charge. Later, after Nasser had been testifying for close to three hours, a Congressman who had just returned to the chamber asked Nasser the very same question that another Congressman had asked an hour earlier. (Except for Tauzin, the members of Congress came and went frequently during the hearings, their movements off camera, leaving to cast a vote in another chamber, to go back to their offices to work on other things or just to take a break.) Nasser began to answer impatiently, "As I already said…" which unleashed the wrath of the Congressman who would not tolerate insolence from a witness. Nasser quickly composed himself and resumed with a more respectful demeanor.

Lesson Learned: Understand what a Congressional hearing is and isn't. *The reason for holding a Congressional hearing is to bring favorable attention on the members of Congress holding the hearing. They will not hesitate to embarrass, even humiliate, a witness for political gain. This circus act should never be confused with a fact-finding exercise. Getting to the truth requires some review of relevant facts, of course. What is focused on and what is ignored, however, is up to the presiding chairman, and to a lesser extent, the other committee members. They decide how to portray the rest of the cast – as villains, incompetents or sympathetic characters. Don't assume because another witness has been cast as villain that you will not also be; there is always room for another villain to be humiliated. Arguing with a committee member or answering in any fashion that can be perceived to be disrespectful of a member of Congress is a quick ticket to being vilified.*

* * *

Media coverage of the hearing's first round was starkly unkind to Firestone, especially Ono. Nasser scored considerably better, though plenty of questions remained for Ford. *TIME* magazine's Daniel Eisenberg called it this way:

> *Watching Masatoshi Ono, CEO of Bridgestone/Firestone, sweat under the nasty glare of Congress during last week's tire-recall hearings, you almost had to feel sorry for the reserved Japanese executive.... Now here he was, the prime suspect in the biggest consumer scare since the Tylenol-tampering case, linked to at least 88 deaths and 250 injuries in the U.S. alone.*

> *"I am more than a little nervous," he said in his tentative English, as three female Japanese interpreters in brightly colored suits hovered nearby. Ono offered a sharp contrast to the carefully scripted performance of Ford boss Jac Nasser, who would later pin the blame squarely on Firestone's tires. He was visibly uncomfortable, expressing regret on one hand, denying any tire defect on the other. And his watered-down apology incited a harsh response. Senator Richard Shelby, Alabama Republican, summed up the general sentiment by asking, "What does it take to put a company on notice that perhaps they've got a defective product out there?"[34]*

One month later, testifying in a grueling, eight-hour deposition for a class-action suit against Firestone, Ono said that his apology before Congress had not been an admission of the company accepting blame for the accidents, but merely an expression of sympathy for those injured or killed in accidents. When pressed by the interviewing lawyer on whether he was denying that Bridgestone/Firestone was at fault for the accidents, Ono replied: "If we are deemed responsible for the accidents, that is another matter. However, there are maybe outside causes that had caused the accidents. Then, I wouldn't say we're responsible for those accidents."[35] The next day Ono retired and returned in disgrace to Japan.[36]

Tauzin's subcommittee called representatives back to testify again the same week. Determined not to be shown up by the brassy

Congressman from Louisiana, McCain turned up the heat in a Senate hearing September 12. McCain said that he wanted to move the focus of the hearings from determining who to blame to deciding what should be done next for the safety of the American people.

Apparently finding this focus on remedy more to his liking, Transportation Secretary Rodney Slater testified for the first time, saying that Congress needed to give federal safety inspectors expanded authority if it wanted to prevent a repeat of the tire disaster. His testimony proved effective in moving the debate away from the criticism of NHTSA that had launched a number of memorable sound bites in the previous week's hearings (including this from Heather Wilson: "Why didn't the watchdog bark? We deserve an answer.")[37]

But the biggest news came when Firestone's John Lampe admitted that there was a defect in at least some of the tires, adding that the Explorer bore part of the blame as well. "We acknowledge there are safety problems and defects in a small percentage of the tires made in our Decatur facility," he said. But, he added, "the tire is only part of the overall safety problems in these accidents. Tires will fail … for a number of reasons. In most cases, the driver can bring the vehicle under safe control."[38]

Lampe testified that the Explorer had a history of rollover accidents and that most of the rollovers did not begin with a tire failure. Lampe also announced that Firestone would recall the additional 1.4 million tires in NHTSA's recent "consumer advisory," and would reimburse customers up to $140 per tire if they chose to replace recalled Firestone tires with tires from a competitive brand.[39]

Nasser disputed the notion that the Explorer shared in the blame for the crashes. "This is a Firestone tire issue," he said, "not a vehicle issue." As proof, he again referenced the "3 million Goodyear tires on Ford Explorers (that had) not had a tread separation problem."[40]

Nasser also drew attention to the testimony from Firestone executives the prior week, when they had admitted having known about abnormally high tread separations claims for certain tires years before Ford asked for such information.

Although I take no personal or professional pleasure in saying it, Firestone failed to share critical claims data with Ford that might have prompted the recall of these bad tires sooner. ... I listened in disbelief as senior Firestone executives not only acknowledged that Firestone had analyzed its claims data, but also identified significant pattern of tread separations as early as 1998. Yet Firestone said nothing to anyone, including the Ford Motor Company.

This is not the candid and frank dialogue that Ford expects in its business relationships. And after Firestone's testimony last week, we expressed Ford's profound disappointment to the head of Bridgestone/Firestone in Japan. It's been said before this morning, my purpose is not to finger point, but simply to tell you that at each step, Ford took the initiative to uncover this problem and find a solution. We agree that we, everyone, needs to do a better job in this area.[41]

The gloves had come off. The two companies were openly at war with each other, exactly what their trial lawyer adversaries wanted. As Nedra Pickler reported for the *Associated Press*, some elected officials seemed to be enjoying the spectacle: "The century-long relationship between Ford and Bridgestone/Firestone unraveled yesterday, with the two companies trading pointed accusations over which is more to blame for scores of fatal accidents..." she wrote. "'It's like tying two cats by the tail and throwing them over the clothesline and letting them claw each other,' observed Sen. Ernest Hollings, D-S.C."[42*]

---

[*] *It was like a bad flashback as I watched televised reports of the appearance before Congress of the CEOs of the Big Three auto companies in November 2008 seeking bailout loans. (Ford's Alan Mulally accompanied the other two CEOs in a show of unity although Ford soon disavowed its need for any Federal assistance.) These hearings, like the ones in 2000-01, provided ample opportunity for grandstanding as each Congressperson tried to outdo the others in berating the auto executives for their ineptness. They found it particularly repugnant that the CEOs had traveled to Washington on private jets. Embarrassed and humiliated, the execs each vowed to sell their company jets. So now, the erstwhile "little guy" plaintiff lawyers continue to operate their private jets while the once mighty automakers do not.*

CHAPTER EIGHT

The Feeding Frenzy Won't Stop

"Firestone seems committed, as a matter of apparently irreversible corporate policy, to stonewalling on the issue of a safety recall of the affected tires.... Instead of moving to resolve the problem, Firestone has chosen to view the resolution of the safety question as suitable for a pitched battle in the courts and in the media.... The subcommittee strongly condemns Firestone's conduct in this matter."
- *U.S. House Commerce Committee's subcommittee on Oversight and Investigations, in its report dated August 16, 1978*

* * *

For Firestone, it was déjà vu. A massive recall, a Congressional rebuke, a badly damaged brand.

At least 35 fatalities and more than 100 injuries had been documented from tread separation accidents on Firestone 500 tires. After a long delay and a stubborn resistance to owning up to the problem tires, Firestone in 1978 conducted the largest tire recall in history – 19.5 million tires. Even after the recall, Firestone continued to deny that there were any problems with its tires, instead blaming poor customer tire maintenance, under inflation and improper repairs.

Cindy Skrzycki of the *Washington Post* noted the eerie parallels between the two tire recall controversies in a story headlined: "'Firestonewalling' Again? Two Decades Later, Echoes of Earlier Testimony."

The similarities are striking – and scary.

139

The recent congressional hearings on the Firestone tire recall could have been held 22 years ago. In May and July of 1978, executives from Firestone Tire and Rubber Co. of Akron, Ohio, sat in front of a House subcommittee for four days, defending a first-generation radial tire called the Firestone 500.

Then, as now, the top officers of the company did not admit to a defect in their product, though there were hundreds of complaints about the tire disintegrating on the rim and 41 deaths. Appearing before Rep. John Moss (D-Calif.), they blamed the tires' problems on bad maintenance and underinflation.

"It's shocking to me they would go through two of these things," said Michael Lemov, who was chief counsel of Moss's Commerce subcommittee on oversight and investigation. "There's no corporate memory or moral suasion from the government. There's probably some of the same people around."[1]

The 1978 recall had nearly bankrupted Firestone, leading to its takeover by Japan's Bridgestone. Now, more than 20 years later, Firestone struggled to complete a tire recall, win back the trust of its customers and try to rebuild its brand. But there still were so many unanswered questions that would stubbornly keep the tire mess in the news.

After the September hearings, Congress quickly passed new legislation that President Clinton signed into law. The TREAD (a forced acronym if there ever was one, standing for Transportation Recall Enhancement, Accountability and Documentation) Act sought to increase tire safety, as well as to increase auto and tire companies' obligations to report to NHTSA all product recalls and replacement actions taken anywhere in the world. And it established criminal penalties for executives of a vehicle manufacturer that intentionally violated the new reporting requirements for a safety-related defect that subsequently caused death or serious bodily injury.

New CEO John Lampe pledged to rebuild the Firestone brand and regain the trust of its customers. Both Ford and Firestone ramped up tire investigations aimed at finding the root cause of the tread separations to head off any reoccurrence in the future.

* * *

A number of pieces of paper of all sizes still hung on the walls of the original Tire Room in the Glass House, including news clippings, lists of replacement tires, contact lists, to-do lists, and the like. One oversize sheet of poster paper ripped from an easel pad had been thumb-tacked to the wall in the days immediately following the recall announcement August 9. On it Ken Zino had scrawled a message in black magic marker, a reminder to the tire team of its priorities:

- "Protect our customers."
- "Protect our business."
- "Protect Firestone."

In the first days after the recall, Ford had seen no choice but to try to protect Firestone from ruin, even if it often seemed to require saving the tire company from its own ineptness. Firestone was Ford's biggest tire supplier. Dropping Firestone was unthinkable – it would mean shutting down for several months or even longer the plants that made the best-selling vehicle in the world, the F-Series pickup, as well as the popular Taurus sedan, the Ranger pickup, the Escape small SUV and, of course, the Explorer. There wasn't a quick and easy way to turn on the spigot of other companies' tire production to replace the millions of tires Firestone supplied Ford. And there certainly wasn't going to be any short-cutting the testing and certification process of introducing new tires onto all these vehicles. Fortunately, there was little reason (at the time) to doubt the quality and durability of Firestone tires not included in the recall. Firestone had made, and continued to make, world-class tires.

But the relationship soon became rocky. The two companies alternatively walked together and knifed each other publicly during the weeks and months following the recall. As much as both Ford and

Firestone wanted to work together to put the recall behind them, their divergent interests kept tearing the two companies apart.

*   *   *

Adversary groups, led by plaintiff attorneys with a wealth of cases against both Ford and Firestone, saw obvious advantage in driving a wedge between the two companies. Journalists, too, relished opportunities to uncover areas of disagreement between automaker and tire supplier. The contrasts between the positions taken by the two companies, and especially the finger-pointing at each other, made the long-running story that much more compelling.

To help increase the cohesiveness between the PR functions at the two companies and ensure consistency of message, Vines offered to send a small contingent of experienced communicators to Nashville to work with Firestone's PR team. After some thought, Karbowiak agreed. Firestone's PR team was overwhelmed by the volume of the media calls and by the complexity of the issues. It would be a while longer before the crisis team from Ketchum was fully up to speed with the tire issues; a mini-team from Ford could help bridge the gap. Zino and two of his media-relations people would take up residence with the Firestone Public Affairs team to better coordinate daily responses to media and help keep both companies "on message."

For awhile, the arrangement served both companies' needs. From Nashville, Zino led a joint conference call for news media just about every day, providing a status update and addressing whatever new issues had surfaced. The often brusque and headstrong Zino understood the delicate nature of his mission and stayed on his best behavior. In fact, his uncharacteristically placid demeanor on the conference calls earned him a new, albeit temporary, nickname from Vines: "Mr. Rogers."

But the arrangement was short-lived. Neither side really trusted the other. The Ford PR contingent was assigned a single large office somewhat removed from the Firestone communicators and the information exchange was less than free-flowing. More fundamentally, there was no way around the fact that each company had its own views and its own self-interests. Three weeks after they arrived in Nashville, the Ford PR people were back in Dearborn, and the visible fissure between the two companies continued to widen.

* * *

Increasingly, the Ford tire team had suspected that Firestone had long known and concealed dangerous defects in a significant population of their tires. Now, Congress had reached the same conclusion. Trial lawyers with cases against Firestone were foaming at their mouths with anticipation; the tire maker would need to put some incredible settlement offers on the table to keep these cases from going to trial. Meanwhile, retail demand for Firestone tires had all but dried up. Tire companies' most profitable business came from the sales of replacement tires to customers who had worn out the tires that came with the vehicle. Sears and other national tire retailers had stopped selling the suspect Firestone tire lines in the days leading up to the recall.

After the recall and with the continuing flood of negative publicity against Firestone, customers in need of new tires were buying other brands.

* * *

When Jason mentioned he planned to agree to a request from CBS's *60 Minutes* to come to Dearborn for a segment on Ford's crisis work, I must admit, my first reaction was: "Are you nuts?" I had some experience working with *60 Minutes* as well as *20/20*, *Inside Edition* and other pre-produced investigative TV series. I was skeptical, to say the least, that we would be given a fair shake. Salacious allegations by plaintiff attorneys and safety advocates, compelling video of sympathetic crash victims and, of course, the close-up look at some purported "smoking gun" document always seemed to make for more emotionally compelling TV than whatever could be served up in defense of the company and its products.

But Jason had already made up his mind. He completely believed in our story and in the crisis management work we were doing. He had spoken at length with executive producer Don Hewitt and came away convinced he wasn't walking into a trap. Vine's gut told him that if he

143

gave *60 Minutes* an exclusive, behind-the-scenes story, Hewitt would treat us fairly. It would be an opportunity to further distance Ford Public Affairs from Firestone's reactionary style of public relations. And, of course, it would be premium exposure for Jason himself, a man with no small ego. All in all, it was a gutsy roll of the dice. And like so often in Jason's career, his instincts were spot on.

Accommodating Leslie Stahl and two separate crews – each with numerous cameramen, lighting experts and producers – was a monumental effort given the stress we were under at the height of the crisis. For two and half insane days, we hosted the television crews – one shooting exclusive B-roll at an Explorer assembly plant in Louisville, at a tire information call center and in the "Tire Room," while the other crew filmed Stahl's every move as she interviewed Nasser several times, as well as Bill Ford and, of course, Jason. Jac also took her for a drive in an Explorer at Ford's Dearborn Proving Grounds, with a shooter and a sound guy in the back seat, and another camera crew shooting from a separate vehicle. Three cameras were manned any time Stahl sat down to talk to an executive, so the piece could later be edited to show the multiple angles that were a *60 Minutes* signature – the shot framing reporter and subject, mixed with close-up shots of each face at various points of the interview, highlighting moments of stress and doubt, or perhaps of candor and vindication. We brought our own videographer to shoot each interview as well, so we would have a complete record of everything that had been said just in case there later was any dispute.

The piece as it aired Oct. 8, 2000, opened with Stahl in Jac's office as he placed a call to a customer who had recently received a new set of tires. The customer was pleased to hear back from the company CEO. To make sure that viewers didn't think this was going to be a puff piece, Stahl's voice as narrator over the footage remarked, "Of course, you wouldn't expect Ford to arrange a call with anyone but a satisfied customer." Then the camera cut to Jac admitting, "We have let them down. We should have known better."

The piece moved to a close-up of a document from Venezuela, the one written by a lower-level Ford engineer in 1997 that spoke of a "tire explosion." Stahl asked Nasser firmly why the company didn't act sooner. Nasser answered without hesitation and only the slightest amount of irritation:

I've said it before. If we had to do it all over again, we could have acted earlier. We would have asked Firestone different questions, we would have looked at other data. But that's a very different situation from saying we ignored the signs.

In every case, I want to repeat this. In every case, when we had an issue anywhere in the world we went into the data, we looked at the data, we asked Firestone for any evidence that would suggest there was a systemic problem. And in every case, the answer came back that there wasn't.[2]

A moment of levity came next in reference to Nasser's widely panned TV commercials. Stahl mentioned that one critic had said that Nasser was so stiff in the commercials, he was like a "cross between Al Gore and Crocodile Dundee." Jac winced good-naturedly and said, "Yeah, that one hurt."

Bill Ford was also featured in the piece, one of a very few interviews he gave during the crisis. He came across as caring deeply about it, even as he had let Nasser direct the effort and be its highly visible leader. And Bill Ford clearly showed concern about the damage the crisis was inflicting on the company that bore his name. "Nothing is more important to me than Ford's reputation," he said.

Stahl drew attention to Bill Ford's unique lineage – as a direct descendant of both Henry Ford and Harvey Firestone. "I keep thinking about your mother. She's a Firestone." Ford nodded, saying "That's what makes this so painful." Then Stahl moved abruptly from this tender irony to a pointed question: "Did that company out-and-out lie to you? That they knew there was a problem and were deceitful?"

"I'm not going to say that; those are strong words," Ford said. "But I will say we did repeatedly ask for data that would enable us to make the right decisions and we didn't get it."[3]

The piece returned to Jason and the Public Affairs team. "The damage control team never rests; dealing with the press is non-stop," Stahl said, capturing the spirit that drove us throughout the crisis. "Vines and his public relations team take the approach to never let an attack, an allegation, or as Vines puts it, misinformation, go unanswered."[4]

Jason wasn't above a little bit of staging for the cameras, bringing his two young sons into the office on the Sunday the CBS crews began filming. Sure enough in the edited piece, the boys made a cameo appearance in Vines' outer office as Stahl voice said, "Even on a Sunday with the kids, Vines hasn't had a day off in 10 weeks, and neither has Nasser." That was the only time I ever saw Jason's boys at work, before, during or after the crisis.

* * *

Just when it looked liked things couldn't get any worse for Firestone, they did. Attorneys representing a Texas woman killed in a 1999 Explorer accident leaked to the media damaging information from the sworn deposition of Bob Martin, Firestone's retired quality assurance vice president. Martin testified that senior Firestone executives, all the way up to CEO Ono, had attended quarterly meetings beginning in 1997 in which claims data indicated tire problems were regularly discussed. Martin's testimony contradicted the testimony Lampe and Wyant had provided Congress just a few weeks earlier. "In sworn testimony and public statements, Bridge-stone/Firestone executives have said the company wasn't aware of potentially fatal tread-separation problems until July...," wrote Jim Healey in *USA Today*. "The information also challenges Bridge-stone/Firestone claims that whatever warning flags existed within the company were cached in the company's finance office, useless to others who might have sounded an alarm."[5]

Healey also described an "unlabeled chart" among the documents Firestone had recently turned over to NHTSA that detailed tread separation problems by production year through August 1996. The chart was likely made no later than early 1997, much earlier than, Firestone executives had testified, anyone at the company had identified any patterns among tread separations. "(The chart) includes handwritten notes that the return rate for tires built at Firestone's Decatur, Ill., factory in 1995 and '96 'looks bad' on (15-inch) tires...."[6]

* * *

146

As Firestone kept getting pushed closer to extinction it reacted exactly like a wounded animal that had been backed into a corner, lashing out with all its remaining energy in a desperate attempt to survive. Firestone attacked its biggest customer with increasingly blunt accusations about the safety and stability of the Ford Explorer.

And suddenly, Firestone's communications work began hitting the mark, catching the Ford Public Affairs team off guard. Two personnel changes greatly enhanced Firestone's ability to communicate effectively in its darkest hour. The first came in the form of a spunky, young, red-haired spokeswoman from Ketchum named Jill Bratina. Firestone had hurriedly hired Ketchum to manage crisis communications after Fleishman-Hillard quit the account. Ketchum clearly had more clout within Firestone than Fleishman had previously, perhaps dictated in the contract it signed with the tire maker. In any event, Firestone executives must have quickly realized what they had in Bratina who soon was being quoted in all the important stories while Karbowiak took a much less visible role. Bratina (who would be named to PR Week's "Top 30 Under 30" list of rising stars for the year 2000[7]) had a sharp wit and strong media relations skills. She understood how to work a story on background or on the record, when to provide a stinging sound bite and when to speak with humility and compassion. Undoubtedly, she was instrumental in framing Firestone's communications strategy and messaging as the company began to do a one-eighty from its earlier missteps shortly after she arrived on the scene. As Firestone grew increasingly combative to Ford, she won our respect as a formidable adversary. When the spotlight of the tire crisis finally began to fade more than a year later, Bratina left Ketchum to serve with distinction as Florida Governor Jeb Bush's Communications Director.[8]

The second change in Firestone's public persona, of course, was at the top of its house. Unlike Ono, John Lampe had no problem communicating to American media, members of Congress or other influentials. A graduate of Kansas State University, Lampe was Midwestern American apple pie. And as a Firestone lifer – he had begun work as a Firestone management trainee in 1973, as his bio states, "changing tires in a Firestone retail store in Cincinnati"[9] – he could speak knowledgably and passionately about all aspects of the tire business in America.

In the October 10 news release announcing his appointment as Bridgestone/Firestone's chairman, CEO and president, Lampe began by apologizing to Firestone's customers. "I want my first act as the new CEO to be a sincere apology to those who have suffered personal losses or who have had problems with Firestone tires," Lampe stated, echoing sentiments his predecessor had tried to express earlier but in a manner that seemed more sincere than Ono had in his contrived performance before Congress. "We can debate over cause and responsibility for there is much that is not known. But that does not change the fact that there have been tragic accidents, and for this I am deeply sorry."[10]

The news release announced "an immediate action plan" with three primary initiatives: "accelerating the recall effort, assembling a new management team and creating new methods to examine product performance data." Including news in an executive appointment release was definitely a step forward for Firestone in its tactical communications. Journalists would find the forward-looking plan with its concrete steps newsworthy and a sharp departure from Firestone's clumsy previous attempts at news management. The release detailed actions Firestone was taking to accelerate tire production and make other tires available as replacements in the recall. "The company is continuing to airlift tires from sister plants overseas and, as previously announced, has made it possible for consumers to obtain replacement tires from competitors." The company now expected the recall to be completed in November, the release stated, much sooner than originally foreseen. Lampe was quoted promising the company would "not rest until we have determined the root cause or causes of the accidents, continuing to work with government agencies and outside experts to ensure that a situation like this never happens again."[11]

As to the "new management team" Lampe was organizing, only one appointment was mentioned in the release: Isao Togashi, senior vice president of tire production and product technology of the parent company, Bridgestone Corp., in Japan had been named to head manufacturing and product development of the U.S. subsidiary. Although Togashi would report to Lampe, he also was appointed vice chairman of Bridgestone/Firestone's board of directors. "In his new management role," the news release stated, "Mr. Togashi will oversee three areas: manufacturing and process controls; research and development; and quality-assurance procedures."[12] Clearly the parent company was sending Togashi to Nashville to keep close watch over Lampe's performance in a critical period. Still, Lampe gave no indications that he was in any way a figurehead American CEO. He would increasingly demonstrate strong leadership and a passionate command of the all aspects of crisis management, including clear and forthright communication.

* * *

On October 12, John Lampe held a news conference in Nashville to detail his plans to rejuvenate the Firestone brand. He also made it clear that he believed that the Explorer owned most of the blame for the rollover crashes that had begun as tread separations. "The thing that makes us curious," he said, "is that the heavy number of (tire) failures are happening on the rear of the Explorer and the majority happen on the left side." The statistical oddity of the over-representation of the left-rear tire in rollover crashes cast suspicion that something specific to the Explorer was contributing to the tread separations. "A tire doesn't have a brain," Lampe said. "A tire doesn't know where it is."[13]

A number of theories were put forward to explain the heightened number of left-rear separations. Some suspected the left-rear tire was stressed by the extra weight associated with the Explorer's gas tank, which was situated under the vehicle's rear left side. One rather odd theory was that the vehicle's exhaust system was heating up the left tire because of its proximity to the tail pipe. Heat was the enemy of the tire, for sure, but in truth the Explorer's tail pipe was not cooking any tires.

Soon we discovered a fact that helped debunk most of these theories: tread separations on other makes and models of SUVs which had been outfitted with the recalled Firestone tires (albeit in much smaller numbers than Explorer) also occurred most frequently on the left rear wheel. It was true for the Toyota 4Runner, Nissan Xterra and Jeep Grand Cherokee. And it was true for the Ford Ranger pickup.[14] Weight could be a factor stressing the tires. You could speculate that a significant percent of the separations occurred on habitually overloaded vehicles, and that if you were to overload an SUV or a pickup truck, the rear tires would likely bear the brunt of the extra weight. But that didn't explain why the rear tire on the left side failed more often than the one on the right. The designs were different for each of these vehicles, so the gas tank and tail pipe theories fell apart. And really so did any of the other theories that tried to blame the Explorer for somehow shredding its tires.

Some of the members of the Ford tire team had their own odd theory: under a summer sun the center of a road was hotter than its shoulders, so the tires on the driver's side of the vehicle would be exposed to more heat than the tires on the passenger side. Roads were built to "crown" in the center so that water would run-off either side. The thicker asphalt grew hotter in the baking summer sun. Sure, many of the accidents had happened on multi-lane, divided highways where the left tires wouldn't be exposed to substantially greater heat than the right tires. But who was to say those tires hadn't already been weakened over time when the vehicle had been driven on hot surface streets?

The "left-rear" mystery would go unsolved for years to come, and would continue to be used by our adversaries as evidence that "something" was wrong with the Explorer.

* * *

I was leaving work one evening when a producer for Detroit talk radio station WWJ called asking for someone to phone in to a program that night to discuss the latest developments in the Firestone crisis. I offered to do it myself and the producer readily agreed.

I arrived home and had a quick dinner with my wife. I asked her to make sure our boys knew not to disturb me when I was talking on the phone as I'd be doing a live radio show. Then I went to my home office, shut the door and turned the radio on. I wanted to listen to the segment leading into mine, so I could reference for the listeners to whatever they'd just been hearing.

As it turned out, the guest being interviewed at that moment was none other than Ralph Hoar, the founder of Ralph Hoar and Associates, a prominent resource group for plaintiff attorneys and an outspoken critic of just about anything any of the auto companies had ever done. (His last name was just too easy to lampoon, so Jason called him simply, "The aptly named one.") Hoar was well into a diatribe about the need to expand the tire recall. Many of the non-recalled Firestone tires were just as dangerous, he said. Further, both Ford and Firestone knew they were dangerous and were conspiring to prevent the recall from being expanded. And the Explorer was a dangerous vehicle, he said, prone to tip over.

I listened carefully, taking down notes on a number of factual errors he had made that had gone uncorrected by the show's host. Then I called the producer at the station, a few minutes earlier than our agreed upon time for me to check in. The producer asked if I had been listening to the show. I had indeed, I said, and was quite anxious to clear the air of the misstatements that might be confusing the station's listeners. Having been caught sand-bagging me by not telling me that I would be following auto safety critic Ralph Hoar, she tried to repair the damage, asking me if I'd be willing to let Hoar join my segment so we could debate the issues together. Sure, I said, as long as I would still have a full segment of time alone with the host after Hoar hung up. That would involve some quick juggling of the schedule, the producer said, but she'd be happy to do it. She seemed surprised that I would be willing to debate Hoar and pleased that she had pulled off a bit of a coup for the station.

For five minutes or so, Hoar and I sparred. I pointed out some errors in what he had said and mentioned several facts and figures showing that the Explorer was indeed a safe vehicle. I said that Ford and Firestone were working closely with the Federal government's safety agency to monitor the performance of tires outside of the recall but to date there was not compelling evidence that the recall needed to be expanded. And I pointed out that Hoar headed a group that received its funding from plaintiff attorneys suing auto and tire makers, so he had a clear financial motive for making accusations against Ford and Firestone. I asked Hoar why he hadn't disclosed the nature of his business to the radio audience. He grew quite defensive, saying that he didn't need to apologize for standing up to big companies that often acted in ways that threatened public safety and so forth. I smiled to myself as he continued to self-righteously describe the work he did, along with the trial lawyers. His identity had been revealed in a manner that would not sit well with most of the station's listeners and he was just digging a deeper hole while using up the last remaining air time we had together. Finally, the host thanked him for calling in and went to a break. A few minutes later, I was back on with the host for several minutes of a calmer exploration of the safety issues I had been discussing. But first I apologized on air for having gotten a bit "worked up" during the previous segment. I had felt my heart race with the adrenaline rush of the live debate with Hoar. "Sometimes I get a little passionate," I said, "especially when someone is attacking the company I work for and its people. No one at Ford would agree to make unsafe products and when I hear someone say that, well, it makes my blood boil a bit."

The next day I was back to work in the Tire Room, fielding calls and updating the massive Q&A. Then my pager vibrated with a text message from Roman Krygier's office asking me to come by to see him. Krygier was an executive vice president in charge of manufacturing. I had been in a large meeting with him once or twice but had never met him personally. Not knowing what he wanted, I finished whatever I was in the middle of and went up to the 12th floor to find his office.

I told his secretary who I was and she smiled and asked me to have a seat in the outer office until he finished his meeting. I continued to rack my brain for what I might have done to get me in trouble with Krygier's manufacturing guys.

Then the secretary told me I could go in. "You're Jon Harmon, right?" Krygier said as he got up from behind his desk and came over to where I was standing. In his late fifties and with his black hair slicked straight back with some sort of gel, he looked a bit like Al Pacino in "Devil's Advocate."

"You're the guy who was on 950 AM last night?" he asked. Yes, I said.

"I was listening to that jerk who was on before you came on," Krygier said. "I had picked up my son, Todd, at the airport and we listened to him as we drove home." Todd Krygier was a recently retired professional hockey player with a well-known mean streak. "We were getting madder and madder as we drove. And then you came on. You put him in his place and you told the truth about the Explorer. You stood up for the company and I just wanted to tell you 'Thanks' for that."

152

Lesson Learned: Remember your home flank in a crisis. The local newspaper and the local news radio stations are important because they reach a good number of your employees. Pay extra attention to ensuring that they cover the crisis with balance and fairness. Oh, and the senior executives might be listening, too.

* * *

The continuing media frenzy was self-perpetuating. If you weren't a political reporter assigned to the 2000 Presidential election (which looked like it would be very closely contested), this was the biggest story of the year. There was tremendous competition among major new organizations to break new developments in the crisis or to provide their own analysis to shed light on the many unresolved issues.

Florida had the unfortunate distinction of having the most Explorer-Firestone fatalities in the nation. So it was not surprising when we learned that the leading news organization in the state, the *Miami Herald*, had endeavored to conduct a thorough statistical analysis of the crashes to try to determine causal factors. What would be surprising, however, was how shoddy the analysis in a highly respected newspaper could be.

The *Herald* had set about to settle the issue of whether an Explorer was more likely to roll over than other SUVs in a tire tread separation accident. This was a matter of growing dispute as Firestone had begun to suggest that the Explorer's stability was the underlying cause of the fatal accidents. While now conceding that Firestone had made "some bad tires," Lampe questioned why tread separations so often became deadly events when they occurred on Ford Explorers. When a tire failed, "a driver should be able to pull over, not roll over," Lampe would say (with Bratina's message coaching fully evident in Lampe's devastatingly simple sound bite).[15] Ford, of course, continued to maintain that the Explorer performed safely on the road and no worse than other SUVs after losing a tire tread at highway speeds.

With the worthy objective of using real-world accident statistics to compare the Explorer to other vehicles, the *Herald* researchers looked to the NHTSA data base. But they immediately ran into a problem – the data that was the most prevalent was also the least trust-worthy. Police and insurance reports for non-fatal accidents were often sketchy. The *Herald* could look at the data for all accidents mentioning a tire failure, but they couldn't isolate accidents caused by a "tread separation" because those words were not reliably used in the accident reports. An analysis of all accident data therefore would include all types of tire failures, including much more common blow-outs.

The researchers needed to look at the smaller population of fatal accidents to meaningfully mine the data for comparisons among various vehicles; Ford researchers had reached the same conclusion. Police reports for fatal accidents were reliable and thorough. The data we quoted to establish Explorer's "real-world safety record" came from the Department of Transportation's Fatality Analysis Reporting System (FARS) records which we normalized in terms of "fatalities per 100 million vehicle miles traveled." Vehicles that had sold well over the years would necessarily be more abundant on the roads than less popular vehicles and therefore involved in more accidents, so we needed to normalize the data. Reporting this "real-world safety record" scaled to 100 million vehicle miles traveled yielded numbers that could be easily grasped by people who weren't statisticians. For example, for 1990 to 1999, Explorer had a "safety record" of 1.1 fatalities per 100 million vehicle miles. SUVs as a whole over this same time period had 1.3 fatalities per 100 million miles. Cars as a class of vehicles had a fatality rate of 1.6 fatalities per 100 million miles.[*] To the news media and to Congress, we continually quoted these numbers to make two points: SUVs were safer than cars, in terms of a person's chances of being killed over 100 million miles of driving, and that Explorer was even safer than an average SUV.[16]

But the *Herald* wanted to dig deeper to focus specifically on roll-over crashes. Knowing that meaningful data mining had to start with a large, robust set of numbers, they began with the 400,000 fatal accidents reported nationwide from 1990-1999 in the FARS system, the same population Ford used for its "real-world safety record" comparisons. The newspaper's researchers wanted to tease out rollover rates for various vehicles in crashes that had been caused by tread separations. But tread separations were rare events for vehicles that

---

[*] *If we had reported the "safety record" as fatalities per million vehicle miles, the numbers would have been .011, .013 and .016, respectively – much more difficult for the average person to comprehend and compare.*

hadn't been equipped with the Firestone tires being recalled, nearly all of which were Explorers. To keep the data sets big enough to make meaningful comparisons among various vehicles, they chose to look at all "tire-related fatal accidents" rather than just fatalities caused by tread separations. Then they would look at what percent of those tire-related fatalities had been rollovers.

When the *Herald* researchers crunched the numbers, they found that the Explorer was much more likely to roll over in a tire-related accident than other vehicles (with the exception of the Ford Ranger pickup which also had been outfitted with the recalled Firestone tires but in smaller numbers).

Demonstrating greater professional integrity than their TV news counterparts, *Herald* reporters Geoff Daugherty and Jay Weaver contacted me before they were up against a deadline so I could help them make sense of what they had found and provide a meaningful comment for their story. After I had promised not to share their study or findings with any news organization until their story had been published, they gave me a detailed review of their work. We had several lengthy phone conversations and email exchanges. In between, I met with Baughman and Grush who were puzzled at the newspaper's results which seemed totally at odds with the safety record as we knew it.

The most astounding part of the *Herald*'s analysis was the contention that "93 percent of Explorers roll over after a tire blows-out." This figure was so absurd to the Ford safety experts that I found it hard to get their serious attention to help me figure out what was wrong with the newspaper's analysis. After pouring over my notes for two days, I found two fundamental flaws in the *Herald* analysis. Then I went to find Grush. He immediately saw the logic of my approach and agreed with my findings. But before I could rub it in to him that the PR guy had cracked the data puzzle before the statistical wizard, Ernie brought me back to earth. "I would have seen that, too, if I had been staring at it for days," he said with a smile. "But I've been pretty busy with other things."

The *Herald* analysis was indeed doubly flawed. The first flaw was the most obvious. Restricting the analysis to fatal accidents was the right approach because it focused on the most robust data. But a study of fatal accidents couldn't yield what they claimed to have found – the likelihood of a vehicle rolling over after a tire failure – because their data didn't include the millions of times tire failures had *not* led to fatal crashes (or any accident at all). The *Herald*'s analysis missed, to paraphrase Lampe, all the times a driver safely "pulled over, not rolled over."

The second flaw was a little more complicated. Rather than looking at all tire-failure related fatalities for each vehicle and determining how many of them had been rollovers, the researchers had started with the number of fatal accidents for each vehicle type and then determined what percent of those fatal crashes had been related to tire failures. (In other words, their analysis was backward. Or more precisely, their basic division was inverted, upside down as it were.) Although this at first seemed a relevant way to determine a range of safety among different vehicles, it was, in fact, misleading.

The *Herald* had found, for example, that a very high percent of the Explorer's fatal accidents had been related to tire failures. But as we had stressed repeatedly, the Explorer had a lower overall rate of fatal crashes (in terms of deaths per 100 million vehicle miles driven) than other SUVs or passenger cars. So Explorer would be doubly penalized in the *Herald*'s math: Explorer's relatively high number of tire-related fatalities (caused by the tires being recalled) would be divided by the relatively small number of Explorer's overall fatalities. Dividing by a smaller number yields a larger result than dividing by a larger number – so Explorer was absurdly penalized in the *Herald*'s analysis for having a better overall safety record than other vehicles.

I quickly called Daugherty and told him I had important information that would shed new light on the analysis. He put me on speaker phone so Weaver could participate as well. I agreed that my comments would be on the record. Then I patiently walked the two reporters through my assessment of their analysis. Not surprisingly, they defended their approach. It was natural that they would want to hold on to the product of weeks of work, particularly when their findings looked to be a major development in the top business story of the year. Later that day, we held another conference call that also included Ernie Grush and the *Herald*'s business editor. Ernie and I slowly went through the flaws in their analysis. The editor informed us that others, including someone from NHTSA, had reviewed the newspaper's findings and agreed that they were significant. The *Miami*

Herald would run the story the next day, he said, but would give prominent play to our objections and to our defense of the Explorer's overall safety record.

The story ran on the *Herald*'s front page October 10 with a headline undoubtedly tempered by our persistent objections: "Tire-related Roll-rate High for Some Fords."

> *Ford's Ranger pickup truck and Explorer SUV roll over more frequently than similar vehicles after a tire failure - an indication that vehicle design may play a role in deaths attributed to faulty Firestone tires, safety experts say.*

> *According to a* Herald *analysis of auto deaths nationwide during the past decade, 51 percent of Rangers flipped over after a tire-related accident, compared to 32 percent of other light trucks in similar crashes. The Explorer performs even more poorly in a tire failure: Ninety-three percent of Explorers roll over after a tire blows out. By contrast, 67 percent of other SUVs rolled over in tire-related crashes.* [17]

The story quoted a crash data expert at NHTSA, Dennis Utter, agreeing that the data appeared to be "pretty significant" and that the *Herald* had taken a "reasonable approach" to its analysis. But he added that he would wait "for the results of NHTSA's own analysis of the same data before drawing conclusions about the link between tire failure and vehicle design." [18]

The story did give prominent play to Ford's perspective:

> *Ford maintains it makes safe vehicles - especially the Explorer. The company attributes the deaths in Explorer rollovers to defective Firestone tires, rather than vehicle design...Ford spokesman Jon Harmon said the number of tire-related rollover fatalities nationwide is relatively small compared with the vehicle's overall safety record. The Explorer's fatality rate regardless of what caused the crash, is 17 percent lower than other mid-sized SUVs.*

*"[The Explorer] is already a safety leader," Harmon
said. "Imagine if you put good tires on it, how safe it would
be.[19]*

After quoting the always available Clarence Ditlow of the Center
for Auto Safety with a predictable rip at both the Explorer and its
Firestone tires, the story summarizes our objections to the study's
methodology.

Ford said the Herald's *approach penalized the company
for making vehicles that are safer than those of competitors.
Because other SUVs have more fatal accidents, Harmon said,
tire-related rollovers look like a comparatively small
problem. At Ford, Harmon said, the overall accident total is
small, and that makes the rollover problem look larger than it
is. ...*

*Harmon also said a greater portion of the Explorer and
Ranger models are equipped with recalled Firestone tires ...
That would mean the Explorer and Ranger would be likely to
have higher tire-fatality rates - not because of a difference in
vehicle design, but because more of them would have faulty
tires.[20]*

So, yes, the story was balanced in the sense that Ford's objections
were prominently featured. But the lead of the story – and its basic
premise – was just plain wrong. An analysis of fatal accident statistics
alone could not indicate the likelihood of a vehicle rolling over after a
tire failure. The upside-down math just compounded the sloppiness.

***Lesson Learned: Closely examine the methodology behind the
analysis.*** *Make sure your own analysis is above reproach and hold
others to the same high standard. Point out mistakes aggressively and
persistently.*

* * *

We might have continued to try to correct the *Miami Herald* story for the record, but we weren't optimistic about our chances of convincing editors to run a retraction in a follow-up story. And, at the very same time, were wrestling with another high-profile newspaper's flawed analysis that we absolutely did feel required a retraction. The *Washington Post* had published a top-of-the-fold front page story October 9 with its own statistical study of accident records. Banner-headlined "Explorer Has Higher Rate of Tire Accidents," the story claimed that Goodyear-equipped Explorers in its study were more than twice as likely to have a "tire-related" accident as were other SUVs. This finding struck right at the heart of Ford's strongest argument that the Explorer's problems were limited to its Firestone tires.

A Washington Post *analysis of national and Florida crash statistics shows ... that the Ford Explorer has a higher rate of tire-related accidents than other sport-utility vehicles, even when the popular SUV is equipped with Goodyear tires. The finding suggests that something about the Explorer may be contributing to these accidents, auto analysts said.*[21]

If Goodyear-equipped Explorers were also prone to deadly tire accidents, it would validate the critics' claims that the Explorer itself was unsafe.

But a couple of things were askew with the *Post*'s analysis. First, there was the miniscule number of Explorer accidents that the *Post* researchers had found in a review of more than 25,000 accident reports in Florida[*] – just 16, a number never mentioned in the lengthy story. Basing broad conclusions on such a small population was questionable at best. Second, a closer look at the 16 reports found that most were not crashes caused by tread separations and it wasn't at all clear if any of them actually involved Goodyear tires.

The *Post* was actively promoting the story, with reporter Daniel Keating appearing on two network television evening news programs and several radio shows. Countless radio stations were picking up the

---

[*] *Police accident reports, maintained at the state level, contained more detail than records in the DOT database. The* Post *researchers chose Florida because it was the state with the most Firestone tread separation complaints.*

summary of the *Post*'s findings as a "rip 'n read." Newspapers in other cities had also picked up the *Post* story. So it was urgent that we quickly act to rebut the story – both to protect the record of those all-important Goodyear tires and to try to discourage other news organizations from conducting their own amateur analyses of accident data.

In the days before the story was published, we had tried to show the *Post* reporters, Keating and Caroline Mayer, that there was strong reason to doubt their conclusions that Goodyear tires on Explorers were also causing accidents. At our urging, Goodyear's senior spokesman had contacted the reporters and told them that Goodyear had no damage claims, accidents, injuries, fatalities or lawsuits in the state of Florida during the years that were the focus of the *Post*'s study.[22] The only mention of this information in the October 9 story was that Goodyear said it had no lawsuits on Explorers in Florida.[23] And a full week before the story ran, Ford had provided the *Post*'s reporters with 1990-99 Department of Transportation FARS data specific to the state of Florida that showed that Explorers had a substantially lower rate of fatal rollovers as well as a lower fatality rate in all types of accidents compared with other similar-sized SUVs. The lower fatality rates for Explorer in Florida were consistent with the national FARS data that Ford had made widely available for the previous two months but inconsistent with the *Post*'s premise of a dangerous Explorer.[24] None of this information was mentioned in the October 9 *Post* story.[25]

It also came to our attention that we had been incorrect in an earlier assertion that one of Ford's Explorer assembly plants had exclusively used Goodyear tires during 1995-97, and that the *Post* had based their study on this assertion. In fact, about 100,000 of the nearly 3 million tires fitted to Explorers at that plant those three years had been Firestones. Since police reports often did not name the brand of tire involved in an accident, the *Post* researchers had tracked Vehicle Identification Numbers in the police reports to find fatal accidents that had involved Explorers built at the plant supposedly using only Goodyear tires.

We quickly made the *Post* aware of the new information that about 4 percent of the tires used at the assembly plant building Explorers had in fact been Firestones – enough to taint the study. We asked to review the 16 accident reports that were at the heart of the newspaper's conclusion that Goodyear-equipped Explorers were prone to tire-related accidents. Soon after we received the fax from the *Post* we noticed that only one of the 16 police reports had identified the brand of tire – and in that one case the report clearly indicated it was a Firestone tire.[26]

Our tire team's hurried investigation into the other 15 accidents further weakened the basis of the *Post*'s shaky premise. Most of the accidents were clearly not caused by tread separation problems and were in no way relevant to a serious analysis of the tire and rollover problems. In one case, an Explorer driver with a flat tire had stopped her vehicle in the roadway, leading to a collision of two vehicles behind her – not exactly the kind of "tire-related accident" supposedly indicative of a problem with the Explorer. Another case involved a motorist who was hurt after she swerved to avoid hitting a cat, then struck a curb causing a tire blow-out, lost control of the vehicle and struck a utility pole. Two cases were Explorer crashes in which the driver was cited by police for intoxication – one for alcohol, cocaine and marijuana, the other for marijuana. In two other instances of a "tire puncture/blowout," the attending police officer cited the driver for failure to properly maintain his vehicle. None of the remaining nine accidents involved a tread separation.[27] As we stated in an issue analysis piece posted on Ford's media website, "A news organization committed to careful and thorough reporting would have thrown out these accident examples as not relevant to any larger point."[28]

With such compelling evidence that the *Washington Post* had reached an erroneous conclusion about the Explorer and its Goodyear tires, we went on the offensive, faxing and emailing our analysis of the issue to every newspaper, wire service, TV and radio station that had picked up the *Post*'s story. We provided a concise response for Ford's customer service call centers to use in helping assure customers who had heard about the issue, especially those with Goodyear tires:

> *This flawed story ignores many facts. In Florida, and nationally, Explorer has a better safety record than other compact SUVs. Florida has a relatively high rate of Firestone tire tread separation accidents. Yet in Florida, and nationally, the rollover fatality rate for Explorer is substantially lower*

than for other compact SUVs. Explorer also has a lower fatality rate for all accident types compared to equivalent SUVs in Florida, and nationally. Explorer is one of the safest vehicles on the road.

Furthermore, Goodyear reports that it knows of not one single claim against Goodyear tires on Explorers in Florida. No lawsuits, no rollovers, no injuries, no fatalities.[29]

On October 11, the *Washington Post* ran a follow-up story on its front page, "Ford Cites Flaws in Explorer Data," focusing on the mistake we had made in assuming the Explorer plant in the study had used only Goodyear tires:

Ford Motor Co. officials said yesterday that a Washington Post *analysis of tire-related accidents involving its Explorer sport-utility vehicle was flawed because a key assumption was not totally reliable. Ford had used the same assumption...*

[The Oct. 9 story's] finding was based on identifying the brand of tire that came as standard equipment on new Explorers by determining which manufacturing plant built the SUV in the mid-1990s. Ford now says that the plant specified as exclusively using Goodyear tires installed Firestone tires on about 4 percent of vehicles they produced during 1995-97, the period covering the Post analysis. ...

"Based on what we know now, it is bad information," said Jason Vines, Ford vice president for communications, who said the new information "repudiates the premise of the analysis."[30]

Other media outlets picked up on the *Post*'s retreat and were less inclined to solely blame Ford for the newspaper's flawed analysis. As Jack Shafer wrote in *Slate* in a column titled "The *Washington Post* Blows the Blowout Story:"

...by Wednesday, Oct. 11, the Post *backed down from its Goodyear-Explorer scoop. The paper could have framed its Page One as a retraction and titled it* "Washington Post Story Rolls Over and Explodes" *or* "Ford produces Evidence that Explorer Not Necessarily a Deathmobile." *Instead of acknowledging that it blew the story, the* Post's *article,* "Ford Cites Flaws in Tire Data," *beats up on the car company for providing bad data.*

In its rush to judge the Explorer a death trap, the Post *engaged in what social scientists call "confirmation bias." The paper and the majority of the press have accepted that the Explorer is deadly. If [the statistical analysis] had somehow exonerated the Explorer, you know the* Post *would have reflexively rejected it. But because the Ford methodology [of identifying Goodyear tires by the assembly plant that built a vehicle in question] confirmed the view that the Explorer kills no matter what rubber it's spinning, the* Post *unquestioningly accepted [it].*[31]

Our media blitz to contain the damage done by the *Washington Post* study did achieve one of our goals: over the many months that the crisis would drag on, no major news organization would again attempt to create news from its own creative statistical analysis of the accident data. While we hadn't succeeded in completely negating the *Herald* and *Post* studies, we had made it clear that the issues were complex and not easily deciphered by amateur number crunchers. And that Ford would vigorously rebut allegations built on shoddy analysis.

Lesson Learned: When a story attacking your company, its people or its products is flat-out wrong, push back immediately, and not just with the offending news outlet. *Get the story corrected there, certainly, but also move quickly to contain and correct the collateral damage from other media coverage. Put a clear and concise reading of the issue on your news media and customer websites and with your call centers. When speaking directly to customers, emphasize your compelling story rather than regurgitating each allegation and your rebuttal in detail.*

*   *   *

Keith Bradsher had us nailed, he thought.

The *New York Times* reporter was convinced that the Explorer could easily be overloaded to the point of being dangerously prone to roll over. He also was sure that vehicle overloading was contributing to the shredding of the Firestone tires. And then David Champion of Consumers Union pointed out to Bradsher that Ford didn't make it easy for customers to know how many pounds of payload – passengers plus cargo – their Explorers could safely carry. Information stamped on a sticker on each Explorer's driver's door jam specified its "gross vehicle weight" (the maximum recommended weight when fully loaded). But it did not specify its "curb weight" (how much that vehicle weighed empty). And there wasn't anywhere for the owner to look up the empty weight of a particular Explorer; it varied significantly depending on which model they had, two-door or four-door; there were two different sized engines available as well, and two-wheel-drive and four-wheel-drive versions. The vehicle's owner manual, Champion told Bradsher, actually instructed the owner to weigh the vehicle for himself. "To obtain correct weights, try taking your vehicle to a shipping company or an inspection station for trucks," it read.[32]

This was ridiculous and Bradsher was calling us out on it. He had driven an Explorer from our press fleet, he told me, and had tried to get it weighed. His story was going to describe the absurd lengths he had to go to weigh the Explorer – the highway weigh stations wouldn't help him; they were set up for much heavier commercial trucks. So he had taken it to a garbage dump, waited in line with a bunch of dump trucks and finally had it weighed. Subtracting that weight from the Gross Vehicle Weight, he calculated that the Explorer he had borrowed had a maximum payload of 1,000 pounds. That didn't seem like enough to Bradsher. Five adult men riding in the SUV could weigh that much or more even before they brought along any luggage or gear. Despite its rugged appearance and the cavernous room for storage between the backseat and the liftgate, he said, the Explorer couldn't carry much weight at all.

But what Bradsher was really keying in on was the lack of useful information Ford was providing Explorer owners. He knew his little adventure with the dump trucks would make good color for the exclusive story he had unearthed through his own reporting. This was Page One material.

When he told me about the lack of information about a specific vehicle's weight as well as the stupid advice in the owner manual, I had to silently agree that we were doing a disservice to our customers. I told Bradsher I'd look into it and have a comment for him shortly.

I walked out into the management parking lot and found my Explorer. The information on the door jam plate and in the owner manual was just as Bradsher had described.

The engineers on the Explorer team were as surprised as I had been at the lack of information we were providing customers. Near as anyone could tell, the door jam data and the owner manual information had carried over year after year without change from the first Explorer. Explorer had been developed off the Ranger pickup truck platform. The idea of taking a vehicle to a weigh station to determine its curb weight sounded like something a truck engineer would have come up with, but no one I talked to owned up to knowing anything about it. In fact, they all agreed that Bradsher was right. We were not providing clear information to our customers.

The relatively low payload figure was easier to explain. Ford likely had the most conservative policy in determining a vehicle's full-loaded maximum weight. It believed in erring on the side of caution, a philosophy evident throughout the company, but especially in Ford Truck.[*]

There was a fair amount of discretion in setting a recommended limit; it was not hard and fast. Picture a family in an outboard boat that is fully loaded down to the last pound as specified on the bright yellow sticker affixed to its inside wall. A bird flies overhead and drops an unwelcome dropping onto the boat's floor. Does it suddenly capsize? Of course not. Obviously there is a safety margin well beyond the limit

---

[*] *This cautiousness was why Ford trucks had a wider margin of error than competitors' trucks in meeting emission standards, making it easier for Ford to commit in 1999 to making its trucks meet the LEV standards. It was why Ford trucks had heavier steel components than its competition, unseen to the customer and therefore not fully valued, that added weight and cost to the truck. And it was why the engineers and finance people were so resistant to making bold promises like the 25 percent fuel economy improvement for Ford's SUVs.*

prescribed on the sticker. It is up to the company to determine the maximum recommended weight. A company's marketing people always want the highest number it can reasonably claim; its lawyers always want a much lower number. At Ford, the lawyers often prevailed.

To their credit, the Truck team readily agreed to change the weight information in the Explorer's owners manual. Fortunately, the upcoming 2002 Explorer was an all-new model and there was still time to rewrite the section in the owner manual and change the information on the door jam. Right up the line to Tom Baughman and Gurminder Bedi, all agreed. Bradsher was more than a little surprised when I called him back, one day after he had brought the weight issue to our attention, and told him that we agreed with his complaint and would provide better information to our customers beginning with the very next model year.

Bradsher's reaction was telling. Although I readily agreed to be quoted giving him the credit for bringing this issue to our attention, he clearly was disappointed. We had acted so fast, agreeing to make a change, before his story had even been published. He could, and did, rightly take credit in his story for effecting change by bringing this issue to our attention. But he clearly would rather have had the story come out ridiculing our lack of transparency and then followed up with another story taking credit for forcing us to make the change.

Headlined "Ford to Include Payload Data in Vehicles," Bradsher's story had become a positive for us. He quoted from me throughout the story describing the change we had committed to as a move toward better communication to our customers.

> *Mr. Harmon said that Ford was making the change in response to inquiries from* The New York Times *about the adequacy of the current manuals, and not because of any concerns that overloading had caused the crashes in Explorers equipped with Firestone tires. 'It wasn't as clear as it could be, as you pointed out – this wasn't a safety issue'* Mr. Harmon said.[33]

A little digging on our part also revealed that the lack of transparency in weight information was typical in the industry for trucks and SUVs. I pointed this out to Bradsher and suggested he speak to the auto trade group in Washington, the Alliance for Automobile Manufacturers. He ended his story by noting that, according to the AMA, it was indeed "common for automakers not to provide information on vehicles' payloads, and to suggest that buyers take vehicles to public scales to weigh them."[34]

We had completely turned around the negative story; Ford would now be seen as among the leaders in the industry in providing transparency to its customers. When I spoke to Bradsher in 2009 for this book's Epilogue and asked him about Ford's PR practice during the crisis, he brought up the weight information episode as the "gold standard" in crisis communications.

"Ford moved so fast to change the manual and took what could have been a Page One story and turned it into a more mundane article about how the company responded to criticism," he told me. "It's one thing to get ahead of the news with what you say but quite another to change policy or enact a fix before a story even comes out. That was a high-water mark. I was very impressed that you were able to move so fast."

Lesson Learned: Do not delay in doing the right thing*. Act quickly and decisively. If the issue was brought to your attention by the news media, give them credit. Don't try to pretend you were going to make the fix anyway.*

CHAPTER NINE

THE BLAME GAME

"It didn't have to be this way."

> - *Third key message mentioned by John Lampe, Firestone CEO, at a June 18, 2001 press briefing previewing points he planned to make at Congressional hearings the next day. The first two messages were "Our tires are safe" and "The Ford Explorer has a design defect."*

* * *

Both Ford and Firestone had taken extraordinary actions to get replacement tires to the market during a critical period when tire shortages created long waiting lists at many dealerships, before newly manufactured tires – from Michelin, Goodyear and Continental-General as well as Firestone – reached the market. Firestone airlifted Bridgestone tires from its parent company's Japanese factories. Ford temporarily shut down three of its assembly plants to free up tires that would have been installed on new vehicles and send them to dealers to be given to customers needing replacements. Hundreds of union workers on temporary layoff who would receive 95 percent of their pay to stay at home voluntarily reported to the factories to help load tires on trucks and rail cars. And Ford paid millions of dollars to produce dozens of tire molds to speed up production of the new tires from various tire manufacturers. By the first of December, more than 95 percent of the recalled tires had been replaced. Those few remaining customers who continued to procrastinate in having their tires replaced could now do so without delay.

* * *

Throughout August, September and October 2000, national and local media covered every conceivable angle of the Firestone tire story. More often than not, each new day brought more front page coverage. Only one other story during this period received more attention: the upcoming U.S. Presidential race between George W. Bush and Al Gore. As the election date drew near, it was obvious that it was going to be very close. Two swing states – Ohio and Florida – were too close to call; how they ended up would tip the balance to the victor on Election Day, November 7.

When the nation woke up the next morning, no President-elect had been declared. Late Tuesday night, Gore had called Bush to congratulate him on his apparent victory, then called Bush back shortly later to say that they'd better wait until the picture crystallized in Florida. Hours rolled into days and then weeks as Florida counted its votes, then recounted them. Unprecedented in American history, the surreal Presidential election over-time period naturally became the focus of news coverage and public discourse. The tire controversy mercifully subsided into the background.

* * *

During this relative lull, Tab Turner scored a huge media placement for his growing rollover crash litigation practice with a 10,000-word cover story in the *New York Sunday Times* magazine in December. Turner wasn't shy about showing writer Michael Winerip his preferred methods of media manipulation. The piece provides a rare look at the tactics trial lawyers had tended to keep out of the public eye.

No one was more responsible than Turner for helping keep the Explorer-Firestone problems atop the national news for so long, to the point that even Ford officials say they've never seen an auto-safety story like it – not the Chevrolet

Corvair in the 1960's, not the Ford Pinto or Firestone 500 tire recall in the 1970's, not the side-mounted gas tank on G.M. pickups in the 1990's.

After a decade of litigating S.U.V. rollovers, Turner has amassed an extraordinary library of Ford internal documents, and he emails them around the nation with gusto, to reporters, Congressional investigators, Nader types and fellow plaintiff attorneys. Throughout the summer and fall, he supplied crucial documents to reporters as they vied to be first to figure out who knew what when at Ford and Firestone concerning defective tires that federal investigators have now linked to 148 deaths, mainly in Explorers.[1]

In an interview for the story, Winerip had asked Vines what he thought of Turner. Jason probably made a mistake in his quick answer, referring to the plaintiff lawyer by his first name. "Every day Tab would take one of those documents and say, 'Here's a little grenade – let me throw it in there.'" The first-name familiarity might have created an impression that the two adversaries chummed around after work together and that the "guerilla war" with the media, as Winerip called it, was just a game to them. Before he had completed his sentence, however, Jason realized his tone was wrong. In his next breath, he made sure Winerip – and his readers – understood what he really thought of Turner, calling him "one of those sharks out there who think they've found the keys to the A.T.M."[2]

Winerip's opus gave plenty of play to Turner's many theories of ill-considered compromises made during the development of the Explorer. But he balanced the accusations with Ford's rebuttals and did not overlook the essential fact of the Explorer's overall safety record:

Which is not to say that the Explorer stands out as particularly rollover-prone among S.U.V.'s. Despite all the horrible publicity, federal fatality data and safety ratings seem to indicate that the Explorer is pretty typical of midsize S.U.V.'s. Jon Harmon, a Ford spokesman, tells reporters that if the bad Firestone tires had been on another S.U.V., "you wouldn't be talking to me; you'd be talking to one of those other companies."[3]

Winerip also dug deeper into the case of the Goodyear tires' stellar performance on 1994 to '96 Explorers which provided damning proof that the Firestone tires owned the blame alone for the tread separations. The Goodyear tires were a pound heavier than the Firestones and, Winerip reported, Ford had plenty of indications in the mid-1990s that the Goodyear tires were more durable. He cited five tread-wear road tests: "The Firestone ATX did markedly poorer than the Goodyear on every test, in some cases wearing out twice as quickly." And he pointed out the Goodyear tires earned a "B" heat resistance rating, while the Firestone tires were rated "C," the lowest acceptable grade.[4]

Why then, Winerip asked, didn't Ford continue to use Goodyear tires beyond 1996? It was simply a matter of money, he wrote, "Goodyear decided it couldn't produce an Explorer tire at the price Ford was willing to pay." Winerip cited a January 1996 letter from Goodyear to C.J. Hole, a Ford purchasing director asking for a price increase to cover rising material costs and the reply from Ford turning down the increase because Goodyear's prices were already "uncompetitive."[5]

"The pricing level disparity between Goodyear and your competitors is a significant concern to us," Hole wrote. Unable to budge Ford, Goodyear stopped making tires for the Explorer. From 1997 until the recall, Ford contracted exclusively with the company that had the cheaper tires, Firestone.

Ford's Harmon says that at the time Ford thought it was getting a comparable quality tire from Firestone at "better value. In retrospect we were wrong."[6]

* * *

Just before Christmas, Firestone released the preliminary results of its "root cause" investigation. The timing was perfect: it allowed the tire company to take an important step toward putting important issues to rest without reopening the media's open-hunting season. The December 18 release addressed perhaps a fundamental question at the center of the crisis: What problems or defects had caused the tire failures? Answering this question with precision was critical to begin putting the controversy behind both companies and answering critics' calls for a greatly expanded recall.

Firestone's preliminary analysis pointed to four causes for the tire failures: the design of the 15" ATX tire had a relatively weak "shoulder," a pelletized rubber process used uniquely at the Decatur plant likely led to inferior adhesion of that plant's tires' steel belts, low inflation pressure in the recalled tires leading to higher running temperatures that would contribute to decreased belt adhesion, and vehicle load levels specified for the Explorer.

The first two causes were admissions on Firestone's part that its tire design and the manufacturing process at the Decatur plant were partially to blame. The revelation that the Decatur plant had used a unique process in applying rubber to the steel belts (using pellets rather than sheets of rubber as was the process in all the other Firestone plants) was particularly important in that it provided an explanation for the Decatur tire failures that did not place blame on the workers there. Up until the release of Firestone's analysis, suspicions abounded that the Decatur tire failures stemmed from poor quality work, or even deliberate sabotage, where labor tensions had persisted. But Firestone's root cause findings largely exonerated the Decatur workers. "The conclusions also absolved workers in Firestone plants of culpability for the tire failures, pinning any flaws in the tires themselves on the company's design and manufacturing processes," wrote Bradsher in the *New York Times*.[7]

The third and fourth causes – tire pressure and loading limits – mentioned in Firestone's news release clearly pointed to Ford sharing the blame for the tire failures. Firestone would continue to insist that Ford had pushed for a tire pressure recommendation for the Explorer (26 psi) that was too low to ensure the tires' durability. This argument ignored two facts. First, Firestone had signed off on the pressure recommendation and there was no evidence that the tire company had ever objected to it – until that early August 2000 weekend in Dearborn. And second, the same pressure recommendation had been

173

given for 2.9 million Goodyear tires equipped on Explorers during the mid-1990s and those tires had performed well, with no reports of tread separation accidents. Similarly, the load limit concern – that an Explorer loaded with passengers and gear was too heavy for the tires to bear – was likewise easily addressed by the solid performance of the Goodyear tires. Again and again, we would stress the comparison to the Goodyear tires, which fortuitously had provided a control group to the problematic Firestone tires.[8]

* * *

As the new year approached, we began preparing for an event that threatened to drag up again all the conspiracy theories against the Explorer, featuring memos seemingly showing a callous Ford Motor Company ignoring warning signs or even willfully designing an unsafe vehicle. The Donna Bailey case was scheduled to go to trial Monday Jan. 8, 2001 in Corpus Christi, Texas. Ford lawyers continued to meet with Tab Turner and the other attorneys representing Bailey, trying to settle the case, but were repeatedly rebuffed. Turner had long wanted to take a winnable Explorer rollover suit to trial because of the enormous publicity it would generate as well as the inflationary pressure a victory would place on Ford in future settlement discussions covering each of his growing inventory of Explorer cases. Ford had prevailed in each of the handful of Explorer cases it had taken to trial. But this case had every advantage Turner could ask for – a sympathetic plaintiff wearing her seatbelt, a driver who hadn't been drinking or asleep at the wheel, a horrible accident with a tragic result. And the case would be tried in a plaintiff-friendly venue.

I dreaded the onset of the Bailey case for another reason. Speaking dispassionately about the safety performance of the Explorer, about the history of its development and about accident statistics in the aggregate, I could continue to maintain some distance from the individual tragedies. Yes, I would speak with genuine compassion for the victims but abstractly and with the knowledge that there were other contributing factors for the crashes. Forty thousand or more people lost their lives every year on American highways, involving every make and model of car and every conceivable circumstance. Every life lost was a tragedy for the families affected.

And yet each of us went on living and working and driving, accepting the risks and keeping a safe mental distance from it all. The Bailey case would threaten to shatter the shell that kept it all impersonal.

Donna Bailey was riding along with two of her friends on March 10, 2000, along an open stretch of Texas highway in a blue 1997 Explorer. They headed for the bluffs of Enchanted Rock north of Austin where they planned to go rock climbing. The tread on one of the Explorer's 15" Firestone Wilderness AT tire began to peel away, then ripped almost completely off, banging violently against the inner wheel well of the vehicle. Inside, the driver was startled by the sudden and loud concussion, and perhaps jerked the steering wheel in the confusion (although the subsequent police report did not cite driver error as a causal factor). In an instant the Explorer rolled over, once and then again and again, finally coming to rest on its roof.

Her friends escaped with minor injuries but Bailey was paralyzed, dangling upside down, suspended by her shoulder belt. The formerly athletic mother of two had become a quadriplegic at the age of 43. Her story received considerable attention in the months after the accident, and especially after the announcement of the recall. Safety advocates calling for a broader recall of tires frequently talked about her case because the Firestone tire responsible for the accident was not part of the original recall.

As the court date neared, national media attention on the Bailey case intensified. Turner's PR firm was calling all of the prominent journalists covering the crisis, offering telephone interviews with Bailey. Or they could come down to Texas and talk to her in person as she lay in bed, forever crippled by the horrible accident. Bailey was more than willing to be interviewed; she wanted to tell her story. She was convinced that Ford and Firestone were absolutely to blame for the crash and should be made to pay dearly for it so that the rollover accidents would stop. She didn't want others to have to wake up each morning to the hell she lived with every day. *TIME* magazine featured a moving story with the ominous headline "A Nasty Turn for Ford?"

Today Bailey is a ventilator-dependent quadriplegic confined to a room at the Institute for Rehabilitation and Research in Houston. In December she turned 44, struggling to learn how to navigate a wheelchair she directs via a breathing tube. Though not a bitter person by nature, she wants justice for missing out on her kids' lives, not to mention her own. So this week, in a Corpus Christi courtroom, Bailey's lawyers will take on Ford Motor Co. and its tire supplier, Bridgestone/Firestone. The charge: that a defective tire--and more important, a defective car--took her livelihood. The principal defendant: the top-selling SUV of the decade, the Ford Explorer. Says lead attorney Tab Turner: "You can't divorce the two. It's a bad tire on a bad car."[9]

TIME's story pointed to the Bailey case as a potential turning point with blame shifting from Firestone to Ford.

Now it looks very much as if the nation's second largest automaker is about to enter an intense public interrogation over the extent to which flaws in the Explorer's design contributed to deaths and injuries like Bailey's....

Ford officials continue to deny vehemently any safety problems with the Explorer. "The Explorer has a phenomenal safety record and the lowest fatality rate in rollovers," says spokesman Jason Vines. The question now is whether that record will be enough to keep Ford above the assault of allegations that are likely to come as Donna Bailey's case goes public.[10]

I dreaded the coming days and weeks, having to travel back and forth from Michigan to Texas to endure the contentious proceedings. Public Affairs people didn't usually attend courthouse trials, but this one was sure to bring out most of the news media covering the Firestone tire crisis. We would need to stay close at hand to have any ability to get our side of the story out. The plaintiff attorneys would be sure to grandstand for the cameras outside the courthouse and continue to make the same accusations we had been diligently knocking down for weeks.

The defense lawyers continued to push for a settlement, but Turner was tightening the screws on Ford Motor Company, itching to bring the case to trial. Still, he had to be pleased by the huge settlement figures Ford was offering. Accepting a settlement much higher than any previous Explorer rollover payout would also have the desired inflationary effect on future discussions with Ford. And there were Donna Bailey's medical bills to consider. Even assuming that the plaintiff prevailed in court with an astronomical award, it might be years before she saw any money from Ford as the automaker would be sure to appeal. And appellate courts frequently reduced the amount of jury awards even when they upheld the lower court's ruling.

Finally, Turner and the other attorneys representing Bailey indicated that she would settle. But there was a catch. She wanted Ford and Firestone executives to visit her in the hospital and apologize. And, the attorneys said, she wanted the apology videotaped. Clearly, Turner was looking for a video advertisement that he could flaunt to demonstrate how he had brought two powerful companies to their knees.

The Ford lawyers balked at this request as a deal breaker. Negotiations resumed. Finally, it was agreed that Ford executives would visit the hospital to meet with Bailey and it would be videotaped but without sound. (Ford was the big gorilla that Turner most wanted to humble. Once he had the agreement from Ford, he didn't press for an in-person visit from Firestone, not wanting any delays to potentially scotch the overall settlement deal. John Lampe would send a hand-written note of apology to Bailey.) It was to be a dignified hospital visit without any theatrics for the video camera.

On Sunday, January 7, three Ford lawyers traveled to the Houston hospital to meet briefly with Bailey, and to humbly offer their condolences for her injuries. A short video, sans sound, of the Ford representatives at Bailey's bedside was distributed to media when the settlement deal was announced the next morning. "The videotape – which has no sound at Ford's request – shows three Ford lawyers, carrying briefcases, walking down a hallway at the hospital and then for about 15 seconds, talking to Ms. Bailey, who is lying in a hospital bed and using a ventilator," the *New York Times* reported. "The video was released by her lawyers to reporters and shown on nationwide television." Terms of the settlement were not disclosed but clearly it hadn't come cheap. "...while the settlement was thought to be very costly for the two companies – people close to the family said the dollar value totaled in the tens of millions... – it enables Ford and

Firestone to avoid what could have been an extremely damaging public trial."[11]

Turner would recall the drama of this hospital visit time and again in countless interviews. He was the David who had brought the Goliath automaker to its knees at the bedside of a paralyzed victim. Indeed, the synopsis for a planned movie version of Adam Penenberg's book, *Tragic Indifference*, uses exactly those terms in describing the film's plot (while inaccurately characterizing the plaintiff's settlement demands):

> *A David v. Goliath story of a lawsuit brought by attorney Tab Turner against the Ford and Firestone corporations for negligence in connection with SUV rollovers and defective tires. The story focuses on the case of Donna Bailey, who became a quadriplegic as a result of a near-fatal accident in a Ford SUV and sought only an admission of guilt and apology from the companies.*[12]

Michael Douglas had signed on to direct the film (with the working title "Blood Highway") and to play the lead role of Tab Turner. Long before we knew of this film project, members of the Ford crisis team in lighter moments had speculated on which actors would play each of us if the tire crisis was made into a movie. Jason decided his own role should be played by Pee Wee Herman, and none of us disagreed.

* * *

Ford had teams of engineers, tire experts, vehicle dynamic experts and safety researchers performing experiments in laboratories and test tracks as part of a massive "root cause analysis" effort. Firestone had its own work stream going. There wasn't much information sharing between the two companies' researchers.

On February 3, Firestone held a conference call for media in which it released the findings of tire expert Dr. Sanjay Govindjee, an associate professor of civil and environmental engineering at the University of California at Berkeley. Govindjee's findings pointed to a combination of factors, rather than a single cause of the tire failures.

"The phenomena of belt separation in these tires resulted from a crack that grew in the rubber between the two belts," Govindjee stated in the report. "This cracking is influenced by a number of factors, including climate, design of the tire, manufacturing differences at Firestone's Decatur plant and usage factors."[13]

The main message in Firestone's conference call was that Govindjee's tire experiments had provided laboratory confirmation for the four-part thesis in the preliminary analysis the tire company had released in December. Heat was the enemy of the tires. Tires operated in hot climates were most vulnerable, as were tires operated at sustained high speeds, in heavily loaded vehicles or at low inflation pressures – all factors that caused substantial heat build-up in the tires. Govindjee also confirmed that the material properties of the rubber between the belts was different for tires built in Decatur than tires from Firestone's other plants.

Lampe praised Govindjee's work and said it was an important step in moving past the isolated incidents of tire failures. Lampe also stressed his firm belief that the now-completed tire recall had been "more than adequate," a pre-emptive against any serious talk of a new, expanded tire recall. "Dr. Govindjee's report is another step forward in assuring that the difficulties we encountered last year with this one particular tire size and type won't happen again," Lampe said. "His report confirms and reinforces our earlier internal findings. It assures me that our company has taken the necessary and appropriate corrective steps to deal with this difficult situation."[14]

Govindjee's report provided the public with the first description of how problem tires began to come apart: Tread separations began as a "fatigue crack" between the tire's two steel belts and spread until the belts came apart. Demands placed on the tires from heavy loading were important in pushing a fatigue crack to grow, he said. On the conference call, the *New York Times'* Bradsher pressed Govindjee about the issue of loading. His story the next day chronicled the tire expert's answer, "'The variable that seems to be most important is the load on the tire – that is, the weight of the vehicle itself,' Mr. Govindjee said...." Bradsher's story included a response from Ford's Ken Zino, who said that the problem was that the tires "were unusually sensitive to the loads on them, and not that the Explorer was too heavy for its tires."[15]

* * *

The ebbs and flows in the uneasy and ultimately severed relationship between Ford and Firestone was a key part of the story that galvanized the news media's attention for so long. By the winter of 2001, the blame game had gone far beyond tiresome; it threatened to sink two proud companies with nearly 100 years of shared heritage. Ford Motor Company's consumer research consistently showed that customers were sick of what they perceived as Ford blaming Firestone and Firestone blaming Ford. They just wanted both companies to own up to their responsibilities and shut up.

It was time to go quiet.

For several weeks, Ford spokespeople held the line and refused to engage when journalists asked for comment on some new accusation. The company would take the high road; that's what customers in the focus groups had said they wanted.

But an odd thing happened. The news media, addicted to the predictable "he said, she said" formula of the Ford-Firestone squabble, neglected to mention in their stories that Ford no longer was attacking Firestone or even defending itself. And rather than participate in a communications détente that might have benefited both companies, Firestone stepped up its acerbic attacks on the Ford Explorer, relishing the opportunity of fighting an opponent who had grown weary of the fight. Consumer research continued to show massive distrust of both companies.

While the American public mostly agreed that the crisis was "a tire issue," not a "vehicle issue," they weren't letting Ford Motor Company off the hook. As one Ford executive explained to other company staffers attending another daily tire meeting: "A customer who goes to McDonald's and gets a bad pickle on his hamburger doesn't want to hear that it's the pickle maker's fault. He wants McDonald's to make it right with no excuses."

* * *

Ford engineers continued to study tires and tire-vehicle interactions, but much of the company geared up for the launch of the all-new 2002 Explorer. As the successor to the best-selling SUV in the world for each of the past 10 years, the new Explorer carried incredible expectations for the company. And the new 2002 Explorer was a worthy successor, with a new independent rear suspension for a greatly improved ride, a fold-down third-row seat, a new all-aluminum V-8 engine and a more spacious interior thanks to a platform that pushed the new Explorer's wheels out two inches wider than the previous Explorers'. It also would feature an array of industry-leading safety technology including electronic stability control, improved brakes and a side curtain airbag with rollover sensors that Ford called the Safety Canopy.[TM 16]

The improved safety features of the upcoming, next-generation Explorer were often mentioned as proof that Ford knew it had problems and was belatedly "fixing" them, such as in Cathy Booth Thomas' January 2001 piece in *TIME* magazine:

> *The 2002 Explorer, which automotive critics acclaim, is Ford's bid to compete against the barrage of new SUV entries hitting the market this year. But as regards the rollover issue, the new model also represents a paradoxical gamble. The company is touting the 2002's safety and environmental enhancements, such as an elaborate air-bag system, wider base and lower center of gravity. Yet the question remains: Why weren't these changes made earlier?*
>
> *That is certainly a focal point of Tab Turner's case...*[17]

Ironically, this line of thinking by safety advocates was hindering the advancement of safety in products sold in America. There was a chilling effect from companies' fears that product liability trial lawyers would succeed in some future trial in convincing jurors to condemn a product on the basis that a company had later introduced improvements in an updated version. For our part, we were adamant in emphasizing that improvements in features and functionality throughout the vehicle represented positive advancements – the Explorer had been a safe vehicle throughout its history and it would be a safety leader going forward.

* * *

During the relative calm in the tire storm throughout the winter of 2001, engineers at Ford, and undoubtedly at Firestone, were growing increasingly uneasy. Ford's root cause work was showing that Firestone Wilderness AT tires not included in the recall were failing in the lab in ways all too similar to the recalled tires. The tire field data – records of lawsuits and claims for personal injury and property damage closely held by Firestone – still indicated that the non-recalled tires had extremely low levels of tread separations, but perhaps it was only a matter of time. The latest data Ford had from Firestone only went through the first nine months of 2000. Meanwhile, the trial lawyer resource groups such as "Safetyforum.com" were quite vocal in calling for an expanded tire recall, citing tires from Firestone's Wilson, N.C., plant as especially troubling. As would be documented in the June 24 *New York Times* front page story (discussed in Chapter 3), the trial lawyers were sitting on additional lawsuits, waiting to file until the most opportune time, and might know of patterns of problems that we hadn't identified.[18]

In a replay of its recalcitrant behavior 12 months earlier, Firestone repeatedly stalled in turning over its field data to Ford. The Ford tire team emphasized the need for the latest data on tire performance to supplement its lab findings to determine if the tire recall needed to be expanded. In the interest of cooperation, Ford would share its tire test lab results with Firestone and with the government's lead vehicle safety agency, NHTSA.

The Ford tire team tested hundreds of tires – Firestone tires of various sizes and models that had been made at each of its plants, as well as tires made by Goodyear and other companies. Tires were placed on a dynamometer that would spin them for hours at various speeds while they were pressed down against the machine's base with a force replicating what a tire felt on a fully loaded Explorer. Friction produced heat and heat was the enemy of the rubber holding the steel belts together. As the fully loaded tires continued to run for hours at high speeds, some of the tires would suddenly rip apart in a violent burst of sheared rubber tread and tiny steel chords. More and more tires were subjected to the sustained torture on the dyno, giving the Ford engineers a more complete understanding of the forces required to detread various types and makes of tires. The picture was becoming clearer.

Meanwhile, Ford vehicle dynamics experts were testing several models of SUVs on a test track in Florida to see how the vehicles handled during and after a tire tread separation. The controlled experiments provided the first thorough look at an SUV's response to this relatively rare type of tire failure. There were no applicable government regulations or company safety standards. So the focus of Ford's study was to see how a number of representative SUVs responded when the driver tried to steer it, with and without braking, after a tread separation.

For the purpose of the experiment, each SUV had one tire that had been prepped with deep cuts to the rubber in its shoulder so that in sustained high speed driving around the test track the tire would be sure to come apart. Each test vehicle was equipped with a pair of outriggers that would allow the vehicle to tip over on two wheels but would prevent any actual rollovers in the tests. Any tip up would count in the study as a dangerous outcome likely leading to a serious, life-threatening crash. The test drivers, of course, were buckled and wore helmets as an added precaution.

Plaintiff attorney Tab Turner had used similar equipment to stage a demonstration of the Explorer's supposed instability. Under no obligation to perform a scientifically rigorous experiment, he intended to showcase the Explorer's tendency to rollover in a dramatic video that could help sway a jury. As compelling as the accident stories were, the only photos or videos invariably were taken after the accident. A staged demonstration would provide priceless footage for the courtroom. Rollovers led to terrible crashes, so an obvious problem in staging a rollover was how to protect the test driver. Turner contracted with a company called Transportation Safety Technologies for the demonstration, in which an old Explorer was equipped with outriggers similar to those that automakers used when testing vehicles in aggressive handling maneuvers during a vehicle's development (and that Ford used in its SUV handling tests at its Florida test track). This undoubtedly was a difficult compromise for Turner to agree to since what he most wanted was to create an indelible image of a rollover crash in the minds of each juror who would see it. A test Explorer tipping up on an outrigger would be far less dramatic to view than an actual rollover.

But to Turner's good fortune, the demonstration accidentally produced just the dramatic footage he had desired. The Explorer that had been equipped with a bad tire spun violently out of control when the tire separated, breaking one of the outriggers which allowed the vehicle to tumble repeatedly off the track and down a shallow embankment. (The outriggers may not have been of adequate strength or been attached incorrectly to the demonstration vehicle.) Fortunately, the test driver was uninjured.

Turner had been boarding his private jet with journalist Winerip when he learned of the test-track mishap. Winerip tells the story of a gleeful Turner instantly realizing the value of the video-taped Explorer rollover in the *Sunday Times* magazine cover story published December 17:

> *That mid-November morning, as he waited ... to take off from Little Rock, the cell phone rang yet again, and it was the head of a test-driving company calling with the latest results. A few months before, Turner hired the Arizona company to run two Explorers through a series of extreme maneuvers. "Howdy, Steve," Turner said. "I had a productive trip. Sorry I missed you, but money always comes first."*
>
> *The jet was taxiing for takeoff. "Oh! How did Mark lose control? . . . Wow! And he's O.K.? . . . Did you get it on video? . . . All right! . . . Let's keep this quiet for now. The last thing we need at this point is one of these media hounds finding out." As the jet climbed upward, Turner put the cell phone down. "Rolled over," he grinned. "Can't do better than that -- that's worth a half-million dollars right there."[19]*

The day after Winerip's story appeared in the *Sunday Times*, Turner gave the videotape of the crashing Explorer to Sharyl Atkinson, who dutifully included it in her piece for the CBS Evening News program, spicing up that day's rather benign news of Firestone's preliminary root cause analysis.

Exclusive video obtained by CBS News offers a dramatic glimpse of the most violent reaction possible to a tread separation. The tests were conducted for lawyers suing Ford.

In the test, the Explorer is fitted with a special outrigger to keep from flipping over. At the moment the tire tread separates, the Explorer appears to swerve drastically out of control. Then something completely unexpected happens: the protective outrigger breaks and the Explorer rolls over.

"The response can be very violent," says Mark Arndt, of Transportation Safety Technologies. "In fact, the response can be so violent, as in this test, that it's not controllable."[20]

* * *

In a two-day meeting at the end of March in Dearborn, Ford engineers and executives met with investigators from NHTSA to discuss the findings of the company's tire and vehicle research and analysis. In controlled experiments on the Ford test track, the Explorer had behaved like other similar-sized SUVs both during and after tire tread separations. The tests showed that each of the SUVs tested continued to drive straight and remain stable after a separation if the driver kept the steering wheel straight and did not brake. However, when the test driver responded to the tire failure with a sharp steering input, and especially if he also braked hard, the vehicle often would tip up sharply on its outriggers, indicating a rollover accident was likely. Each of the SUVs behaved this way – a sudden steering input from the driver after the tread separation would cause the vehicle to veer sharply out of control and a counter steering input would often lift the test vehicle up on its side.

The Ford team presenting the research was careful to point out that the company was not saying that drivers had been at fault in the rollover accidents. The sudden concussion of a tire pelt thumping repeatedly against the vehicle's steel wheel well would be a terrifyingly loud drum beat inside the car and it wouldn't be surprising if drivers reacted by braking hard while trying to steer the vehicle onto the highway shoulder. This natural reaction was exactly the wrong thing to do no matter which SUV they were driving.

At the end of the second day, the NHTSA staffers indicated they understood and did not disagree with Ford's findings that the Explorer had no unique handling characteristics that might make it particularly dangerous in responding to a tread separation.

The meeting also included considerable discussion about Ford's tire failure test on laboratory dynamometers. The tests showed Firestone tires failing sooner and at considerably lower speeds than other brand tires (though still at speeds near or above 100 mph). And the tests showed similar results for Firestone tires of a number of specifications beyond those included in the recall, although the Ford researchers were quick to add that they did not feel the tests alone were conclusive in identifying populations of problem tires. Rather, the lab results should be used in conjunction with real-world tire failure data.

The Ford safety analysts asked the NHTSA staffers for more information about tread separation claims from a variety of manufacturers to help determine some baseline of what might be considered a "normal" failure rate for the tire industry. While confidentiality agreements with the tire makers prevented the NHTSA team from sharing specific claims, they did let the Ford team know that NHTSA had looked at 10 non-Firestone lines of high-volume tires fitted to SUVs and found tread separation claims ranging from zero to about 7 per million tires.

Then the NHTSA investigators told the Ford team to press harder for the latest claims data from Firestone. NHTSA had access to the data but could not share it with Ford, and clearly NHTSA was troubled by what they had seen. The government safety experts gave a strong indication that Wilderness AT tires from Firestone's Wilson plant were particularly troubling but they stressed that they did not yet have a complete picture. Ford's laboratory work and analysis, fitted with the latest claims data, could much more precisely identify suspect populations of tires. (The Firestone tires included in the August 2000 recall were failing in the field in such large numbers as to necessitate a recall before any significant laboratory work had been completed. The other Firestone Wilderness AT tires being scrutinized in the spring of

2001 were failing in much smaller numbers and after longer terms in service.)

One day after concluding the Dearborn meeting with the federal investigators, Ford gave Firestone copies of a thick black binder summarizing its tire and vehicle investigation, the same information Ford had reviewed with NHTSA. And again, Ford pressed Firestone for its most recent claims data. Firestone continued to stall, hoping against hope that it had put the tread separation crisis behind it and could move ahead with bold plans to restore its brand.

* * *

Less than a week later, on April 5, Firestone announced a major image-building advertising campaign, "Making it Right." It would include print ads in major newspapers and trade publications, as well as TV and radio commercials. The news release quoted Lampe in explaining the focus of the campaign:

> *"In the past few months we have carefully examined the way we do business and are making significant changes and enhancements along the way. The 'Making it Right' action plan outlines those enhancements and is an important part of our commitment to restoring public trust in the Firestone brand. We believe in our tires, and we want to prove to the American public they should believe in them as well."*[21]

The print ads were quite simple, featuring a small black-and-white photo of Lampe under the headline "Making It Right: You Have Our Word on That." The body copy emphasized this theme of trust and dependability: "We'll do whatever it takes, however long it takes, to win your trust.... In the role of watchdogs, a new team of top technical and quality control managers has been assembled to continuously analyze tire and safety data. They'll act to uncover issues before they become problems."[22]

Although the ads themselves were not particularly well received, there was no denying that the Firestone brand under Lampe was demonstrating remarkable resilience. Against all odds, he was determined to save the Firestone name. He believed that the time was right to begin putting the problems in the rear view mirror (note how the ad copy begins with a promise to fix what had gone wrong and then shifts to a promise to work to prevent future problems). To Lampe's thinking, Firestone had taken more than its fair share of the blame. And he steadily stepped up the rhetoric questioning the Ford Explorer's role in the tread separation accidents. Congressman Billy Tauzin planned to hold another round of hearings in June and Lampe wanted the focus to be on the Explorer.

* * *

We weren't out of the woods yet by any means, but that didn't stop some inside Ford from declaring victory. An in-depth cover story April 28 in the *National Journal*, headlined "Blowout," examined and contrasted the lobbying efforts by Firestone and Ford in connection with the Congressional hearings the previous fall. The story lambasted Firestone for its inconsistent work on Capital Hill, while giving the Ford team high marks. "After watching both chief executives testify, [Congressman Ed] Bryant says he knew the damage to Bridgestone/Firestone was severe. 'The contrast was really there.'...'Ford ate our lunch,' says a lobbyist for the [tire maker]."[23]

There were many specific details in the 6,000-word story that made it obvious that the reporter, Shawn Zeller, had been well informed by a source inside our Washington office. And, in fact, Ford's vice president of Governmental Affairs was singled out for the highest praise. "The situation at Ford was much different [from the confusion at Firestone, thoroughly chronicled earlier in the story]," Zeller wrote. "The automaker benefited from a large Washington government affairs staff headed by Janet Mullins Grissom, a former State Department aide... An experienced Washington player, Grissom saw what was coming."[24] It didn't strike me as particularly helpful for a Ford executive to so overtly engage in self-promotion in Washington just before a new round of hearings was set to kick off. But what did I know about matters inside the Beltway?

I read the rest of the story incredulously. Then I brought the magazine into Jason's office and waved it at him. He looked at what I was holding, then turned back to his computer screen, feigning disinterest. He obviously had already read the piece. "You'd think in a story that long there'd be some mention of who had tried her hardest to keep Jac from testifying," he said at last.[*]

* * *

On May 11, 2001, Firestone finally turned over its claims data for the final three months of 2000. And there it was – claims for Wilson-built tires jumped sharply from the levels in the previous data. Although still far below the claims rates for the Decatur-built tires in the original recall, both 15" and 16" Wilson tires were involved in an unsettling number of injury accidents. And a number of other types of Firestone tires showed an increasing level of claims in the latest data.

Staying quiet was no longer an option for Ford; more tires would have to be replaced. Millions of more tires.

But Firestone would certainly not agree that an expanded recall was justified. Even in the latest data, the failure rates in terms of claims per million tires were far lower than the tires that had been recalled. Where would it end? It was not possible to guarantee that there would be no tread separations in any population of millions of tires, each driven for tens of thousands of miles, particularly when proper customer maintenance was necessary for the tire's robust performance. Firestone management continued to believe that incidents of improper inflation by customers explained the tread separations on tires not included in the recall.

Ford executives and key members of the tire team quietly made preparations to meet with Firestone and with NHTSA. Ford would press Firestone to voluntarily recall a huge new population of tires. But if Firestone refused, Ford would have to replace the tires on its own. With the heat of summer approaching, it would be irresponsible to delay in replacing suspect tires.

But before the Ford team could meet with Firestone, Keith Bradsher broke a story that would infuriate the tire maker and

---

[*] *Indeed the only reference to the issue is this passage: "The one point on which [Firestone's] lobbyists were persuasive was their recommendation that Ono testify. At the time, having the CEO appear before Congress seemed like a deft PR move, especially given that Ford CEO Nasser was expressing reluctance to testify."[25]*

precipitate the final break-up of the two companies' historic relationship.

On Friday, May 18, the front page of the *New York Times* featured
a story headlined "Ford is Said to Consider Seeking Recalls of More
Tires." Bradsher's piece citing unnamed sources at Ford and NHTSA
who said that the automaker was close to announcing a replacement
campaign of millions more Firestone Wilderness AT tires.

> *The new problems were identified by Ford statisticians a
> month ago, after an exhaustive review of data on many
> brands of tires used on many kinds of vehicles, people close
> to the review said. ...Ford hopes to make a final decision on
> whether to seek a further recall by the end of the month, and
> perhaps as soon as this weekend, two people close to the
> review said.*

> *Jill Bratina, a spokeswoman for Bridgestone/Firestone
> Inc., said that the tire maker had not been in discussions with
> Ford about any kind of broader recall.*[26]

The story made it clear that another recall would be a bitter pill for
Firestone to swallow.

> *Last month, the company... began the biggest advertising
> campaign in its history, in hopes of regaining consumers'
> confidence in the Firestone brand. Its sales of replacement
> tires are down sharply, and Bridgestone's stock remains more
> than 40 percent lower than a year ago.*

> *If a new recall included all tires with problem rates that
> are above average by a statistically significant margin – the
> broadest action under consideration by Ford – it would
> involve even more tires than were recalled in August.*[27]

We could only imagine the reaction to the revelations in
Bradsher's story at Firestone's headquarters in Nashville. Carlos
Mazzorin, Ford's vice president in charge of Purchasing, called John
Lampe requesting a meeting in Dearborn the following day to discuss

Ford's analysis of tire claims data in conjunction with its laboratory and vehicle field testing. Lampe said he couldn't get his team together that quickly. Mazzorin offered to fly down to Nashville. The Ford representatives could come down later that same day, or on Saturday, whatever would work best for the Firestone team. Lampe said he wouldn't be prepared to meet with Ford until Wednesday of the following week. Mazzorin insisted on meeting sooner, and eventually they agreed to meet in Nashville on the following Monday.

Clearly it was not going to be a pleasant social call.

On Monday, May 21, Mazzorin and two other executives, Richard Parry-Jones and Sue Cischke, who had succeeded Helen Petrauskas as head of Environmental and Safety Engineering, flew to Nashville on a corporate jet. Lampe met them at the airport and brought them to Firestone's head office where they went directly to an executive conference room. Parry-Jones led a detailed technical analysis both of the dynamometer tire experiments and the real-world tire claims data. Taken together, it was evident that there were serious concerns about a number of Wilderness AT tires that had not been included in the recall. Lampe and other Firestone executives asked several questions about Ford's methodology which Parry-Jones and Cischke answered.

Then Lampe switched gears. He wanted to know about the Explorer. Lampe especially questioned its stability after a tire tread separation. Again, it was Parry-Jones who responded. Parry-Jones had received considerable acclaim, first in Europe and subsequently in North America, as one of the most brilliant technical minds in the auto industry in the complex field of vehicle dynamics. He patiently explained the thorough testing Ford had done with Explorers and other SUVs to study their handling characteristics during and after a tread separation. All of the SUVs had responded similarly, he said. All remained safe and stable if the driver did not steer sharply after the separation. But all showed a similar tendency to spin out of control if a driver turned sharply to the left after a right rear tread separation, or sharply to the right following a left rear separation. The various SUVs were no different in their response to these driver inputs. Further, there was no practical way for an automaker to design a vehicle to remain completely controllable during a catastrophic tread separation and still have plenty of maneuverability during the everyday circumstance of driving on four good tires. The only way to reduce the tread separation accidents, Parry-Jones said, was to replace tires prone to tread separation.

Lampe abruptly ended the meeting, and handed Parry-Jones a letter to Nasser. In the letter, which obviously had been prepared before the Ford executives had arrived in Nashville, Lampe said that Firestone had decided to terminate its 97-year-old relationship. The letter, in its entirety, read:

Today, I am informing you that Bridgestone/Firestone, Inc. is ending its tire supply relationship with the Ford Motor Company. While we will honor our existing contractual obligations to you, we will not enter into any new tire sales agreements in the Americas with Ford beginning today.

Business relationships, like personal ones, are built upon trust and mutual respect. We have come to the conclusion that we can no longer supply tires to Ford since the basic foundation of our relationship has been seriously eroded. This is not a decision we make lightly after almost 100 years of history. But we must look to the future and the best interests of our company, our employees and our other customers.

Our analysis suggests that there are significant safety issues with a substantial segment of Ford Explorers. We have made your staff aware of our concerns. They have steadfastly refused to acknowledge those issues.

We have always said that in order to insure the safety of the driving public, it is crucial that there be a true sharing of information concerning the vehicle as well as the tires. You simply are not willing to do that. We believe you are attempting to divert scrutiny of your vehicle by casting doubt on the quality of Firestone tires. These tires are safe, and as we have said before, when we have a problem, we will acknowledge that problem and fix it. We expect you to do the same.

I wish you and the Ford Motor Company continued success and regret that we cannot continue our relationship going forward.[28]

Lampe did not mention to the Ford executives that Firestone already had distributed the letter to the newswire services and the television networks as a preemptive move against Ford's call for a massive, new tire recall that had been foretold by the *New York Times*. Nor did Lampe mention the meetings Firestone had recently held with NHTSA in which the tire maker was given clear indication that the safety agency was leaning strongly toward ordering a second recall of millions of Wilderness tires manufactured at Firestone's Wilson plant, a recall that would have had devastating consequences for Firestone.

Soon after we learned of Lampe's letter, we hastily drafted a short statement to make sure media and the public understood what really had led to Firestone's action: "We are deeply disappointed that upon hearing and seeing (Ford's latest) analysis of Firestone Wilderness AT tires, Firestone decided not to work together for the safety of our shared customers, which is the only issue that matters." In a story headlined "Firestone Dumps Ford," CNN included that statement and noted: "Many safety advocates have pushed for Firestone to expand its recall ... and according to published reports last week, Ford officials were weighing whether to push Firestone to expand the recall of tires as well...." With some on-background guidance from us, CNN predicted that "Nasser will present the findings of its latest analysis to Congress Tuesday, reportedly along with the details of the expanded recall."[29]

The next morning, we put out the word that we would hold a news conference that afternoon in the media center on the first floor of the Glass House. We didn't worry at all about the media turn-out even on such short notice; reporters were anxiously waiting for Ford's next move. Nasser confirmed the stunning news that Ford would take it upon itself to replace about 13 million Wilderness AT tires, tires that Firestone had refused to recall. "We simply do not have enough confidence in the future performance of these tires keeping our customers safe," he said.[30] "Ford's decision to replace an enormous number of tires over the supplier's objections, at a cost that Ford estimated at \$3 billion, is unheard of in the auto industry," Bradsher reported in the *New York Times.*[31]

Firestone responded with a statement of its own declaring that its tires were safe and that Ford was undertaking the replacement campaign in an attempt to create a "smokescreen" to cover up the Explorer's safety problems.[32] To the Ford management team, it was ludicrous that the company would spend billions of dollars to voluntarily replace tires – and in the process dredge up a story that had mostly gone away – as some sort of "smokescreen."

The two companies were now openly at war. Bradsher could scarcely hide his amazement as he chronicled what had transpired over the previous few days in his analysis piece in the *Times* May 24:

> *Instead of standing shoulder to shoulder as they face hundreds of lawsuits, further Congressional hearings and public criticism, Ford and Firestone have been playing elaborate games, refusing to speak to each other's executives and secretly telling regulators about safety problems with the other company's products.*
>
> *Now they are publicly denouncing each other every few hours. Firestone released statistical analyses today purporting to show that the Ford Explorer is more likely to roll over than other sport utility vehicles when a tire fails, a day after Ford released an analysis showing that Explorers were less likely to roll over. Ford and Firestone presented Congressional investigators this afternoon with reports blaming each other's products for crashes that have killed more than 100 people in Explorers, mostly in the summers of 1999 and 2000.*
>
> *"Both presentations raised more questions than they answered, and we will be requesting additional documents," said Ken Johnson, a spokesman for Representative Billy Tauzin, the Louisiana Republican who is chairman of the Energy and Commerce Committee and has led the Congressional investigation. "It's getting ugly. They've gone from shouting to shooting."[33]*

* * *

Meanwhile, Tab Turner continued to peddle to major media his conspiracy theories about compromises Ford had made in the development of the Explorer. *TIME* magazine assigned five writers over several months the task of sorting through the various allegations and making some sense of them. The dramatic events in Nashville provided a perfect news peg for *TIME*'s feature story:

> *In the most spectacular corporate crack-up in recent memory, consumers hardly knew whom to trust or root for last week. First, Bridgestone/Firestone CEO John Lampe brought the tire maker's 95-year-old business with Ford Motor Co. to a screeching halt over what Lampe called "significant concerns" about the safety of the Ford Explorer. One day later, Ford said it would replace 13 million Firestone Wilderness AT tires—mounted mainly on Explorers—that were excluded from Firestone's sweeping 6.5 million tire recall last August. Firestone admitted that those tires were no good but maintains that everything else on the road today is safe....*

> *Ford is clearly trying to pin the damage on Firestone, and vice versa. But a five-month investigation by* TIME *of Ford documents, which the company prepared for investigators and government lawyers, shows Ford's engineers were wrestling with the stability and handling of the Explorer even before it hit the market in 1990... Previously undisclosed memos and emails show the extent to which the engineers were juggling decisions about the Explorer's suspension systems, tire pressure, weight and steering characteristics, plus its height and width, all of which could factor into a vehicle's stability.[34]*

The *TIME* writers largely succeeded in taking a complex subject – engineering trade-offs in balancing several competing objectives – and making it understandable for their readers. "No company sets out to design an unsafe vehicle. But creating a car involves making trade-offs

195

among engineering, manufacturing, safety, sales and advertising components as well as responding to consumer and competitive pressures. It is a wildly expensive process that takes five years or so to complete."[35]

The article cited two Ford memos written 12 months before the Explorer would first go on sale in April 1990 in which engineers fret over a prototype's performance in a stability test featuring emergency handling procedures. "Of course, prototypes are early versions of vehicles that are built so that designers can get the bugs out. And Ford says it got the bugs out," the article's authors stated as they strove to be fair and balanced: "'In developing any product you go through variations,' says Ford spokesman Jon Harmon. 'Then you test them until they meet standards.' He adds that the Explorer has proved to be among the safest vehicles in its class."[36]

But the next sentence in the story was simply incorrect: "It's not a particularly safe class, compared with cars."[37] In the interest of simplification, *TIME* got it wrong, confusing two sets of statistics: overall fatality rates that consistently showed SUVs as being safer than passenger cars, and fatality rates specifically for rollover accidents in which SUVs indeed had elevated numbers.

It was a common mistake that we often saw in the media coverage. SUVs certainly were involved in more rollovers than cars. And rollovers were often fatal crashes. But cars were involved in more frontal and side collisions than SUVs (the higher seating position of the SUV driver afforded better visibility enabling them to avoid accidents). And SUVs tended to be larger and heavier than cars, providing increased occupant protection when a crash did occur. Crashes from frontal and side collisions, too, were often fatal crashes. All told, you were more likely to die during a million miles of car driving than in a million miles of SUV driving. Reporters often brushed off this explanation, saying, "Maybe, but we're writing about rollovers."

At that point, if I had worked with the writer before, I might ask to go off the record. "Listen," I would say, not wanting to be quoted saying something that might sound callous but that was important for the journalist to understand, "it doesn't matter how you die. No fatality is worse than another fatality. Your story is wrong if it leads readers to the conclusion that they would be safer trading in their SUVs for a car.

In fact, they will be somewhat *more likely* to be killed. Our job as an automaker is to reduce the overall likelihood of any kind of fatality in any number of foreseeable types of accidents. Focusing on one type of accident without paying attention to all other types of accidents would be irresponsible."

Lesson Learned: Understand thoroughly the subtleties of your story. *Don't let journalists jump to inaccurate conclusions in the interest of simplicity. Whenever possible, find a way to make your points simple. But don't compromise the truth in the interest of "dumbing it down," and don't let others get away with it either.*

* * *

We knew we didn't want to repeat one of the key mistakes of the first tire recall – failing to provide the data that defined the population of tires needing to be recalled. It wasn't just elevated failure rates. Ford's tire team had made considerable progress over the past few months in advancing the science of understanding tire tread separations and their effect on vehicle dynamics. It was time to present our findings and to relate them directly to Ford's decision to replace millions of tires that Firestone insisted were perfectly safe.

Nasser would open the news conference to set the stage. Richard Parry-Jones and Tom Baughman would then take the media through a detailed PowerPoint that I was creating that would explain why certain tires were prone to the separations and what effects tread separations had on various SUVs being driven at highway speeds. The discussion should be thorough, complete and a bit dull. We wanted the journalists to walk away feeling their questions had been thoroughly answered and to understand that we had conducted a serious and rigorous scientific study of the core issues.

But we also wanted to include something memorable with just enough visual interest to be featured in all the television news coverage. Something that would focus the attention of the journalists, along with their readers and viewers, on the tires and away from the Explorer. We would thoroughly explain in the PowerPoint why the Firestone tires were failing and how the Explorer and other SUVs responded to tread separations. But we needed to reinforce the emphasis on the problem tires with a strong visual.

We had made plenty of videotapes of tires running on dynamometers, spinning and spinning until they suddenly ripped apart. This was a good start. But the videos had no sound, so they were a bit sterile. And the video of an exploding Firestone tire didn't mean much unless you also watched a companion video of the tests of Goodyear or other durable tires performing well on the dyno. We needed to bring all that together.

I explained to Parry-Jones what I thought we needed to make just the right impression: a split-screen video that would show two tires side-by-side, each of dynos performing the same test cycle. We would put microphones in the dyno boxes to record sound. Richard agreed to the idea, although he was plainly irritated by the concept of having to provide an interesting visual for the media and the public. "You already are making all the slides for kindergartners," he said disapprovingly. He was referring to the large up or down arrows labeled "stronger" or "increased failure rate" that I had added to each slide featuring a chart so a non-technical audience could instantly tell if trends on the graphs were good or bad. The data should stand for itself, Parry-Jones had thought. But he let us keep the arrows and the simple language in the slides' headings.

We were busy both days of the weekend before our news conference tracking down pieces of information and data points to complete the PowerPoint, which despite our best intentions at brevity would grow to 33 slides. So I chose not to go to the lab where the dyno runs Sunday would be videotaped, a decision I would soon deeply regret. The engineers and video director were instructed to run the tests just like they were conducted during actual testing over the course of two hours or so – with each tire feeling the equivalent weight of its share of a fully loaded Explorer and "exercised" for consecutive 10-minute increments at ever-increasing speeds.

The tests were run and edited down to a single split screen, a Firestone tire of the type that Ford was now replacing and a similar spec Goodyear tire, side by side on identical dynos. A whirring sound of the spinning tires continued for a few seconds, then changed pitch slightly as the dyno speed increased past 90 mph. Again the sound changed slightly as the speed increased again, a digital read-out indicating that each tire was now being run at 100 mph. A digital clock kept track of the time the tires' torture test had lasted – as the edited tape featured only a few seconds at each speed. Another step up in speed, and then in just a few seconds the Firestone tire began to get angry, shaking and shredding pieces of rubber before a loud *BANG!* burst out from that side of the video screen. The tread pelt from the Firestone tire ripped off the rest of the tire and smashed violently against the remote camera inside the wire cage surrounding the dyno. The camera angle was left askew as the tire carcass began to slow down, the operator having turned off that dyno. Meanwhile, the Goodyear tire continued to spin, a bit of a blur at that speed, but clearly still holding together well.

Everyone who saw the video was captivated by it. We smiled broadly knowing we had the visual that would run on every network's news. And then a horrible thing happened. The video continued to run, stepping the Goodyear tire through the next level of speed on the dyno torture test, then time-lapsed to an even higher speed. And before we knew it, we watched the Goodyear tire begin to shake and tremble, and soon it, too, had thrown its pelt. To the engineers this was the obvious conclusion to the dyno test – you ran it until the tire inevitably failed. The test showed that it had taken a higher speed and additional time on the dyno to bring about the death of the Goodyear tire of the same age and specifications as the Firestone tire.

But I saw it differently. Continuing to run the test to include the destruction of the Goodyear tire severely weakened the visual power of the demonstration. It showed the Goodyear tire to be mortal; worse it came apart in a very similar fashion as the Firestone tire. Previously, the Firestone tire had appeared to be sinisterly flawed, capable of suddenly exploding in a terrible manner. Now we had been shown that the same fate could happen to the Goodyear tire; albeit at a higher speed and longer cumulative time on the dyno.

We debated cutting the tape to end after the destruction of the Firestone tire. But Parry-Jones was adamantly against it. It was one thing if we had ceased running the test as we'd planned. Now that the test had been allowed to run longer, and to be captured on video, we had a problem. Clearly we could not destroy any portion of the original tape; with all the litigation pending we were prohibited from destroying relevant evidence that plaintiffs would have a right to review. But Parry-Jones didn't even want us to shorten the already edited tape. Showing and releasing the shortened tape to the media might expose the company to questions about the rest of the tape and we might have to later come forward sheepishly with the rest of the tape showing the shredding of the Goodyear tire. On the other hand, the test should have ended when the first tire shredded. As long as we didn't alter the image of either of the tests up until that point, editing the tape to end there wouldn't be duplicitous, would it?

We decided against showing any of it to the media. I was sick to my stomach, knowing I should have personally supervised the production of the video. But I also was convinced that there wasn't a plaintiff attorney in the country who wouldn't have edited and released the tape. And I didn't think they would have been wrong to do it. But once again, Ford made the conservative, cautious choice.

Lesson learned: Make sure critical projects are executed properly even if that requires you to supervise them yourself when you are immersed in other responsibilities.

Lesson learned: Stay on the moral high ground, absolutely. But don't confuse integrity with scrupulosity. Do the right thing always, but don't tie your own hands behind your back unnecessarily.

At the news conference, Nasser declared that we had acted in our customer's interest in deciding to replace millions of tires that Firestone refused to replace. Parry-Jones and Baughman led a detailed technical discussion of the science of tire and vehicle testing. They went through the PowerPoint dutifully. The Firestone tires, both those recalled earlier and those Ford was now replacing, ran considerably hotter than Goodyear tires under a variety of loads and a variety of inflation pressures, just as they would experience in the real world of customer use. For example, the rubber on a Firestone tire under a fully loaded Explorer and inflated to only 18 psi reached 170°F in the test, compared to about 140°F for a Goodyear tire subjected to the same treatment. Heat was the enemy of the tires. "Running at a relatively cool temperature is a tire's first line of defense against a tread separation," read the large heading on the slide. The second line of defense was a relatively large "wedge" (a tiny piece of rubber inserted

200

where the tire's steel belts came together inside the tire's "shoulder") that would safely absorb the flexing energy of a loaded tire under stress. The Ford team had cut up hundreds of tires, measuring their wedges: Decatur-built Firestone tires had the smallest wedges at an average of 1.1 mm; the wedges from tires at Firestone's other plants averaged between 1.2 and 1.6 mm; the wedges for Goodyear tires came in at 1.7 mm. Finally, the third line of defense was a tire's "peel strength" – the resistance its steel belts put up to forces trying to pull them apart. Again, Decatur tires were the weakest; the best of Firestone's tires were about equal to the Goodyear tires in peel strength. The Firestone tires Ford had tested were significantly more prone to separation than were the Goodyear tires and these three variables showed why: Goodyear tires ran cooler, had bigger wedges and more peel strength than most of the Firestone tires.[38]

Parry-Jones also described the results of dynamic testing of the Explorer and other similar-sized SUVs. Numerous charts depicted the "under steer" characteristics of 10 different SUVs – included expensive European models such as the BMW X5 and Mercedes ML320, as well as the Explorer's more traditional competition, the Chevy Blazer and Jeep Grand Cherokee. The Explorer performed pretty much like all the other SUVs before, during and after a tread separation. This was not to say that tread separations were always routine events on the test track. "A tread separation alters the handling of all vehicles dramatically," one of the slides read. "Explorers, like every other vehicle we have tested, cannot deal with a tread separation well enough to avoid a small but significant risk of loss of control with the treadless tire."[39]

When Parry-Jones had finished going through the PowerPoint, he and Baughman dutifully answered the reporters' questions. It was all very thorough and reasonable and technically sound. But there was no emotion. And we were not rewarded with the blanket of sympathetic coverage we had once envisioned.

Lesson Learned: There is a need for analytic purity and thoroughness in a complex story. But you need something visually interesting and emotionally engaging to break through to viewers and readers. Journalists and their editors screen out the dull even when it is factually important.

CHAPTER TEN

CASE CLOSED?

"There are two modes of establishing our reputation: to be praised by honest men, and to be abused by rogues. It is best, however, to secure the former, because it will invariably be accompanied by the latter."

- *Charles Caleb Colton (1780-1832)*

* * *

The feud between Ford and Firestone had gone from ill-advised to ridiculous. There seemed no way out of a vicious cycle. Firestone's accusations provided credibility to the plaintiff attorneys' "experts" who charged that the Explorer was as much to blame as the tires. NHTSA was taking a more cautious and deliberative stance, but other authorities in the U.S. and abroad had seemingly made their decision, as *Consumeraffairs.com* noted:

> *Early in the week, Bridgestone/Firestone announced it would no longer sell tires to Ford, adopting what might be described as the "You can't fire me, I quit" approach. Sure enough, the next day Ford announced it was eliminating Firestone tires from most models and offered to replace <u>all</u> 13 million Wilderness AT tires on Ford vehicles....*

> *But Ford's dramatic action was followed by a report from Venezuela saying that consumer protection officials*

there were considering recommending a ban on the Explorer, blaming design problems with the vehicle for a string of accidents. Officials said there have been 25 deaths in Explorer rollovers since May 2000, when Ford replaced Firestone AT tires on all Explorers in Venezuela.

The National Highway Traffic Safety Administration is investigating but says it doesn't expect to reach a conclusion until August. In Congress, Rep. W.J. "Billy" Tauzin (R-La.) says the House Commerce Committee, which he chairs, will hold hearings on the dispute next month.[1]

Shortly after Tauzin opened the new round of hearings, the Congressman sent a letter to NHTSA asking the safety agency to broaden its tire investigation to look into accusations about the stability of the Ford Explorer. "...the scope of your investigation appears to have always avoided one of the key questions posed by last year's controversy: whether the problem with the Firestone tires is solely a tire issue, or whether it is a tire-vehicle application issue," Tauzin wrote.[2]

In written testimony submitted to Tauzin, Lampe had two simple messages: the additional tire recall was ill-advised and the focus of future investigations should be on the Explorer. "The recall of more of our tires is not necessary and will not increase customer safety," he said. "There is something wrong with the Ford Explorer."[3]

Nasser was direct in his rebuttal: "This is a tire problem and only a tire problem."[4] Another recall was necessary because consumers had lost faith in the Firestone tires, he said.

Firestone tipped off Tauzin's investigators to another seemingly stunning development: some of the tires Ford planned to use as replacements in the massive expanded recall had failure rates far higher than some of the Firestone tires to be recalled. But this sensational factoid was altogether misleading, as we would explain first to Tauzin's investigators and then to the media: the failure rates for some of the replacement tires were based on data populations too small to be meaningful, and Ford was basing its decision to replace more tires not only on failure rates in the claims data but also on its laboratory testing. The Firestone tires came apart on the dynamometer at lower speeds than the replacement tires.

But Tauzin was not interested in a calm, informed examination of the issue. Reveling in his place once again at the center of national media attention, he made the most of the questionable data on the replacement tires. "Ford is going to replace recalled tires with tires that have a worse record," he said. "One of the tires has a claim rate of 124 per million, well in excess of Ford's five in one million."[5]

Earlier, when pressed on what Ford considered the "normal" failure rate of good tires, Nasser had given the "five per million" figure, but quickly added that decisions on which tires to replace should also factor in laboratory testing when available.

We were careful not to call Tauzin out in the media. But we were growing tired of his political theatrics and sometimes our irritation came through in our quotes. "We've tested more tires than anybody in the history of mankind for an automaker," Vines said in interview with *Fleet Owner* magazine. "We, of course, will continue to work with Mr. Tauzin. We hope he's armed with enough facts to make good decisions."[6]

* * *

On June 28, Firestone announced the closing of its Decatur plant, citing lost business from Ford. "This has nothing to do with the quality and commitment of our Decatur employees," said John McQuade, Bridgestone/Firestone's vice president – Manufacturing Operations. "This has everything to do with capacity."[7]

* * *

As the summer rolled on, it became increasingly obvious to us that we had done the right thing in pushing Firestone to recall the additional Wilderness AT tires and then, following Firestone's May 21 action to "fire" Ford as a customer, in replacing them on our own. NHTSA investigators told us privately that they were becoming convinced that the additional tires needed to be replaced but that they could not order a recall until a number of additional process steps had

205

been completed. Meanwhile, Ford continued to replace the tires in question at the company's own considerable expense.

On July 19, NHTSA asked Firestone to "voluntarily" recall the tires (indicating that the safety agency was close to completing findings that would trigger a mandatory recall). Firestone refused.[8]

NHTSA issued a news release later that day that made it clear that Firestone's truculence was not going to win out. "The agency has completed its defect investigation into the tires in question... Firestone was asked to recall some of the tires and they refused to do so. Therefore, NHTSA will issue an initial defect decision, the next step toward a forced recall."[9]

Firestone didn't blink. "Taking more of our tires off the road is not the solution. It doesn't solve the real problem: the vehicle," Lampe told the *Los Angeles Times*.[10]

Although we didn't want to be quoted in stories about the NHTSA-Firestone stalemate, we made sure on background journalists understood that Ford was already replacing the tires NHTSA and Firestone were arguing over. And that Ford would expect to be reimbursed if and when NHTSA found the tires defective. *L.A. Times* writer Terril Yue Jones captured our position perfectly: "The impact on consumers of a wider recall is unclear because many of the tires in question already are being replaced by Ford... However, if Bridgestone/Firestone is forced to expand its recall, it might have to reimburse Ford for the $2.1-billion cost of the auto maker's recall."[11]

* * *

It would be another two-and-half months before NHTSA finally released its "initial" defect decisions. Such is the nature of government agency process. But when the day finally arrived, the news was almost worth the wait. For the frazzled people in Ford's Glass House tire rooms, Oct. 4, 2001 was a day of sweet redemption.

NHTSA's findings amounted to an almost total victory for Ford and bitter pills for both Firestone and the plaintiff lawyers to swallow. The agency declared a safety defect in 3.5 million Wilderness AT tires not included in its previous recalls, and ordered Firestone to immediately recall them.[12] Since Ford had already replaced most of these tires on its own over the past five months, NHTSA's action did not have much practical effect for consumers. But it did clear the way for Ford to demand reimbursement from Firestone, perhaps with a little thank-you for initiating a replacement program before the heat of another summer set in, thus preventing an undeterminable number of accidents. (Neither reimbursement nor thank-you were forthcoming from Firestone. Finally, in 2005, after much legal wrangling, Firestone quietly agreed to pay Ford the paltry sum of $240 million to settle all outstanding financial obligations for the August 2000 tire recall and Ford's May 2001 tire replacement program.)[13]

There was one other important piece of news from NHTSA. The agency had found that the Explorer was not inherently to blame for the tread separation rollover crashes, a finding that infuriated both Firestone and the trial lawyers with suits against Ford.

The tread separations at issue in this investigation reduce the ability of a driver to control the vehicle, particularly where the failure occurs on a rear tire and at high speeds, and can lead to a crash. The likelihood of such a crash, and of injuries or fatalities, is far greater when the tread separation occurs on an SUV than when it occurs on a pickup truck. Claims and complaint data indicate that a tread separation on an Explorer is no more likely to lead to a crash than on other SUVs.[14]

When asked for comment, we deliberately tried to temper our jubilation to avoid coming across as gloating. "I guess the facts finally won out," Jason said, "NHTSA's statements vindicate what Ford analysis has said all along."[15]

Likewise, Lampe stated Firestone's reaction clearly and unemotionally: "We do not agree with NHTSA's findings," he said. "Our testing and science show our tires perform extremely well."[16]

But there was no missing the significance of the day's news to both companies. "U.S. blames the tires, not Ford's Explorers," proclaimed the banner headline across the top of the front page of the *Detroit Free Press* the next morning:

In a victory, long-awaited by Ford Motor Co., the federal government ordered Bridgestone/Firestone Inc. to recall 3.5 million more tires Thursday and said the design of the Ford Explorer did not contribute to sometimes fatal rollovers that occurred after tread separations.

The National Highway Traffic Safety Administration said that a tread separation on an Explorer is "no more likely to lead to a crash than other SUVs."[17]

A few days later, every member of Ford's tire team received a framed copy of that *Free Press* story on a matte that had been personally autographed by Parry-Jones, Baughman and three other engineering executives, with the inscription: "TRUTH PREVAILS: From you, it demanded outrageous hours, torturous work, lost weekends, neglect of friends and family... Our appreciation for a job well done!"

* * *

Two other framed artifacts would join that *Free Press* story on a wall in my office and stay with me for years to come through several moves to different roles and different offices. The first was an editorial cartoon by the *Free Press'* Mike Thompson which ran a few days after the NHTSA announcement. It depicts a nerdy scientist in a white lab coat emblazoned "NHTSA" speaking to a corporate executive in a blue pin-striped suit with "Ford" in script on his lapel. A ripped-up tire hangs from a rope fastened around the exec's collar. The caption reads: "You can remove that millstone ... I mean Firestone ... around your neck."

The other piece of framed journalistic art on my office wall contained another *Free Press* front page, this one with a banner headline in even bigger type than the October 5 paper. "U.S. Clears Explorer," declared the story from Feb. 13, 2002 on the occasion of NHTSA's even more definitive ruling exonerating the Explorer. In the months following NHTSA's October release of its "initial findings" in its safety investigation, Firestone and a chorus of trial lawyers and safety advocates had continually badgered the safety agency to open a full-scale investigation into the Explorer's design and handling characteristics. After a thorough review of relevant facts, NHTSA found no persuasive case against the best-selling SUV. The *Free Press* story begins with a taut summary that captured just what the NHTSA ruling meant to us:

> *After more than 18 months, two tire recalls and thousands of hours of verbal warfare, the world's most popular sport-utility vehicle – the Ford Explorer – has been vindicated by the National Highway Traffic Safety Administration.*
>
> *The federal regulatory agency refused to open a safety defect investigation on the Explorer.*[18]

* * *

Looking back at the crisis and especially at the many accusations about Ford and the Explorer, I believe several conclusions are inescapable:

Firestone certainly "made some bad tires," as Lampe admitted to Congress. And the tire company's executives knew a great deal about the Wilderness tire defects long before telling Ford or NHTSA.

Throughout its run from 1990 to the present day, the Ford Explorer has been a safe vehicle compared with other SUVs, and compared to passenger cars in general, of the same time period. It was no more likely to roll over following a tread separation than other similar-sized SUVs. Looking at DOT data on fatal rollover crashes, the Explorer had a considerably lower fatality rate per 100 million vehicle miles than its closest contemporary, the Chevrolet Blazer.[19] If Chevrolet rather than Ford had equipped its best-selling SUV with the Firestone tires involved in the recalls of 2000-2001, it is likely that General Motors would have been engulfed in crisis instead of Ford, and one could speculate that there might have been a higher incidence of fatal rollover crashes stemming from the tread separations.

Neither the management of Ford nor its product engineers were engaged in a deliberate conspiracy to disregard passenger safety in the development of the Explorer. They made a series of decisions related to trade-offs in fuel economy and ride quality, while always meeting or exceeding Federal safety standards as well as Ford's own safety standards. Some of those trade-offs involved setting the tire air inflation recommendation, with Firestone's concurrence, at the relatively low 26 psi. This level of inflation was chosen to help provide a cushier ride to address a common complaint among Explorer owners that the truck-based Explorer's ride quality was uncomfortably stiff. However, this relatively low inflation pressure provided only a small margin of protection against under-inflation by Explorer owners. The Firestone Wilderness AT tires were not particularly well designed, and combined with manufacturing process problems, especially at the Decatur plant, they were especially sensitive to the damaging effects of chronic heat build-up. When operated in hot climates and driven at high speeds or overloaded for sustained periods, these sensitive tires were prone to tread separation – a type of tire failure that was quite rare among other tires on other vehicles.

In the United States and around the world over more than 10 years, more than 300 people died and hundreds more suffered severe injuries in Explorer rollover crashes that began with a Firestone tread separation. An awful, mind-numbing number of accidents, even in the context of the more than 40,000 fatal vehicle crashes each and every year in the U.S. alone. Each of these crashes is a sudden and horrible tragedy for the people involved, their families and their friends.

* * *

One nagging question remained. Why had so many of the Firestone tread separations on Explorers led to fatal rollover crashes? Or, using Lampe's words, why were so many Explorer drivers experiencing tread separations unable to "pull over" safely and instead "rolled over," often with tragic consequences?

The all-too easy answer from the trial lawyers was that the Explorer was dangerously tippy, its balance easily upset by what should have been just an annoying occurrence, a tire failure. But that answer didn't hold up to serious scrutiny. Again and again, Ford engineers and vehicle dynamics experts put Explorers to the test and found the vehicle to perform at least as well as other similar-sized SUVs before, during and after a simulated tread separation. NHTSA reviewed the results of these tests and found their conclusions compelling. The SUVs all performed about the same during and after the tread separation. When drivers did nothing after the separation other than to let off the accelerator pedal, the SUVs continued straight down the test track until they gradually came to a stop. Only when the test driver reacted to the separation by braking and tugging sharply on the steering wheel, did the SUVs react wildly, especially if the driver steered hard to the right in the case of a left rear failure, or hard to the left in the case of a right rear failure. This was true for all the SUVs tested.

On all vehicles tested, rear tire separations were more difficult to control than front separations, the opposite of what one might expect. Here's why: Losing the tread from a tire significantly reduces the grip of that tire relative to the other three tires. The still-inflated treadless tire's smooth surface provides very little "lateral adhesion" (sideways grip). During braking, the weight of the vehicle shifts to the front tires, temporarily "unloading" weight from the rear tires which reduces their grip on the road. So the problem of lack of grip for a detreaded tire is exacerbated for a rear tire during braking. Losing grip in the rear makes a vehicle "loose" in NASCAR racing parlance, that is, susceptible to "over steer" (fish-tailing). That can lead to the loss of control of any vehicle, and in SUVs in particular, a significant chance of a deadly rollover crash.

So the theory was that most of the rollover crashes occurred when a driver responded to the loud bang of a tire pelt smashing on the inside of the vehicle's wheel well by braking hard and steering sharply in the opposite direction. Undoubtedly, many of the crashes happened just this way.

But no explanation adequately addressed the strange statistical phenomenon that had led to many Explorer conspiracy theories: an unusually high percentage of the reported tire tread separations on Explorers occurred on the left rear wheel. Lampe himself had cited this fact in testimony before Congress as evidence that the Explorer itself was somehow to blame for the Firestone tread separations. "A tire doesn't know where it is on a vehicle," Lampe had said.[20] The four tires on any vehicle were made in exactly the same way, so one would expect to find about half of the tread separations occurring on the right side and the other half on the left.

The theory that gained the most traction in explaining the relatively high percentage of left rear tire separations on the Explorer was advanced by Sanjay Govindjee, the tire expert Firestone had hired to determine root causes. The Explorer, he said, had an "uneven weight distribution that puts an extra load on the left rear tire." But Govindjee conceded that he hadn't yet determined if that relatively small extra load was a factor at all in the tire separation cases. Not to mention that the extent of the extra load would vary considerably depending on where occupants sat and how far right or left in the space behind the back seat any cargo was stowed.[21]

We kept knocking down Govindjee's theory by pointing out that tread separations on other makes and models of SUVs which had been outfitted with the recalled Firestone tires (albeit in much smaller numbers than Explorer) also occurred most frequently on the left rear wheel.

But we didn't know why that was.

We weren't even sure that a disproportionate number of left rear tires were separating on each of these SUVs, only that more *accidents* had been caused by a left-rear separation. Claims for tire failures that didn't lead to accidents were not nearly comprehensive so an analysis of tread separation incidents in which the driver had safely "pulled over" could not accurately be made with the information available. But it was clear that when it came to separations that had caused a crash, an unusually high number had occurred on the left rear wheel, no matter which SUV you studied. Why?

It wasn't until after the crisis had long faded from the media spotlight, Congress had moved on to other concerns and Ford and Firestone executives had mostly satisfied the plaintiff attorneys' desire for their depositions that Tom Baughman came up with a theory that might solve the riddle.

After he retired from Ford in 2003, Baughman pieced together some of what he'd heard from the company's root cause analysis project with some of his own observations. The tires might have separated in different ways depending on whether they were fitted on the driver side or passenger side of the vehicle, although this pattern hadn't been identified on the test track. For testing purposes, deep cuts were made in the tire's shoulder that would ensure that the tire would peel apart when driven at high speed on the track. In these tests, the tires ripped apart the same way just about every time. But in the real world, they may have separated differently depending on which

212

side of the vehicle they'd been mounted. Once Baughman understood this, he quickly surmised why some tread separations were so unsettling to the vehicle.

Right- and left-side separations were different precisely because all the Firestone tires were made the same way – instead of half being made for the right side and half for the left. The steel belts, shoulders and treads of the tire were built onto the rest of the tire as it was spun counter-clockwise on a spindle. The tire maker applied the hot rubber, the first steel belts, an adhesive layer, the second steel belt and more rubber in bands and pieces that were wrapped sequentially around the tire. Just like a roll of toilet paper is wrapped around a spinning cardboard tube.

Prior to a tread separation, heat build-up caused cracks in the shoulder of the tire, and if the cracks spread to the belts and across the other shoulder of the tire, it became weak and susceptible to being torn right off the tire by the centrifugal force of the spinning tire. So tread separations tended to happen at high speeds, when the centrifugal force was strong enough to rip the tread off, tearing the two steel belts apart.

But the separations were very different depending on which side of the vehicle they occurred. On the right side, a separated pelt of tread and steel belt ripped cleanly off and out behind the vehicle. This left a still-inflated but horribly bald tire with greatly reduced ability to grip the road. Startled drivers could easily get in trouble in this situation, but most of the time they were able to safely control the vehicle to a stop. But if the separation occurred on a tire on the left side, the pealing pelt couldn't slip cleanly off. It came off a bit, was run over by the tire, ripped off a bit more, was run over again and so forth until it, too, ripped apart from rest of the tire. This rapid sequence of events could be very unsettling to any SUV and lead to a violent crash.

To understand this better, hold a roll of toilet paper so that the loose end is on the bottom hanging back toward you. Roll it forward on the floor. The paper flows right off the roll. That's what happened when a tire on the right separated.

Now take the roll and flip it over so the loose piece is on top, still pointed back at you. Again, roll it forward on the ground. The paper tries to come off but it bunches, rolling over itself again and again.

When a tire on the left side of a vehicle began to separate, the tread pelt at first could not come freely off the tire. It bunched up, was

213

rolled over, got somewhat bigger before it was rolled over, again and again. Of course, this all happened very quickly if the vehicle was traveling at 70 mph or so. In an instant the tire tread and steel belt became a sizeable obstruction for the tire to bounce over, up and down, up and down, perhaps lifting the vehicle somewhat while exerting drag on that wheel. (Think of a shopping cart moving forward. If you step on the left rear wheel and keep it from spinning, the cart will veer sharply to the left.) The driver trying to control his SUV that was suddenly headed to the left would naturally steer hard to the right. And remember that the worst thing you could do with a left rear separation was to steer sharply to the right.

That situation would be difficult to control. And that could explain why so many of the Explorer rollovers were caused by a left rear tire separation. (Ford today disputes this theory, favoring the explanation that drivers' sudden steering impulses toward the shoulder off the right side of a highway explain the left-rear crashes.)

Knowing this might have changed the way Firestone made its tires. If the people running a tire company knew that some of the tires it was making were prone to tread separations, as Firestone executives almost certainly did by the late '90s, maybe earlier, they could have built two types of tires. Tires for the right side of the vehicle would be built the standard way, and labeled accordingly. But tires for the left side would be built on a spindle spinning clockwise instead of counterclockwise. They would be clearly labeled for application on the left side of the vehicle. That would ensure that tires suffering tread separations on either side of a vehicle would peel off cleanly and fall away. Auto mechanics and tire store employees would be trained to make sure right-hand tires went on the right side and lefts on the left, like shoes, and owners would need to be instructed as well, particularly if they were going to rotate their own tires.

Much more practical would be to design and build robust, high-quality tires that didn't run as hot as the recalled Firestone tires did, had larger wedges and greater peel strength. Tires that would almost never suffer tread separations even after many years and tens of thousands of miles of use. Like those Goodyear tires that Ford had foolishly stopped buying when they had seemed costly compared to the Firestones.

But all that is hindsight now.

CHAPTER ELEVEN

Full Circle

"The CEO must relentlessly hold the senior team accountable for executing and delivering on promises made and remind the organization that the most inspirational visions amount to nothing without superior execution. The CEO's job is to make sure that the plan is executable and is executed."

- *Leslie Gaines-Ross,* CEO Capital.[1]

"You can't build a reputation on what you are going to do."

- *Henry Ford (1863 - 1947)*

* * *

Throughout the Firestone tire ordeal, one ray of hope shown ahead for the Explorer nameplate. We looked forward with great anticipation to the launch of the 2002 Explorer, code-named U152. The new vehicle – both the Explorer and its fraternal twin, the Mercury Mountaineer – featured significant upgrades to better compete in the midsized SUV market that had changed considerably over the years since the original Explorer first defined it.

The U152 would be the first Explorer to feature an optional third row bench seat to extend its appeal as a family vehicle for those who thought minivans were, well, dorky. To accommodate functional third row seating, the new Explorer would have a longer wheelbase and a wider wheel track. And it would feature a much improved suspension that delivered greater ride comfort and enhanced handling ability. The new independent rear suspension would also allow the rear floor of the new Explorer to be lowered by seven inches, which was needed to accommodate that new fold-flat third row seat.[2] But the independent rear suspension was controversial within the company because it added significant costs that would be difficult to recover through pricing.

The U152 would feature the latest advancements in new safety technologies as optional equipment. These included electronic stability control – a computerized set of sensors and gyroscopes that could detect the beginning of vehicle instability and intervene by automatically applying a small amount of brake force on whichever wheel needed to be slowed to return the vehicle to a more stable path. (Think again of that moving shopping cart but with a suspension system in the form of a set of springs on each wheel assembly. If you suddenly push hard in a forward motion on the left side of the handle bar, the cart not only darts to the right but also leans down on its right side as the force of its weight is shifted to the right wheels. Now you rub your shoe against the left rear wheel to slow it down; the cart will not only correct back to the left but will level out as the weight becomes more evenly balanced.) Another advancement was electronic brake force distribution which would apply an extra amount of force on the brakes if the driver pushed down suddenly on the brake pedal, as in a panic stop, but with insufficient force to engage full stopping power. Together with other active safety features already standard on the Explorer, such as electronic anti-lock brakes, these new technologies would help drivers avoid crashes.

The new Explorer also would feature an optional new Safety Canopy system featuring large side curtain air bags fitted with special rollover sensors – the airbags would inflate only for an instant in the case of a side collision but would remain inflated for as long as six seconds if the vehicle began to roll over. Explorer would be the first vehicle on the market to have rollover activated side curtain air bags.[3]

Of course, Ford Public Affairs wanted the new safety technologies to be included on all new Explorers as standard equipment. But each of the new systems was expensive and the U152 Explorer's base price would already be rather high. Four years later, as the cost of the electronics fell, Ford would make electronic stability control and brake assist standard on 2006 Explorer, along with front seat side airbags.[4]

Lesson Learned: Put safety first. *Whenever possible, push to make advanced safety features standard. However, recognize that affordability is a legitimate concern. The safest product in the world protects no one if it is priced so high that no one buys it.*

* * *

We held the media introduction for the U152 Explorer and Mountaineer in November 2000 in Arizona. The location allowed us to offer journalists a unique combination of driving conditions in a relatively compact day-and-a-half program that was sensitive to their busy schedules. Journalists would arrive at the Phoenix airport and drive in the previous generation 2001 Explorers over a variety of road surfaces to help give them a baseline of comparison for the new-and-improved model.

Then they would receive a short overview of the new Explorer and pair up two to a vehicle, heading out on the drive course we had planned for them. This enabled one journalist to drive and one to navigate, with frequent opportunities for driver swaps at pre-arranged stops where, of course, we offered comfort food and bathrooms. We had several rules in setting up media ride n' drives, including never letting a journalist get hungry or have a distressed bladder. They would often joke about the frequent feedings but we knew better than to give them reasons to complain.

Keith Bradsher joined us for the first time on a vehicle drive program. As a business writer for the *New York Times*, Bradsher did not write product reviews. But with his continuing focus on SUVs, Bradsher was keenly interested in the new '02 Explorer. So we invited him to participate in the drive program and he readily accepted. Bradsher would be able to experience the Explorer launch first-hand as well as interview Ford executives on the program. We paired him up with Dale Claudepierre, the chief program engineer for the new Explorer (and who we affectionately called "the man with three first names"). Not thinking it prudent to leave Bradsher and the sometimes loose-lipped Claudepierre together in the same vehicle for several hours, I rode with them as well.

Soon Bradsher said he wanted to experience riding in the third row and I took the wheel. Bradsher would describe our drive, with

217

perhaps a little embellishment, in his anti-SUV book *High and Mighty* in a chapter called "Seducing the Press:"

> *When Harmon's turn came to drive, Claudepierre soon began needling him for only going a few miles per hour over the speed limit – a clear sign of inadequate virility among auto engineers... Harmon drove faster, cars whistling past us in the opposite direction on the public road. Claudepierre was still not satisfied, saying the rigidity of the vehicle could only be fully appreciated at speeds far above what traffic engineers recommended on speed limit signs....*

> *Harmon did step on it and when we crested the next rise, the vehicle almost became airborne. On the downhill side of the rise, a police officer was just climbing out of his patrol car with a radar gun preparing to catch speeders making exactly Harmon's mistake. Harmon violently mashed the brake pedal. Had we not all been wearing our seat belts – a requirement on press junkets – we would have been plastered on the inner surface of the windshield. The police officer did not get his radar gun up in time; Harmon narrowly escaped a ticket and drove more cautiously after that and Claudepierre kept quiet.*[5]

Lesson Learned: Do not allow an executive to goad you into unsafe behavior, *particularly when you're with a prominent journalist who has a fixation on safety and is operating under the suspicion that your product is unsafe.*

The drive would take the journalists through the town of Sedona and surrounding central Arizona before they stopped for the evening at a resort called "Enchantment," where we had a dinner prepared at a campsite surrounded by the red rock cliffs. In his book, Bradsher would make note of the overabundance of good food and drink on the Explorer "junket." At the end of the first day's driving, he wrote, "...we went into a large heated tent where chefs served a gourmet meal of venison and other local delicacies accompanied by a selection of excellent wines. We waddled back stuffed to our hotel suites where it was hard to think critical thoughts of SUVs."[6]

Lesson Learned: Make a product launch an enjoyable experience for journalists without going overboard. *Serious journalists will not be bribed (or bullied) into writing good reviews of inferior products, but they will complain incessantly if you don't make them comfortable. Note that this journalist felt it necessary to resist any inclination to be favorably impressed by our hospitality, to the point of expressing, at least whimsically, his desire to conjure "critical thoughts of SUVs" before setting about the serious work of writing his story.*

* * *

Drive impression stories of the new '02 Explorer in nearly all the media outlets that had participated in the Sedona program were strongly favorable. They especially noted improvements in the SUV's ride quality as well as the new available safety technology.

Production of the U152 Explorer began slowly at first, as planned, and then ramped up at the two dedicated assembly plants with a smooth production launch. Initial quality measures were all very strong. We breathed a collective sigh of relief, knowing the eyes of the world were closely watching this launch. In January 2001, the new model went on sale. We already had a nice bank of dealer orders and the initial customer reaction was encouraging.

Too soon after the media launch, I was back at my second office in the Glass House dealing again with tire issues. The month of May would bring the big break-up with Firestone and our additional tire replacement program. During the summer I split time working on tire issues and my real job leading Ford Truck Public Affairs.

* * *

Not all corporate jets are airborne mini-palaces for pampered executives wanting to avoid the hassle of traveling commercial. Companies often maintain regular routes for their private aircraft to ferry personnel to remote locations not accessible by commercial air travel. Twice a week, a Ford jet configured to comfortably carry up to

219

52 people flew from Detroit to Havasu City, Arizona, near the company's massive Arizona Proving Grounds. Engineers and others working on truck and SUV development programs would get on the "milk run" to APG and return later in the week to Dearborn. The company jet typically continued on from Havasu City to Long Beach, Calif., near the company's Premier Automotive Group Headquarters in Irvine, a west-coast Glass House of sorts for the Lincoln Mercury, Jaguar, Aston Martin, Land Rover and Volvo brands. A contingent of sales and marketing types could be counted on to take the extra leg to California.

On board that Ford jet one otherwise unremarkable Tuesday morning in September, I chatted with Whitney Said, a bright, young up-and-comer who we had recently appointed to be Public Affairs launch manager for the 2003 Expedition. Whitney was part of the team I led; she and I were traveling to Long Beach with several engineers from the Expedition program. We were to drive from the airport three hours east through the southern California desert to a remote location near Borrego Springs where Ford maintained a semi-secret test site for SUV development. We were to drive in the deep sand in a number of prototype Expeditions along with competitor vehicles to understand the new, big Ford SUV's capabilities so that Whitney could plan a dramatic ride n' drive event for the motoring press the following spring. It was good to get away from the daily grind; we had been looking forward to escaping from the office for a few days to go off-roading with the Expedition team.

As we made our approach toward the tiny air field at Havasu City, the pilot took our plane through an extra 360-degree circle above the mountains. "He must have missed his approach," I said to Whitney. Just then, the Ford flight attendant – a cheerful and patient woman who always took care of us with grace and good humor – snapped the glass of water out of my hand without a word and took it away as she ambled up the center aisle to the front of the jet. "Someone seems a little stressed out," I said. Whitney just shrugged.

We touched down a few minutes later. As we taxied in, the flight attendant took the PA system's mike and spoke to us, her voice clearly shaken. "The captain has an announcement to make," was all she said.

"I regret to tell you that we have received some disturbing news," the pilot said. "The World Trade Center in New York has been attacked by aircraft and the Pentagon has been bombed. I don't have any other details. But the FAA has grounded all flights in the United States. This will terminate our flight today. I have no other information about when we might resume the flight…"

We disembarked the plane, bewildered by what we'd just heard, cell phones pressed against our ears trying to find out what was going on. I reached Mary at home in our living room watching the television news. She told me what had happened, two jets had flown right into the World Trade Center towers. Then she gasped, describing how the second tower was collapsing, "just like the Hudson's building." A few weeks earlier local TV news had repeatedly shown the abandoned historic Hudson building in Detroit being razed through a carefully planned implosion that brought it straight down without harming the surrounding buildings. She began to cry.

The world changed that day, of course. We would continue on in rental cars westward for four or five hours to Borrego Springs where we'd test drive the Expeditions as planned, killing time, really, until the day would come when flights would resume and we could fly home to be with loved ones. For a time, it seemed the terrorists had won. They had succeeded in shaking American confidence. Although the country came together in a patriotic swell of emotion and resilience not foreseen by the 19 hate-filled hijackers and countless others involved in the plot, they did succeed in dealing a crushing blow to many sectors of the U.S. economy. Airlines, cruise liners, hotels and others in the travel industry suffered greatly in the aftermath of September 11; so did the auto industry. In the turmoil and uncertainty that followed the attacks, sales of big-ticket consumer items, such as automobiles, virtually ceased, threatening to bring the overall economy to a standstill.

Within days, General Motors responded with an unprecedented sales incentive program, dubbed "Keep America Rolling." With zero percent financing for up to five years on its entire vehicle lineup, the GM program was designed not only to resuscitate GM auto sales but to jump start the entire U.S. economy. Ford and Chrysler followed suit matching the generous incentives, but it was General Motors that rightly received credit for demonstrating leadership in a moment of crisis with an innovative program that was as much about patriotism as affordability. "All around Detroit American flags are flying. But it is

221

the General Motors Corp. that has wrapped itself in Old Glory," wrote *Forbes*'s Robyn Meredith, an insightful, engaging reporter who was married to Keith Bradsher. "Eight days after the terrorist attacks GM unveiled its 'Keep America Rolling' plan, offering car buyers free financing for up to five years. That eye-catching discount, good through Oct. 31, is worth, on average, $3,600 per vehicle..."[7]

GM's marketing plan was a strategic master-stroke in that it not only kept the company's factories open but at terms considerably less expensive than those faced by its domestic competition. Just before the September 11 attacks, Chrysler had lowered sticker prices up and down its lineup by an average of about 1 percent in an attempt to avoid succumbing to the latest round of expensive consumer rebates the other automakers had begun. "GM hadn't dropped sticker prices. So the 0% loans are substituting in effect for rebates," Meredith wrote. "It's already stealing sales from its rivals. In September GM's sales dropped just 2.9%, not the 15% some analysts had feared. Ford took one day to match GM's free financing offer but couldn't change advertisements as quickly. Its sales fell 9.9%."[8]

Already having a difficult year, Ford had to absorb the cost of the massive incentive program at the same time revenues were declining with weak sales performance. For the two-year period 2001-02, Ford would lose a staggering $6.4 billion.[9]

* * *

On October 30, Bill Ford fired Jac Nasser, along with Jason Vines and David Murphy, the vice president - Human Resources. Although no reason was officially offered for the firings, the Firestone debacle clearly was high on a long list of woes, along with widespread quality problems and a controversial, cold-blooded employee evaluation program championed by Nasser and implemented by Murphy.

"Speculation about Nasser's future had accelerated in recent months as the company lurched from one crisis to another," wrote Terril Jones in the *Los Angeles Times*. "Even before the recall of Firestone-brand tires burst into the news in August 2000, quality problems had plagued the launches of the Ford Focus sedan and Escape sport-utility vehicle, triggering multiple recalls."[10]

The day before the firings, Nasser had gamely taken part in a media photo-op commemorating the start of production of Ford's new small electric vehicle, even as rumors of his demise circulated among the press. When a reporter asked him to name the main challenges Ford would face in 2002, Nasser replied, "You have three or four hours?"[11]

But, more than any other single factor, the decision to pursue the expanded tire recall in May 2001 ultimately cost Nasser his job. The costs of the recall weighed on a weakened Ford; just as great was the psychic impact on an emotionally exhausted workforce within the company and at its dealerships. And although NHTSA would ultimately declare the tires in that second recall defective, Ford's decision to replace seemingly any tires that had a higher than average failure rate put it on dangerous ground as a mass manufacturer of complex consumer goods. If any batch of production that resulted in an above average defect rate was subject to recall, it potentially meant that nearly half of everything ever built should be recalled, a proposition that no one other than a plaintiff lawyer would find tenable.

Against all odds, Lampe and Karbowiak were still gainfully employed at Firestone and had outlasted Nasser and Vines at Ford.

As CEO and President, in addition to his role as Chairman, Bill Ford began holding employee meetings to refocus the company on its core business. Dubbed "Backed to Basics," it was a backlash against the ambitious transformation Nasser had envisioned for Ford to become the "world's leading consumer company."

But Bill Ford had neither the temperament nor expertise to lead the company's operations. He had been well-suited to the role of Chairman, taking a long view and setting an inspiring vision, while Nasser had directed the day-to-day business of the company. Many in the company had seen Nasser as an ego-maniacal tyrant and, in the end, most had bid him good-riddance, but the strong hand of an experienced CEO would soon be sorely missed. It would be nearly five years later, in September 2006, that Bill Ford would finally act, hiring Alan Mulally from Boeing to step in as CEO and implement another iteration of a perennial Ford turnaround plan. Those five years were not kind to Ford Motor Company.

*   *   *

In January 2002, Ford laid off 35,000 employees, in what consultant Challenger, Gray and Christmas would later include at number five on its list of the biggest layoffs in corporate America from 1993 to 2008.[12] Of course, the term "layoff" was anachronistic. Long gone were the days when thousands of workers would be temporarily laid off in a cyclical downturn that might last several months or a couple of years before call-backs came. These dismissed workers would never be rehired and Ford would never again employ more than 300,000 people worldwide.

*   *   *

One bright light stood apart from Ford's gloomy sales tallies in 2002. The new 2002 Explorer was a hit. Sales of the new-and-improved SUV steadily grew from the difficult days following the September 11 attacks and kept growing throughout the following year. In August 2002, Ford sold more than 51,000 Explorers in the United States – the best sales month ever for any SUV by any automaker. It was more than a high-water mark for Ford's iconic sport utility; it was sweet vindication for the besieged nameplate. And it was validation for those in marketing, sales and public relations that our efforts on behalf of the Explorer had, in the end, been worth it.

The *Detroit News* ran a banner headline September 5 across the top of its front page: "Resilient Explorer rides high again." In his story, Mark Truby chronicled the unlikely restoration of the Explorer back to the top of the sales charts. "After the Firestone tire controversy erupted two years ago, some marketing experts labeled the Explorer damaged goods and advised Ford Motor Co. to rename its best-selling SUV," Truby wrote. "Consumers, after all, had been bombarded with images of mangled Explorers and questions about the popular sport utility vehicle's safety performance. Now with the recall of millions of tires behind it, the once-tarnished Explorer is arguably more popular than ever."[13]

The story detailed the Explorer's sales resurgence, quoting Ford's sales analyst George Pipas: "If ever there was a comeback kid – it's the Explorer. It really ran through a public relations gauntlet." The resilience of the Explorer brand was remarkable, Truby said: "With the exception of Tylenol, which rebounded from an ugly package-tampering controversy, it is nearly unheard of for a consumer product to pass through a blizzard of negative publicity and safety questions virtually untarnished."[14]

*   *   *

But the huge losses weighed heavily on Ford. As the company struggled, it became increasingly difficult to live up to the ideals of socially responsible leadership. With money scarce, Ford's powerful Finance staff choked off projects they saw as unnecessary or imprudent. Additional burdens were placed on the various vehicle teams by requiring them to find offsets within their own tight budgets to overcome rising material costs throughout the company. Worse, the first vehicle team adopting a new technology was required to bear the burden of the development cost of the technology, even if it would also be used by many other vehicle teams in the future. This was a strong deterrent to innovation. It was ridiculous to charge an individual vehicle team to develop technologies that would benefit the corporation broadly. So it should not have been surprising when the vehicle teams began to drop plans for many of the new features. But Finance refused to budge. The 25 percent fuel economy commitment had been a particularly nettlesome irritant to the "beanies," as the arrogant Finance people were known to the rest of the company, and now they used their power to ensure its failure.

One vehicle program after another backed off some of the advanced technologies delivering relatively small amounts of improved fuel efficiency. Fewer and fewer new parts would be made of light-weight but costlier materials such as aluminum and magnesium. With each small defection, achievement of the fuel economy commitment became more tenuous. Then the lynch-pin of the commitment, the U251 Explorer to be launched in the fall of 2005, fell completely off the tracks. This was the program once envisioned by Gurminder Bedi to be a "27.5 mpg Explorer" (a fully capable SUV achieving the fuel economy mark that passenger car fleets were required to meet). It was to include a mild-hybrid powertrain, light-weight materials and other innovations. When the U251 team declared

225

they would no longer achieve the fuel economy level we had booked, and the senior management of Ford allowed them to slide, the "25 in 5" fuel economy commitment was dead. It was only a matter of time before we would have to concede publicly that we weren't going to make it.

Our communications strategy was to wait until well after Ford's Centennial celebration in June 2003 to provide the update that we might not fully achieve the 25 percent gain by the end of 2005 as promised. There were some who wanted to wait quite a bit longer. After all, if something caused gas prices to spike high enough to change consumer buying behavior – hurting sales of our biggest, most gas-thirsty SUVs and perhaps increasing demand for the new Escape small SUV that would soon include a hybrid model – we might achieve the 25 percent gain across our SUV fleet despite ourselves.

That debate soon became moot. At the New York Auto Show, in April 2003, Ford's vice president heading Product Creation, Phil Martens inelegantly let the cat out of the bag. During a series of interviews, Martens forgot that we had not yet publicly conceded defeat against the SUV fuel economy objective. Stories about Ford backing off its fuel economy commitment drowned out any other news the company tried to make at the auto show. Far worse, the broken promise would be brought up incessantly over the following months and years, a constant drag on the company's reputation. The company had gone from being seen as an environmental and safety leader among auto companies to being labeled a liar, an untrustworthy pariah.

The chorus of boos from the environmentalists was deafening. "What Ford is doing is telling the American people that we can't trust Ford's commitments," said the Sierra Club's Dan Becker, one of the most respected and level-headed environmental spokespersons. "Bill Ford's claims to being an environmentalist ring hollow if Ford repudiates the most important environmental commitment it's made in recent years."[15]

Inside the company, the tide had turned against what many in the Engineering and Finance communities saw as reckless activism by Public Affairs. The company should never have been boxed into a rigid commitment, according to the new conventional wisdom, and Public Affairs in particular was guilty of making promises the company couldn't afford to keep.

But with the further passage of time, it is clear that the failure was not in allowing Public Affairs to co-opt the company's decision-making processes to sign up to an untenable commitment. Rather, a collective failure of will allowed the company to walk away from a commitment it could have kept. When gasoline prices spiked in the summer of 2008 to more than $4.50 a gallon and consumers altogether stopped buying fuel-thirsty, truck-based SUVs, no matter how low the price was slashed, did anyone at Ford still believe they had made the right decision to walk away from the SUV fuel economy commitment?

Incredibly, we made matters worse by poorly communicating our failure. Repeating the mistake Firestone had made in August 2000 when it had refused to release the data that defined the recalled population of tires, we did not quantify the fuel economy improvements we still were on track to achieve. Media simply reported that Ford was backing off its promise to improve the fuel economy of its SUVs by 25 percent by 2005. To the public, the impression was that we hadn't improved our SUV's fuel economy at all. Toward the end of 2005, I worked with Ford's fuel economy programmers and sales analysts to determine exactly what our improvement had been over the base of our 2000 model year SUV fleet fuel economy. The answer? A 17.9 percent improvement, far off the mark promised but clearly a substantial improvement that we weren't getting credit for. But it was too late. We'd been bludgeoned for two-and-a-half years about our broken promise and no one at Ford had the stomach to bring it up all over again. The public perception remained that our SUVs were no more fuel efficient than they had been at the turn of the millennium.

Lesson Learned: Even when you lose control of your message, keep your head in the game. *There will be times when the news leaks before you are ready to announce it. Chances are good that what the media reports won't be "on message." Monitor coverage closely and follow-up with those who will continue to cover the issue, providing specific details or data to support your version of the story. You can't undo a leak but you needn't settle for someone else's interpretation of your story.*

* * *

227

In June 2003, Ford celebrated its Centennial. For several days, the Dearborn campus surrounding Ford's WHQ Glass House transformed into a sentimental, nostalgic tribute to Henry Ford and the company he founded in 1903. This was more than just one company's milestone; it was the 100th anniversary of the founding of the one company that unquestionably had had the most profound impact on American life in the 20th century: The moving assembly line that revolutionized mass production. The Model T – the car that "put the world on wheels." The five-dollar work day that led to the creation of a middle class in America. Ford's rapid conversion of a massive assembly plant at Willow Run to produce B-24 bombers to help win World War II that cemented Detroit's war-time reputation as The Arsenal of Democracy. The Mustang. The Taurus. The Explorer. And, yes, the Edsel and the Pinto.

Retirees, car club fanatics and history buffs traveled to Dearborn. We hosted media from all over the world. They gathered on a track of land a little larger than Disney's Magic Kingdom to walk through historic and futuristic technology exhibits, ride in Model T's, watch fireworks and listen to concerts. One night it was Toby Keith, the mega-popular country star renowned for his musical endorsements of Ford's F-150 pickup truck. Another night featured an up-and-coming pop star with an unusual name, Beyonce Knowles, performing for the first time in concert without the group Destiny's Child.

Just on the other side of Michigan Avenue, the spectacular collection of Americana old Henry Ford had created, Greenfield Village and the Henry Ford Museum, attracted record numbers of visitors. You could see Greenfield Museum from my 10th floor office on the south side of the Glass House, where I now led Ford's Global News Bureau, or from the adjoining conference room, where we had gathered three years earlier to watch the Congressional hearings on C-Span. It was Saturday, June 14, the second-to-last day of our Centennial celebration. The blinds in the conference room were drawn up so my team and I could see out the window, but we weren't looking out toward Greenfield Village. Further to the east, in a vacant lot across Michigan Avenue, a small band of protesters were struggling to inflate some sort of big, green, oddly shaped hot-air balloon. We weren't sure what the point of the balloon was, but we were watching them carefully. Two environmental activist groups, the notorious

Rainforest Action Network and the somewhat less radical Global Exchange, had earlier let it be known that they planned to interrupt Ford's Centennial celebration in protest of the company's broken promise on SUV fuel economy improvement. Four years earlier, the same two groups had spread mayhem in downtown Seattle to protest a meeting there by the World Trade Organization.[16] The last thing we wanted at our Centennial celebration was some sort of violent act in the name of righteous environmentalism. We were working closely with our security details but mostly we hoped to ignore them.

Eventually, the gas-powered flame had heated enough air that the giant rubber blob began to rise up a little and take form. First as a lumpy, green mound. Then as a large reptile struggling to lift up its head. And finally as a taut, fully-inflated dinosaur rising up in the air above the parking lot as several college-aged men and women struggled with ropes to control it in the unpredictable summer breezes.

"Here it is," one of my managers said as she stared into the computer screen in front of her; "a release that explains what they're doing over there." She read from a news release issued by Rainforest Action Network. "Inflating a 100-foot balloon across from Ford headquarters, environmental and human rights advocates today called Ford a 'corporate dinosaur' and urged the company to make more efficient vehicles to avoid extinction.'"[17]

We nodded, slowly getting the strained connection.

Words written across the dinosaur's belly stated: "I love guzzling gas." Although quite a handful for the activists to control in the wind, it was by no means 100 feet tall. On the ground, the gas burner continued to spew forth a large blue and yellow flame, left unattended by the earth-lovers so intent on protesting our greenhouse gas emissions.

Our Centennial guests largely ignored the RAN protesters. So did the media. By Sunday they were gone.

EPILOGUE

CRISIS COMMUNICATIONS IN A WORLD OF NEW MEDIA

"In today's world, where ideas are increasingly displacing the physical in the production of economic value, competition for reputation becomes a significant driving force, propelling our economy forward."
- *Alan Greenspan, former chairman of the Federal Reserve*

* * *

Ford's flippant PR vice president Jason Vines, Ketchum wunderkind Jill Bratina and *New York Times* Detroit Bureau Chief and anti-SUV jihadist Keith Bradsher each played outsized roles in the epic Ford-Firestone crisis. Each helped shape the words and stories that came out of the crisis. And each has gone on to take on new career challenges:

- Soon after being fired from Ford, Vines was named to the top PR job at Chrysler Group. He surprised many in the industry who didn't think he'd last long at DaimlerChrysler working for the famously serious-minded Germans. Vines paired well with Dieter Zetsche, helping the Chrysler CEO earn high marks with employees, the motoring press and analysts. But when Daimler dumped Chrysler, its new owner, private equity fund Cerberus, didn't feel compelled to provide much information to the public and Vines soon quit. He was hired by global soft-ware firm Compuware to head PR and marketing, but stayed only a year. Next was an even shorter stint at Forgotten Harvest, a

231

Detroit-based non-profit, where he headed PR and fundraising. As this book went to press in July 2009, Vines was making news again, having made the unlikely move to Christian book publisher Zondervan, as VP-Communications. Rumors are rampant that there is at least one more act in Vines' long-running career in the auto industry.

- Jill Bratina joined the Firestone crisis team as a young but already respected member of Ketchum's crisis practice. Soon she became the company's primary spokesperson. As the crisis wore on, Firestone hired Bratina from the agency and named her director – Public Affairs. Later, she left the tire company to become communications director for Florida Governor Jeb Bush. She then joined Public Strategies, a Washington-based PR agency, as managing director. Bratina currently is responsible for Volkswagen's North American communications.

- Keith Bradsher's many articles for the *New York Times* sharply questioning the safety and environmental impacts of SUVs provided most of the grist for *High and Mighty: SUVs – The World's Most Dangerous Vehicles and How They Got That Way*. The book would win an award from the New York Public Library for excellence in journalism. In 2002, Bradsher left Detroit to become the *Times'* chief correspondent in Hong Kong, covering finance and business news in China and southeast Asia. He received a Society of Publishers in Asia award for his coverage of avian flu.

In the spring of 2009, I caught up with these three interesting characters for their reflections and insights on the crisis management implications of today's communications dynamic rapidly being transformed by social media from Facebook to Twitter.

* * *

The media "feeding frenzy" that defined the prolonged Firestone crisis grew directly out of a new development that even highly experienced corporate communicators weren't really prepared for – the media-savvy corporate adversary and the adversary network.

"Everyone was just pushing around documents," Bradsher noted. "There were so many memos and documents and they could be used to tell very different stories depending on who you were speaking to. I tried to step back and see the bigger picture but it wasn't always easy to do." Many news organizations demonstrated little skepticism in accepting the documents as proof of corporate malfeasance.

"The plaintiff attorneys were very aggressive," the veteran *New York Times* writer continued. "They kept the crisis in the news with a steady dribble of memos."

And the plaintiff attorneys didn't hesitate to stray from the truth in explaining the significance of the memos, Vines says, which put the onus on the corporate communicators to persuade news organizations to at least question the salacious stories they were being fed.

"Defending a company in such an environment is a thankless job," says Vines. "Our greatest successes weren't what you read in the papers, but what you didn't read. The hardest work is playing defense – correcting misinformation, adding balance – before a story comes out. And in knocking down stories completely that are just flat-out wrong. You don't get credit for what people don't see and read, but that is often the most important part of the job."

Bratina, too, remembers the daily challenge of hustling to provide journalists with context to the leaked memos. "We were constantly being faxed a document [by a journalist] at 4:00 or 4:30 in the afternoon," she says. "We'd have to pull people together from all over to meet quickly to try to understand what the document meant and what our response should be, and in time to meet the reporter's deadline. We knew the stories were going to run, with or without our comment."

When I asked Bradsher what the two companies could have done better to combat each day's new set of allegations, he had a radical suggestion.

"Crisis experts will tell you that it's best to get out all the bad news out at once, as quickly as possible," he said. "But this was a crisis that had an almost unlimited amount of bad news. Perhaps early on you could have published all the accusations that you might expect the plaintiff attorneys to throw out there, along with your rebuttals, before they had a chance to make news with all the memos."

It seems like a crazy idea: making a public record of every allegation you can imagine *before* your adversaries can. Few companies would contemplate such an action in self-confessing transparency. But what if Ford had somehow published a version of the "Explorer Myths and Facts" (included as the Appendix in this book) in the first week of the recall in August 2000? We would have had to call it something else, perhaps "Distortions You May Hear About the Explorer" since the allegations hadn't yet become myths. Most of the allegations that would be fed to media over the coming months already had been made in Explorer cases that never had gone to trial and hence had never been written about (and, therefore, were arguably newsworthy). So with help from company lawyers, Ford Public Affairs could conceivably have published a similar document before plaintiff attorneys could begin the drip-drip-drip of leaked documents that would feed the news cycle for so long.

While we never even considered such a radical action, it might prove to be just the right approach for an agile and confident company facing some future crisis. If the company had strong suspicions that adversaries would soon take a series of allegations public – and the company had strong factual rebuttals for each charge – it might shut down the conspiracy theories even before they came to light.

* * *

Why were the adversary groups able to keep the story alive so long?

"The appetite for the story was extraordinary," Bradsher says. "It went on and on. News judgment wasn't simply based solely on some utilitarian calculation of what factors were contributing most to the numbers of crash deaths annually. Part of me felt that there were much bigger, broader stories that didn't receive the same attention because they couldn't be litigated." Bradsher was convinced, for example, that crashes involving relatively heavy SUVs and lighter passenger cars were leading to fatalities on a much larger scale than the tire accidents were. He was frustrated when his periodic stories in the *Times* on the issue of "compatibility" between SUVs and cars did not lead to other news organizations following suit. Meanwhile, the tire story would not go away.

"The *New York Times* has to pay attention to the news cycle just like other newspapers. Clearly the Explorer-Firestone matter was a story that affected public attitudes on many issues, not just tires, and so it had to be covered comprehensively."

And there was a unique aspect to this crisis that made it irresistible. "One of the things that made the crisis such a big story," Bratina says, "was the conflict between Ford and Firestone."

As plaintiff attorneys, safety advocates and politicians saw the fissure growing between the two companies, they could hardly believe their good fortune. They gleefully drove their own wedges into the cracks and then stood back and watched the chaos. To their delight, each company seemingly responded by trying to destroy the other.

Both companies could see it happening, too, of course. So why couldn't we stop fighting each other?

"Ford and Firestone should have stayed aligned. Customers didn't appreciate all the in-fighting," Vines says. "We knew from customer research that it alienated them." He's quick to add: "I put the blame on Firestone. They saw they were going down and they decided to take down Ford with them."

Not surprisingly, Bratina has a very different perspective. "We knew the facts were on our side, but they weren't getting communicated in the media," she says. "In order to protect our reputation, we had to tell our side of the story. John Lampe set and led that strategy. He was an incredible leader at a difficult time. I would follow John anywhere into battle. Without his leadership and ability to take on risk, and get others to take on appropriate risk, we wouldn't have come through the crisis as we did."*

Each company was pulled in the direction of its own unique interests – legal, political and reputational. And, clearly, neither company trusted the other. Each company surely would have been better served by a joint defense strategy. But at the end of the day,

---

*It should also be made clear that Bratina takes issue with my assessment that she was the critical difference-maker in Firestone's new-and-improved communications. She credits the whole Firestone crisis team, beginning with Lampe, for the company's sharper, more effective messaging as the crisis went on. "I was part of a really smart team," Bratina says.

each company believed in its own story far more than in the other's and believed that its own version of the truth would win out. We were all naive in that way, believing that truth would necessarily win out with the news media, or Congress, or in the court of public opinion. How well you are able to tell your story is important, too. Sometimes the deck is stacked impossibly against you, because you have only the lifeless weight of the facts on your side and it can't measure up to the emotional weight of a compelling accusation accompanied by some striking visuals. It's hard to play defense well without a compelling visual or a pull on the heart-strings.

"The plaintiff attorneys worked hard to put the focus on the victims," Bradsher says. "They were especially aggressive in working to schedule interviews with Donna Bailey. It's difficult for a company to respond in a story of an interview with a paraplegic."

*　*　*

The rise of social media – blogs, Facebook, texting, Twitter and the like – clearly is changing the practice of crisis communications management. Whether you call these communication forums "new media" or "consumer-generated media" or "peer-to-peer media," they are all about empowering subpopulations of the public to turn to each other for information, opinion and context. Social media aren't necessarily displacing traditional mass media channels but they are reducing the direct influence of the mass media. Social media react to news as it is reported, instantly providing meaning within the group, amplifying or dismissing the news, and connecting it to other bits of news and opinion. The line between verifiable news and gossip disappears; rumor and innuendo often are trumpeted at least as vigorously as any piece of "legitimate" news.

Social media also provide a quick and unfiltered take on an event as it is happening, with a virtually unlimited number of potential "citizen journalists" on the spot, each with a camera and video cam in the form of their cell phone, quickly uploading images and commentary. This puts even more pressure on traditional media to quickly post breaking news accounts from an accident scene or other visible manifestation of an emerging crisis, often before "official commentary" is available or even sought.

These are troubling developments for the corporate communicator, to say the least. "The Internet is the greatest and the most destructive communication tool ever," Vines says in characteristically blunt language. "It allows ordinary people to disseminate information around the globe. Unfortunately it also can be used to spread disinformation and lies. And it provides adversaries with more venues to get out false information or statements taken totally out of its context."

Bradsher agrees that the rise of social media puts additional pressure on corporate communicators. "The importance of the blogosphere has increased dramatically and that does make it more difficult for companies to communicate effectively," he says. "On the one hand, a company can put statements and press releases up on its own website, by-passing the media and explaining its perspective directly to the public. But on the other hand, it is more difficult to make a complex issue understandable because you no longer have a relatively small number of journalists to explain your issue."

"New media" are also making life difficult for the old-guard mass media in another way, of course. *Craigslist* and other Internet sites have siphoned off much of a newspaper's most dependable income in the form of classified advertising. Meanwhile, newspapers' income from display advertising as well as from paid subscriptions, have fallen with each drop in readership. Fewer and fewer people find a daily newspaper indispensable as more and more turn to news aggregators – like Yahoo! – for short, snappy and instantly accessible news. Of course, the aggregators need to aggregate from some primary sources of information. The lines between hard news, feature news and gossip continue to fade; so do the controls for accuracy and fairness that we quaintly continue to expect in the information we absorb. As newspapers shut down and newsrooms shrink under tremendous financial pressure, professional journalists exert smaller influence on developing stories as they are conveyed to the public.

"It's sad," Vines says. "There are fewer and fewer pros out there who really check their facts and look to get it right. We saw the beginnings of this during the Firestone crisis. Speed was the Number One metric. Media would put out a story and continually update it. There was less reservation of going with a story that might be too rushed. The Internet takes news to the lowest common denominator. Speed is first. Accuracy is a distant second. I hope it's still second."

Bratina also noted that the disappearing breed of the experienced professional journalist makes it harder for the corporate communicator to patiently take a few influential journalists through complex and nuanced issues. "Back then [in 2000-01] you could have detailed conversations with the key journalists, walk them through an issue or just talk to them about what they were working on and thinking about as they developed stories. Each major news organization had experienced reporters dedicated to the crisis story who were deeply immersed in the issues and in many cases deeply experienced in the automotive industry. So they were less likely to get something completely wrong and you were more able to work with them as they worked through complicated issues."

The sense of loss within the profession of journalism is even more acutely felt by Bradsher. "The number of professional journalists is shrinking drastically," he says. "There simply are fewer people covering companies than there were earlier in the decade. News organizations have made severe cuts. So there are far fewer news organizations that can cover a story like the tire crisis and stay with it. Most news organizations will just focus on local news and pick up national stories from the wires. And even the national journalists are becoming less knowledgeable on any subject – since there are only half as many journalists to cover the same ground. They each have to cover twice as much, so they can't go very deep."

How might the Firestone crisis have played out differently with today's pervasive social media?

"It all would have been even more publicly adversarial with an even greater focus on the in-fighting between the companies," Bratina says. "It all goes to what drove the story then and what would fuel it in social media today – conflict. It would have amplified the pressure on all of us. The plaintiffs bar, the NGOs and others would have been using social media to put more pressure on the two companies. And cooler heads and thinking might have really lost out in all the noise on Twitter and Facebook."

So how should corporate communicators deal with bloggers and other significant voices in the social media?

"You have to embrace legitimate bloggers," says Vines. "Treat them like real media, not 'new media.' It's about mutual respect. But you also have to be prepared to call out bad bloggers. Use your company's blog or website to tell the truth and show how some bloggers are misleading people – call them out for what they are."

Future reputational challenges will be immense for large companies and their communicators. Corporate adversary groups, networked against common enemies, will use social media, along with anti-corporate-leaning media such as Air America, the *Huffington Post*, *Daily Kos* and various liberal commentators on cable TV networks from Keith Olbermann to Rachel Maddow. This new "Fifth Estate" will see a righteous mission in keeping big corporations honest. How can corporate PR push for balance in such an environment?

"Give them factual information and your perspective." Vines says. "If they ignore it or use it incorrectly, knowingly or unknowingly, correct them personally. If they continue to avoid the truth, nail them very publicly by showing – in a step-by-step manner – how badly they disseminate information…. Factually expose their links to one another. For example, the same PR firm that perpetuated the Alar hoax was behind both the "What Would Jesus Drive" campaign and Ariana Huffington's anti-SUV campaign [that accused SUV owners of supporting terrorism by driving fuel-thirsty vehicles]." In each of the two anti-SUV campaigns Vines mentions, controversial ads were created to generate publicity with very little actual ad spend. Though overt in the practice of media manipulation, the campaigns were quite effective. Few of the media reports were critical in any way.[1]

* * *

Another new development in the media dynamic that Bradsher is keenly attuned to is the rapid growth in government-controlled and government-sponsored media. "In China, Xinhua and *China Daily* cover everything, but you have to remember that their coverage is always guided by censorship," he says. "From Al Jazeera in the Gulf States to the BBC, there are plenty of examples of state-supported media. They will get even more important as private news organizations become more constrained in their reporting budgets. This is not a good trend for people who believe in the importance of a free press."

Tight restrictions in government-controlled media have long been evident in Venezuela. Shortly after Mike Moran joined the crisis team there in 2000, he and the Ford of Venezuela Public Affairs people wanted to view the CBS broadcast of the *60 Minutes* program dealing with the Firestone crisis. But it was not available among the state-censored channels for public consumption. The Ford contingent traveled to Caracas to the studio of Globovision as guests of the only non-government-controlled news network. There they were able to view a private screening of the live CBS broadcast so they could be ready to answer media questions that might arise from the program. Much more recently, in May 2009, a Venezuelan police raid of a residence of Globovision President Guillermo Zuloaga made inter-national news. Zuloaga claimed that the Hugo Chavez government was attempting to "shut us up" after Globovision had criticized the government's slow response to aid victims following a moderate earthquake earlier in the month.[2]

In June 2009, the Iranian government drew global condemnation for its crackdown on protests following the official announcement of highly questionable results of the country's presidential election. Already having blocked most outside media broadcasts to and from Iran, the government shut down social networking sites Facebook and Twitter, and disabled cell phone transmissions. Protesters had used social media to organize massive protests despite government prohibitions. Even with the massive government censorship, images of police brutality toward peaceful protestors made it to the Internet, drawing further outrage against the Iranian government.

As I spoke with Bradsher about the twin chilling effects on media – budget cuts that were decimating the abilities of news organizations to report comprehensively and the specter of state-controlled media all over the globe – I thought of another question for him. I wanted to ask him about the *New York Times'* own precarious financial performance and the possibility the "old gray lady" might have to turn to the U.S. Federal government for its own bailout loan to survive, thereby becoming yet another casualty in the global trend toward state-supported media. But as one who loves to read news that is printed on paper and deeply appreciates the societal value of a proud, world-class news organization, even a left-tilting one like the *New York Times*, I couldn't ask him that. I just couldn't do it.

APPENDIX

Myths and Facts

In the spring of 2001, I condensed my voluminous Q&A into the following "Myths and Facts" summary that we began to distribute to media who continued to ask many of the same questions over and over. We later posted the document on the Ford Media Website.

Making this document widely available accomplished several positive outcomes for Ford. Clearly it was a time saver for the Public Affairs team, saving us countless hours that we'd been spending answering the same questions. More importantly, it helped ensure consistency in coverage of contentious allegations. But there was a third positive result as well: We undoubtedly were able to avoid quite a few repetitive negative stories when we could point journalists to a published document. Emphasizing that a story has already been thoroughly covered, and the allegation discredited, can help end the cycle of stories that adversaries will continue to try to perpetuate.

Ford Explorer and the Firestone Tire Replacement Program: Myths & Facts[1]

Myth: SUVs are unsafe because they roll over. SUV owners would be better off driving cars.

Fact: That's false. Advances in safety technology have made all types of passenger vehicles safer than the vehicles on the road a generation ago. And Ford's analysis of federal and state government safety data shows that, overall, SUVs are even safer than passenger cars. That's because SUVs are involved in fewer accidents, SUV drivers often have better lines of sight and SUVs are more visible to

241

other drivers. Also, SUV occupants are often better protected when they are involved in collisions.

Although SUVs are involved in more rollover crashes than passenger cars, there is a greater risk of fatality in a passenger car in frontal, side and rear impacts. As a result, SUVs are safer overall.

SUVs do handle differently. That is a key reason that the different handling characteristics are printed on a label appearing on the visor of every SUV all automakers build.

Leading edge safety technology available later this year on the 2002 Ford Explorer, including AdvanceTrac^{TM} electronic stability control and Ford's new Safety Canopy^{TM} will further reduce the risk of a rollover and serious injury or death if a rollover accident occurs. But a buckled safety belt is still the best and primary line of defense for any adult occupant in a serious accident. Children should of course be in the proper restraint system (child seat, booster seat, etc.) until they are large enough to use adult safety belts.

Myth: The Ford Explorer is more prone to roll over than other SUVs.
Fact: Not true. Ford's analysis of safety data from the U.S. Department of Transportation confirms that over the past 10 years Explorer consistently ranks among the safest vehicles in its class. The fatality rate for passenger cars is 1.5 per 100 million miles of vehicle travel. The rate for compact SUVs is lower: 1.3 per 100 million miles. And the Explorer is even lower at 1.1 per 100 million miles.

Focusing on rollover accidents alone, the Explorer is safer than competitive SUVs. Ford analysis of government safety data reveals that the Explorer line is involved in 19 percent fewer fatal rollovers than other similar SUVs. And, state safety data, which covers fatal and non-fatal rollovers, show that Explorers are involved in 16 percent fewer rollovers than competitive SUVs.

Myth: Ford launched this tire replacement effort to shift blame away from the Explorer. Something is wrong with the Explorer, but Ford wants people to think it's "just a tire issue."
Fact: Not true. Ford Motor Company is replacing these tires because its number one priority is to ensure the safety of our customers and

their families. Ford's concern is the Wilderness AT tire. The facts are as follows:

First, Ford fitted both Firestone tires and Goodyear tires on Explorers beginning in 1995 and through the 1997 model year. And the difference in performance is dramatic. For the roughly 3 million Firestone tires equipped on about 500,000 Explorers, Firestone's own claims database shows that there have been 1,183 claims of tread separation. For the 3 million Goodyear tires on another 500,000 Explorers (that have traveled more than 25 billion miles), there have been only two minor claims of tread separation according to claims information supplied by Goodyear. The performance on the Firestone AT tires on Explorer is 600 times worse than Goodyear tires on Explorer. This remains the only apples-to-apples comparison in this issue. If the vehicle was the issue, or at the very least a contributing factor, the tread separations between the Firestone and Goodyear tires would be in the same ballpark. They are not even close. That's why Ford is replacing the Firestone Wilderness AT tires.

Second, when Ford engineers tested the Wilderness AT tires over the past nine months, they found that the tires were more sensitive to stresses and consistently failed at higher rates, at lower speeds and lighter loads than other tires tested, including the Goodyear tires used on Explorer.

Third, the failure rates of Firestone Wilderness AT tires differ dramatically based on the plant in which they were made. If the vehicle were the cause of these separations, the tire plant location would not make a difference in rate of tread separations reported.

Finally, Firestone CEO John Lampe testified last year before Congress under oath and said the following: "We made some bad tires and we take full responsibility for those." When a Senator asked, "Are bad tires equated to be tires that have defects of some kind," Mr. Lampe responded, "Yes, sir."

Myth: The Firestone tires performed far better on the Ranger than the Explorer. That's proof that the Explorer is part of the reason for these tire failures.

Fact: The tires have performed better on Ranger, however the Firestone tread separation claims on Ranger are still higher than average. And, importantly, the Firestone tread separation claims on Ranger are higher than Goodyear claims on Explorer.

In the June 11, 2001-dated issue of *BusinessWeek*, Brian O'Neill, president of the Insurance Institute for Highway Safety, was asked about the Explorer-Ranger comparison. He said, "It's an apples-to-oranges comparison that has no validity in my opinion."

Ford agrees with Mr. O'Neill. Tires used on any SUV perform differently compared with tires installed on a pickup. The two vehicles are used differently. SUVs typically weigh more, and frequently are more heavily loaded, putting more stress on the tires. A sensitive tire, like we have discovered with the Wilderness AT, will not perform as well under these conditions.

Nevertheless, the larger-than-average numbers of tread separation claims for Firestone tires on Rangers *are* proof – proof that these tires should be replaced. This is why Wilderness AT tires on Ranger are part of Ford's replacement campaign.

Myth: Even if the Explorer does not cause the tread separation, it certainly is more likely to roll over as a result of the tread separation.

Fact: Not true. Ford has conducted many tests comparing Explorer with competitive SUVs and we have shared our findings with the National Highway Traffic Safety Administration. By inducing a tread separation at speeds approaching 70 mph on Explorer and competitive vehicles, with various load conditions, the Explorer's performance before, during and after a tread separation was found to be typical of other SUVs. This exhaustive study was shared with NHTSA and Firestone in March 2001.

The real-world accident experience shows when a Firestone tire separated on an Explorer, a rollover accident occurred on average less than 7 percent of the time. This information is based on Firestone's own claims data. Government data show Explorer and competitive SUVs have similar rollover experience in tire-related accidents.

Unfortunately, Firestone tires on Explorer have separated with far greater frequency than tires on other SUVs and, of course, Goodyear tires on Explorer. The two known Goodyear tire separations, out of about 3 million Goodyear tires in service on Explorers over the last six years, did not result in any accidents, rollovers or injuries.

Myth: *Safetyforum* **says that when tires fail on Explorers the results are four times more likely to produce catastrophic rollover than when they fail on other SUVs.**

Fact: Ford's analysis of government data show that the Explorer has a considerably better safety record than other SUVs both in terms of fatal crashes and fatal rollover crashes. *Safetyforum* is misinterpreting data by using unverified reports for a variety of manufacturers. It's also misleading because it compares the Explorer to all light trucks and not just competitive SUVs.

Ford and the U.S. government use tire makers' claims data, not this collection of unverified reports. Even *Safetyforum*, which is a plaintiff's attorney resource organization, says they do not take into account the tire model in their analysis. The fact is that Ford's testing shows Explorers perform like other SUVs before, during and after a tire tread separation, and real world safety data show that Explorer is among the safest vehicles on the road year after year.

Myth: Internal memos show that Ford knew about the instability of the Explorer years ago and did nothing.

Fact: That's just plain wrong. The Explorer team sought to develop a safe vehicle, recognizing that safety performance among the leaders in its class would help it to become the sales leader. And that's just what they accomplished, over the past 10 years Explorer consistently has ranked among the safest vehicles in its class based on Ford's analysis of the Federal government's real world database of crash statistics. And Explorer has been the best-selling SUV in the world each year.

Memos from engineers working on the original Explorer show them working hard to make it a safety leader, and sweating over small changes necessary for prototype vehicles to pass Ford's stringent internal safety tests that ensure safe, predictable vehicle responses in severe handling maneuvers. And yes, from time to time, they debated among themselves in their search for the optimum solutions. That is what our engineers get paid to do. If any version of those prototypes didn't pass every stringent test, changes were made until they did. That's exactly why prototypes are built. By the time the first Explorer was driven by the first customer on a real road, the vehicle had passed all of Ford's internal safety tests.

Myth: Ford has spent a lot of time looking at tires as the root cause of the problem and has done little to evaluate Explorer handling due to tire separation and rollover. It seems odd that Ford has relied solely on government data for its analysis.

Fact: While important, government data is not the only part of the evaluation of the Explorer. On March 28 and 29, 2001, Ford presented NHTSA with an exhaustive analysis of Explorer. (This technical analysis is available from NHTSA.) The analysis included stringent on-road and computer-aided testing of the Explorer and comparative SUVs in its class. The analysis dissected the performance of every major component of the Explorer that has anything to do with ride and handling, including emergency handling maneuvers and tread separation of the tires. Contrary to recent Firestone charges, it is a fact that Firestone received this thorough analysis from Ford on March 30, 2001.

The conclusion: Before, during and after a tread separation, the Explorer controllability is typical of comparative SUVs. Bring in the government's data and these conclusions are consistent in the real world where analysis of statistics from the U.S. Department of Transportation shows that over the past 10 years Explorer consistently ranks among the safest vehicles in its class. The fatality rate for passenger cars is 1.5 per 100 million miles of vehicle travel. The rate for compact SUVs is lower – 1.3 per 100 million miles. And the Explorer is even lower at 1.1 per 100 million miles. Likewise, focusing solely on rollover accidents, the Explorer is safer than its competition. Government figures reveal that Explorers are involved in 19 percent fewer fatal rollovers than other competitive SUVs. The same is true for single-vehicle rollover accidents – Explorer is safer than other similar-sized SUVs.

Myth: Explorer 26 psi recommended tire pressure is too low. That's why the tires failed.

Fact: Not true. The 2.9 million Goodyear tires performing at world-class levels on Ford Explorers convincingly disprove this myth. The recommended tire pressure for the Goodyear tires also was and, importantly, still is 26 psi. Yet the Goodyear tires are not showing the same tread separation problems. If tire pressure were really the issue, why isn't it an issue for the Goodyear tires? In addition, the extensive analysis by Ford and Firestone's independent experts show that inflation pressure generally does not cause tread separations on robust tires unless the tire is operated substantially below 26 psi.

Incidentally, the 16-inch Wilderness AT tires in the replacement program have a recommended pressure of 30 psi. Ford's analysis of Firestone's latest claims data (May 2001) showed increasing failure rates for the 16-inch tires similar to the failure rates of the 15-inch tires made in the same plant.

Myth: Ford told Firestone to decrease tire pressure to 26 psi so the vehicle could pass Ford's handling exercises and/or reduce the center of gravity. That increased the heat of the tire and caused these tread separations.

Fact: Not true. Working with Firestone, Ford engineers selected the recommended tire pressure for Explorer to optimize numerous vehicle and tire characteristics including ride quality and handling. The tire pressure selected, 26 psi is not unusual. Dozens of other competitive light trucks, SUVs, and passenger cars run on similar sized (15-inch) tires specified at 26 psi. Ford did not recommend 26 psi to lower the Explorer's center of gravity, since tire pressure has nothing to do with a vehicle's center of gravity. A 4 psi decrease (30 psi to 26 psi) lowers the center of gravity by 90 thousands of an inch (about the thickness of a nickel.)

As was said earlier, the 16-inch Wilderness AT tires in the replacement program have a recommended pressure of 30 psi. Ford's analysis of Firestone's latest claims data (May 2001) showed increasing failure rates for the 16-inch tires similar to the failure rates of the 15-inch tires made in the same plant.

Myth: Firestone never agreed with Ford's recommended 26 psi tire pressure.

Fact: Firestone consistently supported Ford's recommended inflation pressure, at least until NHTSA opened its investigation in May 2000. In fact, Firestone delivered tires and paid warranty claims on those tires, year after year, under the 26 psi specification. In addition, the catalogs that Firestone issued to its dealers and customers from 1993 through 2000 state that Firestone, not just Ford, recommended 26 psi on the 15-inch tires. Furthermore, Firestone CEO Masatoshi Ono, told the *Wall Street Journal* on August 18, 2000, that "we do not believe Ford's recommendation of 26 psi [pounds per square inch] for our tires was a mistake." Firestone approved the 26 psi recommendation in December 1989, prior to Explorer production. Goodyear also concurred in the recommendation when Ford bought Goodyear tires for Explorer.

Myth: Tires cannot tell where they have been placed on a vehicle. Yet most of the Firestone tread separations on Explorer occurred on the left rear tire. That's a sign it's the vehicle that is causing this.

Fact: False. Firestone claim data shows the same pattern for nearly all trucks and SUVs. It's consistent for GM and Daimler-Chrysler vehicles as well as Ford vehicles, the rear tires have more tread separation claims for property damage or injury than the front tires and the left rear tire tread separation claims outnumber the right rear tire tread separation claims.

Myth: Ford knew, or should have known, last summer that the recall should have been wider and are only now reluctantly replacing all the Wilderness AT tires.

Fact: Not true. Ford didn't have all the information last summer that it has today. Last summer, Ford's review of the Firestone claims data showed alarming failure rates for Firestone 15-inch ATX and Decatur-built 15-inch Wilderness AT tires. And so Ford urged Firestone to recall those tires. The Firestone claims data available to Ford at the time showed other Firestone Wilderness AT tires performing at world-class levels with no crashes, no rollovers, no injuries and no fatalities.

Since last August, Ford has invested nearly 100,000 people-hours studying tires, testing tires on rigs, pouring over field analysis and conducting tire design case studies. Then, after repeated requests, Ford obtained on May 11, 2001, additional claims data from Firestone, another piece of the puzzle that confirmed Ford's research and analysis. That data showed significantly increasing failure rates for some Wilderness AT tires and raised serious questions about the long-term durability of all of the non-recalled Wilderness AT tires. Once it obtained this information, Ford did not wait and took this preventive action to protect its customers.

Myth: Ford replaced the 16-inch Wilderness AT tires overseas more than a year ago. That's proof Ford knew about the problem before last summer.

Fact: False. Ford had not, in fact, found the same failure pattern in the U.S. as it had in the overseas locations where unique usage and environmental conditions existed. Nor did Ford see the same failure pattern in the U.S. that it saw overseas. However, more recently we have seen warning signs in the U.S. that led Ford to take this action as a precautionary measure.

Myth: Ford should not have accepted "C" temperature-rated tires from Firestone. They are only tested to 85 mph.

Fact: The Firestone Wilderness AT tires are, in fact, certified to 112 mph at full vehicle loads.

The confusion is that there are two different tests used to rate tire characteristics. One test, for temperature rating, is run on a test drum with huge loads placed on the tire – far greater than the tires experience in the real world even when the vehicle is fully loaded. The 85-mph threshold a tire must pass on the test drum to be certified actually translates to speeds significantly higher in on-road usage by our customers.

A "C" temperature-rated tire is an appropriate tire for a vehicle if the tire is well manufactured and meets the performance criteria set by the automaker. Tires certified with a "C" temperature label have passed a stringent government standard, and are therefore determined to be fully acceptable. In fact, there are millions of "C" tires on some GM, Toyota and Nissan SUVs and light trucks and these tires appear to have performed well.

There is a separate test that certifies tires for a speed rating. This test is run at higher speeds and full vehicle loads. All Wilderness AT tires are speed rated "S" and are certified to 112 mph, substantially higher than the top speed of an Explorer.

249

Myth: The other companies are not replacing Firestone Wilderness AT tires on their vehicles. That means the tires are fine.

Fact: That is a decision that the other automakers have to make. Ford conducted extensive vehicle and tire testing, analyzed Firestone field data and discussed findings with NHTSA. Ford concluded that there was a growing risk of additional tire failures in the future and decided to replace all Wilderness AT tires on Ford vehicles as a precautionary measure.

Other auto companies may be using different types of Firestone Wilderness tires having different specifications. It is interesting to note that days after supporting their use of Firestone tires, some of these manufacturers acknowledged that they are replacing Firestone tires on future vehicle production.

Myths & Facts About Actions in Venezuela

Myth: The Explorer is still rolling over at high rates in Venezuela. And they now have Goodyear tires. That's more proof that the problem is not the tire.

Fact: Absolutely false. For one thing, there has been no attempt to make any connection between these accident reports and tire failures. For another, many of these reports of "Explorer rollovers" have actually been other vehicles misreported as Ford Explorers. Other accidents mentioned include an Explorer in heavy traffic that was rear-ended by a large truck and then sandwiched between two heavy vehicles. The vehicle did not roll over, it was not in any way a tire-related incident and, thankfully, the occupants walked away with only scratches. No one, including Firestone, should make claims or allegations based on this data that is, at best, clearly flawed.

Newly obtained data from the Venezuelan transportation authority, SETRA, show that most SUV accidents in Venezuela involve vehicles other than Explorers. In the period 2000 to 2001, there were 701 accidents reported involving SUVs, but only 9 percent involved Explorers.

This data involves both fatal and non-fatal accidents in ten Venezuelan states. Two other competitors' SUVs had more fatal accidents than Explorers in Venezuela. The data was gathered and analyzed from traffic reports in the SETRA records.

The fact is Explorer, in addition to being a very popular SUV in Venezuela, has one of the safest records of any SUV in the country. Explorer's safety record in Venezuela is consistent with its performance in the U.S. where the DOT accident data confirms that Explorer is among the safest vehicles in its class.

Myth: Venezuela may ban the sale of Explorer and that's more proof that it is a dangerous vehicle.

Fact: The misinformed accusations by one Venezuelan investigator, acting on the flawed data mentioned above, does not change the fact that Explorer is a safe vehicle. The investigator has failed to substantiate any of his theories, which do not withstand any serious technical review. The Venezuelan National Assembly established an independent Technical Commission to review the investigator's allegations. Ford has been working closely with the Technical Commission and has shared its testing and analysis with them. This data and analysis disproves the investigator's allegations, including suggestions that electromagnetic interference or aerodynamic turbulence were causing vehicle rollovers.

We would expect the Venezuelan governmental agencies to act responsibly, not on a misrepresentation of hearsay.

251

NOTES

Preface

1   David Halberstam, *The Reckoning* (New York: Morrow, 1986).

Chapter One: Pride Before the Fall

1   Margot Roosevelt, "How Green Was My SUV," *TIME* magazine, Aug. 6, 2000.

2   "The Inside Edition of GM v. NBC," Communications and Media Law, *New York Law Journal*, April 2, 1993.

3   Ibid.

4   Pearce's Power Keeps Growing," *Ward's Auto World*, January 1996.

5   Roosevelt.

6   Paul Eisenstein, "Publisher's Letter," August 2000 *The Car Connection*.

7   Jeffrey McCracken, "Ford Posts $1.19 Billion Loss," *Wall Street Journal*, April 22, 2006.

8   Bernard Simon, "Automakers suffer as drivers downsize," *Financial Times*, May 12, 2005.

9   "Ford Ranks As 'Most Admired' Automotive Company," Ford press release, February 1999.

10 GM Annual Report: 2000. Market share in the U.S. was 27.8%, down 1 percentage point from 1999.

11 "Ford To Top GM's Global Production In 2005," Autoparts Report, June 10, 1999 citing a report by AutoFacts (a division of Pricewaterhouse Coopers).

12 "Ford: It's Worse Than You Think," by Joann Muller with Kathleen Kerwin and David Welch in Detroit, Pamela L. Moore and Diane Brady in New York, *BusinessWeek* cover story, June 25, 2001.

13 CBS Evening News, March 11, 2003.
http://www.cbsnews.com/stories/2003/03/11/eveningnews/main543605.s
html

14 "Who Killed the Electric Car?" 2006, Sony Pictures,
www.whokilledtheelectriccar.com/

15 "Ford, Nasser to Run Ford Motor Co." *Automotive Industries*, Oct. 1,
1998.

16 James R. Healey, "Big Three breaks ranks: Safety, pollution squabbles
divide U.S. automakers," *USA Today* Feb. 6, 1998.

17 Ibid.

18 Helen Petrauskas, Ford vice president – Environment and Safety
Engineering in *Issues in Science and Technology Online*, Spring 2001.
http://www.issues.org/17.3/index.html

19 "If a belted occupant is in a rollover accident, his chances of survival are
ten times higher than unbelted occupants." – Sue Cischke, Testimony
Before the Commerce, Science and Transportation Committee, U.S.
Senate, Feb. 26, 2003.
http://media.ford.com/article_display.cfm?article_id=14618

20 Jim Mateja, "Ford's Free Trunk Release Lacks Impact of GM's $50
System," *Ward's AutoWorld*, Spring 1999.
http://www.autoworld.com/news/Ford/TrunkRelease_Winner.htm

21 *Connecting With Society* (Ford Corporate Citizenship Report: 2000),
pp.81-82.

22 "Sport Utility Vehicle Case Study," *Connecting With Society* (Ford
Corporate Citizenship Report: 2000), p 82.

23 Eisenstein, editor and publisher, *The Car Connection*,
http://www.thecarconnection.com/index.asp
http://blog.vehiclevoice.com/2005/11/time_for_suv_jihad.html

24 Book jacket notes for *High and Mighty: SUVs – The World's Most
Dangerous Vehicles and How They Got That Way*, by Keith Bradsher,
(New York: Public Affairs, 2002).

25 David Lee, "Ford Commits To Major SUV Fuel Economy Gains,"
AutoWorld.com, July 2000.
http://www.autoworld.com/apps/news/FullStory.asp?id=45

26 National Public Radio, preview of live webcast of Jac Nasser's National
Press Club speech, July 27, 2000
http://www.npr.org/programs/npc/2000/000727.jnasser.html

Chapter Two: Rumblings Around the World

1   Al Tompkins, "Breaking the Big One: How KHOU Did It," *The Poynter Institute on-line*, Oct. 11, 2000.

2   Ibid.

3   Alicia Shepard, "Local Heroes," *American Journalism Review*, December 2000. http://ajr.org/Article.asp?id=507

4   KHOU "The Defenders" broadcast, Feb. 9, 2000.

5   Tompkins.

6   KHOU "The Defenders" broadcast, Feb. 9, 2000.

7   Ibid.

8   Ibid.

9   Tompkins.

10 Timeline from Public Citizen's "Chronology of Firestone/Ford Knowledge of Tire Safety Defect;" www.citizen.org/autosafety/articles.cfm?ID=5336

11 Ibid.

12 Ibid.

13 "Venezuela to Ban Sale of Ford Explorer," CNN transcript, May 25, 2001. http://transcripts.cnn.com/TRANSCRIPTS/0105/25/tonight.09.html

14 Ford news conference Aug. 24, 2000: CNN transcript, aired Aug. 24, 2000. http://transcripts.cnn.com/TRANSCRIPTS/0008/24/bn.01.html

15 Testimony of Bridgestone/Firestone Before the Senate Commerce Committee, Sept. 12, 2000.

16 U.S. Department of Transportation (DOT) Fatality Analysis Reporting System (FARS) data. http://www-fars.nhtsa.dot.gov/Main/index.aspx

17 Ibid.

18 Public Citizen timeline.

Chapter Three: Showdown in Dearborn

1   Timeline from Public Citizen's "Chronology of Firestone/Ford Knowledge of Tire Safety Defect; www.citizen.org/autosafety/articles.cfm?ID=5336

2   Ibid.

3   "Bridgestone/Firestone's Bob Martin to Retire," *Business Wire*, March 31, 2000. http://www.allbusiness.com/automotive/automotive-trade-motor-vehicle/6414240-1.html

4   Keith Bradsher, "S.U.V. Tire Defects Were Known in '96 But Not Reported," *New York Times*, June 24, 2001, page A1.

5   Ibid.

6   Ibid.

7   Ibid.

8   Ibid.

9   Public Citizen timeline.

10 "Burst tire precipitated Concorde crash, says report," CNN.com, Aug. 31, 2000. http://edition.cnn.com/2000/WORLD/europe/08/31/france.concorde.02/

11 "Firestone Tire Tread Separation," Strategic Safety, Aug. 3, 2000. http://www.kraftlaw.com/ArticleArchive/FirestoneTires/StrategicSafety/firestone_tire_tread_separation.htm

12 Healey, "More Deaths Linked to Tires," *USA Today*, August 2, 2000. http://asp.usatoday.com/money/consumer/autos/mauto716.htm

13 Firestone statement, August 3, 2000. www.usatoday.com/money/consumer/autos/mauto728.htm

14 Dates and stories mentioned taken from *USAToday.com*'s "Index of Firestone Tire Stories." http://www.usatoday.com/money/consumer/autos/mauto731.htm

Chapter Four: Day of Reckoning

1   Transcript of CNN live broadcast August 9, 2000. http://transcripts.cnn.com/TRANSCRIPTS/0008/09/bn.07.html

2   Wikipedia: Ford Ranger. http://en.wikipedia.org/wiki/Ford_Ranger

3   Sherrie Gossett, "The CBS 'Cold Case' Files," *Accuracy in Media*, May 13, 2005. http://www.aim.org/media-monitor/the-cbs-cold-case-files/

4   "Ford Explorer Rollover and Recall History," Ford Explorer Rollover.com http://www.fordexplorerrollover.com/rollover_history.cfm

5   "Ford Motor Company Statement in Response to Firestone's Recall," Aug. 9, 2000 http://www.prnewswire.com/cgi-bin/stories.pl?ACCT=104&STORY=/www/story/08-09-2000/0001286554&EDATE=

6   Transcript of CNN live broadcast August 9, 2000. http://transcripts.cnn.com/TRANSCRIPTS/0008/09/bn.07.html

7   Shepard.

8   Ibid.

9   Transcript of CNN live broadcast August 9, 2000. http://transcripts.cnn.com/TRANSCRIPTS/0008/09/bn.07.html

10   Ibid.

11   "Helen Petrauskas," *American Woman Motorscene*, 2000. http://www.theautochannel.com/mania/women/oldawm/awm09952.html

12   Transcript of CNN live broadcast August 9, 2000. http://transcripts.cnn.com/TRANSCRIPTS/0008/09/bn.07.html

13   Bill Poorman, Michigan Public Radio, interviewing Sean Kane for "Marketplace," August 14, 2000. http://marketplace.publicradio.org/shows/2000/08/14_mpp.html

Chapter Five: Media Feeding Frenzy

1   Alex Frew McMillan, "A long wait for new tires," CNN.com, Aug. 11, 2000 http://money.cnn.com/2000/08/11/home_auto/q_tiretime/

2   "Q&A," *USA Today*, Aug. 10, 2000.

3   Kevin McDermott, "Blame for tire defects is touchy point at factory," *St. Louis Post Dispatch*, Aug. 23, 2000.

4   Myron Levin, "Illinois Firestone Plant Torn by Labor Tension, Tire Recall," *Los Angeles Times*, Aug. 12, 2000.

5   James Cox and Sumiko Oshima, "In Tokyo, fingers point at Ford," *USA Today*, Aug. 10. 2000.
    http://www.usatoday.com/money/consumer/autos/mauto735.htm

6   Robert Simison, "Behind the Wheel: For Ford CEO Nasser, Damage Control Is The New 'Job One,'" *Wall Street Journal*, Sept. 11, 2000, page A1.

7   Joann Muller, "Ford: A Crisis of Confidence," *BusinessWeek*, Sept. 8, 2000. http://www.businessweek.com/2000/00_38/b3699191.htm

8   David Kiley, "Venezuela Investigates Ford, Tires," *USA Today*, Aug. 29, 2000, http://www.usatoday.com/money/consumer/autos/mauto791.htm

9   "Ford Motor Company Talks About Tire Controversy," CNN Transcripts, Aug. 29, 2000.
    http://transcripts.cnn.com/TRANSCRIPTS/0008/29/se.03.html

10 "Road Troubles," *Jim Lehrer NewsHour* transcript, Aug. 29, 2000.
    http://www.pbs.org/newshour/bb/transportation/july-dec00/tires_8-29a.html

11 Thinkexist.com encyclopedia of quotations.
    http://thinkexist.com/quotes/ralph_hoar

12 "Ford Takes Out Ads to Reassure Customers," CNN.com, Aug. 13, 2000. http://archives.cnn.com/2000/US/08/13/firestone.02/index.html

13 Mac Gordon, "Ford dealers Dig In During the Firestone SUV Tire Recall Fiasco," *Ward's Dealer Business*, October 2000.
    http://wardsdealer.com/ar/auto_ford_dealers_dig/

14 Jay Leno, "Tonight Show," Aug. 12, 2000 and Oct. 13, 2000 – quoted on *Edmunds.com* http://townhall.edmunds.com/direct/view/.ee94abc/119 and about.com http://humor.about.com/library/quote/blquip081200.htm

15 David Letterman on the CBS "Late Show" Aug. 31, 2000
    http://lateshow.cbs.com/latenight/lateshow/top_ten/index/php/20000831.phtml

16 Tom Fitzgerald, "Top of the Sixth," *San Francisco Chronicle*, Oct. 13, 2000. http://www.sfgate.com/cgi-bin/article.cgi?f=/c/a/2000/10/13/SP65299.DTL&hw=harbaugh&sn=408&sc=086

17 Drew Winter, "Together Again in the Headlines," *Ward's AutoWorld*, Oct. 1, 2000.
    http://wardsautoworld.com/ar/auto_together_again_headlines/

Chapter Six:
Trial Lawyers Seize Control of the News Cycle

1 Tab Turner interview from PBS' "Frontline," (not dated).
http://www.pbs.org/wgbh/pages/frontline/shows/rollover/interviews/turner.html

2 Tab Turner's biography as featured on the website of his law firm, Turner & Associates. http://www.tturner.com/profile.html

3 "Judge Cuts Award in Fatal Crash Suit," *New York Times*, August 26, 1995.
http://query.nytimes.com/gst/fullpage.html?res=990CEEDA1F3CF935A1575BC0A963958260

4 Eric Freedman, "Court Cuts Bronco II Defect Award," *Automotive News*, October 1998.
http://findarticles.com/p/articles/mi_hb6674/is_199810/ai_n26644870

5 Bart Jones, "Jury clears Consumer Union of liability in Isuzu case," Associated Press, April 7, 2000.

6 "Judge Cuts Award in Fatal Crash Suit," *New York Times*, August 26, 1995.
http://query.nytimes.com/gst/fullpage.html?res=990CEEDA1F3CF935A1575BC0A963958260

7 Michael Winerip, "What's Tab Turner Got Against Ford?" *The Sunday New York Times* magazine, December 17, 2000.

8 Explorer safety data originates from Department of Transportation's Fatality Analysis Reporting System (FARS) and can be found at numerous sites, including the Appendix of this book: "Ford Explorer and the Firestone Tire Replacement Program: Myths & Facts."

9 Turner & Associates website. http://www.tturner.com/profile.html

10 Adam Penenberg, *Tragic Indifference: One Man's Battle With the Auto Industry Over the Dangers of SUVs*, (New York: Harper Collins, 2003).

11 Ted Frank, "Rollover Economics: Arbitrary and Capricious Prod-uct Liability Regimes," American Enterprise Institute for Public Policy Research, Jan. 4, 2007
http://www.aei.org/publications/pubID.25395/pub_detail.asp

12 As the Public Affairs manager at Ford in charge of legal matters in the mid-'90s, I had many dealings with these two journalists. See also

"Overlawyered: Chronicling the High Costs of Our Legal System; Myron Levin and the *Los Angeles Times* does it again." http://www.overlawyered.com/2005/08/myron_levin_and_the_los_angel e.html and, alternatively, "Myth Buster!: How Corporations Abuse Our Civil Justice System." http://www.centerjd.org/free/mythbusters-free/MB_discoveryabuse.htm and "Lawyers Wonder Who Is Responsible for Sept. 11," by Milo Geylin, *Wall Street Journal*, Oct. 18, 2001, page B1.

13 Frank.

14 Ibid.

15 Howard Kurtz, "Rather Concedes Papers Are Suspect," *Washington Post*, Sept. 16, 2004. http://www.washingtonpost.com/wp-dyn/articles/A24633-2004Sep15.html

16 John Greenwald, "Inside the Ford/Firestone Fight," *TIME* magazine, May 29, 2001. http://www.time.com/time/business/article/0,8599,128198,00.html

17 Frank.

18 NHTSA Consumer Advisory, Sept. 1, 2000. http://cars.spancity.com/_src_/advisory/advisory_nhtsa_200009_fireston e.html

19 "Ford Statement on NHTSA Firestone Tire Consumer Advisory," Sept. 1, 2000. http://www.prnewswire.com/cgi-bin/stories.pl?ACCT=104&STORY=/www/story/09-01-2000/0001303564&EDATE

20 Kathryn Kranhold and Erin White, "The Perils and Potential Rewards of Crisis Managing for Firestone," *Wall Street Journal*, p. B1, Sept, 8, 2000.

21 Ibid.

22 James O'Rourke, "Bridgestone/Firestone, Inc. and Ford Motor Company: How a Product Safety Crisis Ended a 100-Year Relationship," University of Notre Dame, Corporate Reputation Review, Volume 4, Number 3, page 7. http://reputationinstitute.com/crr/V04/ORourke.pdf

23 "Is Firestone's Clock Ticking?" CNN Money, Sept. 8, 2000. http://money.cnn.com/2000/09/08/companies/firestone_brand/index.htm

24 Daniel Eisenberg, "Firestone's Rough Road," *TIME* magazine, Sept. 10, 2000. http://www.time.com/time/magazine/article/0,9171,54426-1,00.html

25 Kranhold and White.

26 Tim Aeppel, Claire Ansberry, Milo Geylin and Robert Simison, "Road Signs: How Ford, Firestone Let the Warnings Slide By As Debacle Developed," Sept. 6, 2000 *Wall Street Journal*, page A1. http://www.stern.nyu.edu/om/courses/summer03/cafo_grad/pinedo/tqm/ford-firestone/ford-firestone-9-6.pdf

27 Ibid.

Chapter Seven: Congressional Circus Act

1 Stephen Power and Timothy Aeppel, "Executives at Ford, Firestone Will Field Questions From House on Tire-Test Data," *Wall Street Journal*, Sept. 18, 2000.

2 Sheldon Rampton, "Ketchum tackles Corporate Responsibility," Center for Media and Democracy. http://www.prwatch.org/prwissues/2002Q3/ketchum.html

3 O'Rourke.

4 Teresa Lindeman, "Bridgestone/Firestone Becomes Latest lesson for Public Relations Industry," *Pittsburgh Post-Gazette*, Nov. 16, 2000.

5 Ibid.

6 John Chartier, "Companies try to pin blame on each other, but others say both are at fault," CNN-FN on-line, Sept. 6, 2000. http://money.cnn.com/2000/09/06/companies/bridgestone_ford/

7 "Congressional Hearings Likely," *Consumeraffairs.com*, Aug. 24, 2000. http://www.consumeraffairs.com/news/firestone_mccain.html

8 "Ford Statement of Congressional Hearings," Aug. 30, 2000. http://www.prnewswire.com/cgi-bin/stories.pl?ACCT=104&STORY=/www/story/08-30-2000/0001301890&EDATE=

9 Kiley, "Ford CEO Changes Mind, Says He Will Testify," *USA Today*, Sept. 1, 2000. http://www.usatoday.com/money/consumer/autos/mauto800.htm

10 Aeppel and Joe White, "Bridgestone/Firestone Fretted About Replacements," *Wall Street Journal*, Sept. 6, 2000.

11 Ibid.

12 Ibid.

13 House Commerce Committee Hearing, Sept. 6, 2000. PBS: http://www.pbs.org/newshour/bb/transportation/july-dec00/tires_9-06.html

14 CNN transcript of House Committee Hearings, Sept. 6, 2000. http://transcripts.cnn.com/TRANSCRIPTS/0009/06/se.08.html

15 Earle Eldridge, "Legislators: NHTSA "Apparently Asleep," *USA Today*, Sept. 7, 2000. http://www.usatoday.com/money/consumer/autos/mauto813.htm

16 Ibid.

17 "Rough Road," CNN coverage of the House hearings, Sept. 6, 2000 http://www.pbs.org/newshour/bb/transportation/july-dec00/tires_9-06.html

18 Ibid.

19 Eldridge.

20 House Commerce Committee Hearing, Sept. 6, 2000. PBS: http://www.pbs.org/newshour/bb/transportation/july-dec00/tires_9-06.html

21 "Firestone, Ford Under Fire," CNN Money, Sept. 6, 2000.

http://money.cnn.com/2000/09/06/companies/bridgestone_ford/

22 Ibid.

23 Robert Simison and Stephen Power, "Firestone Knew of Tire Safety Problems," *Wall Street Journal*, Sept. 7, 2000.

24 Ibid.

25 Ibid.

26 "Firestone, Ford Under Fire," CNN Money, Sept. 6, 2000. http://money.cnn.com/2000/09/06/companies/bridgestone_ford/.

27 CNN Transcripts, Jac Nasser testimony to House Commerce subcommittee, Sept. 6, 2000. http://transcripts.cnn.com/TRANSCRIPTS/0009/06/se.09.html

28 Ibid.

29 Ibid.

30 Ibid.

31 Ibid.

32 Ibid.

33 Ibid.

34 Eisenberg.

35 "Firestone CEO Says Apology Doesn't Mean Fault," Associated Press, October 10, 2000. http://bankrupt.com/CAR_Public/001011.MBX

36 Dan Ackman, "Top Of The News: Bridgestone's Ono Out Of The Fire," *Forbes.com*, October 10, 2000. http://www.forbes.com/2000/10/10/1010topnews.html

37 Highway safety head undergoes baptism by Firestone," CNN, Sept. 11, 2000. http://usgovinfo.about.com/gi/dynamic/offsite.htm?site=http://www.cnn.com/2000/US/09/11/sue.bailey.profile/index.html

38 "New fire on tire recall," CNN Money, Sept. 12, 2000. http://money.cnn.com/2000/09/12/companies/firestone_ford/

39 Ibid.

40 Ibid.

41 "Ford CEO Jacques Nasser Addresses Senate Commerce Committee on Firestone Tire Recall," CNN, Sept. 12, 2000. http://transcripts.cnn.com/TRANSCRIPTS/0009/12/se.04.html

42 Nedra Pickler, "Ford, Firestone blame each other in tire deaths," Associated Press, Sept.13, 2000. http://community.seattletimes.nwsource.com/archive/?date=20000913&slug=4042242

Chapter Eight: The Feeding Frenzy Won't Stop

1 Cindy Skrzycki, "'Firestonewalling' Again? Two Decades Later, Echoes of Earlier Testimony," *Washington Post*, Sept. 12, 2000. http://www.johnemossfoundation.org/wp-dyn.htm

2 CBS *60 Minutes* broadcast, Oct. 8, 2000.

3 Ibid.

4 Ibid.

5 Healey, "Firestone may have known of trouble in '94," *USA Today*, October 4, 2000. http://www.usatoday.com/money/consumer/autos/mauto870.htm

6 Ibid.

7 Jill Bratina bio on Public Strategies, Inc. website. http://www.pstrategies.com/personprofile.php?eid=168

8 Ibid.

9 Resume: John T. Lampe, *BusinessWeek*, April 30, 2001. http://www.businessweek.com/magazine/content/01_18/b3730084.htm

10 "John T. Lampe Named Chief Executive Officer of Bridgestone/Firestone," Bridgestone/Firestone news release, Oct. 10, 2000. http://www.prnewswire.com/cgi-bin/stories.pl?ACCT=104&STORY=/www/story/10-10-2000/0001334462&EDATE=

11 Ibid.

12 Ibid.

13 "American New Boss at Firestone," United Press International, Oct 11, 2000.

14 Bradsher, "Questions Raised about Ford Explorer's Margin of Safety," *New York Times*, Sept. 16, 2000. http://query.nytimes.com/gst/fullpage.html?res=9900E1D61138F935A2575AC0A9669C8B63&sec=&spon=&pagewanted=all and "Ford Explorer and the Firestone Tire Replacement Program: Myths & Facts," Appendix.

15 Testimony of John T. Lampe before Congress, June 19, 2001.

16 Ford calculations based on Department of Transportation Fatality Analysis Reporting System (FARS) data 1990-99. Released repeatedly by Ford beginning October 2000, also included in PowerPoint presentation prepared for Richard Parry-Jones for use in Ford news conference June 15, 2001.

17 Geoff Dougherty and Jay Weaver, "Tire-related Roll-Rate High for Some Fords," *Miami Herald*, October 10, 2000. Page. A1.

18 Ibid.

19 Ibid.

20 Ibid.

21 Dan Keating and Caroline Mayer, "Explorer has Higher Rate of Tire Accidents," *Washington Post*, Oct. 9, 2000. Page A1.

22 Jon Harmon and Ken Zino, "Errors in Oct. 9 *Washington Post* story: A case study of careless analysis," posted on Ford's Media Website, www.media.ford.com October 2000.

23 Keating and Mayer, Oct. 9, 2000.

24 Harmon and Zino.

25 Keating and Mayer, Oct. 9, 2000.

26 Harmon and Zino.

27 Ibid.

28 Ibid.

29 Harmon, "Response to *Washington Post* Story," prepared for use by Ford's Media Information Center and Customer Service Center, October 2000.

30 Keating and Mayer, "Ford Cites Flaws in Explorer Tire Data," *Washington Post*, Oct. 11, 2000. Page A1.

31 Jack Shafer, "The *Washington Post* Blows the Blowout Story," *Slate*, October 11, 2000. http://www.slate.com/id/1006255/

32 Bradsher, "Ford to Include Payload Data in Vehicles," *New York Times*, November 7, 2000. http://query.nytimes.com/gst/fullpage.html?res=9404E5D61339F934A35 752C1A9669C8B63&sec=&spon=&pagewanted=1

33 Ibid.

34 Ibid.

Chapter Nine: The Blame Game

1 Winerip.

2 Ibid.

3 Ibid.

4   Ibid.

5   Ibid.

6   Ibid.

7   Bradsher, "Firestone Engineers Offer a List of Causes for Faulty Tires," *New York Times*, Dec. 18, 2000.

8   "Ford CEO Jacques Nasser Addresses the Senate Commerce Committee on Firestone Tire Recall," Sept. 12, 2000. CNN transcript http://transcripts.cnn.com/TRANSCRIPTS/0009/12/se.04.html

9   Cathy Booth Thomas, "A Nasty Turn for Ford?" *TIME* magazine, Jan. 7, 2001

10   Ibid.

11   Winerip, "Ford and Firestone Settle Explorer Suit Over Tire Crash," *New York Times*, Jan. 9, 2001. http://query.nytimes.com/gst/fullpage.html?res=9404EFDF133AF93AA 35752C0A9679C8B63

12   "Tragic Indifference" movie preview site at Hollywood.com. http://www.hollywood.com/movie/Tragic_Indifference/3462877

13   "Firestone Announces the Completion of the Independent Expert's Analysis: Dr. Sanjay Govindjee Confirms No Single Factor Findings Shared with Public," Firestone news release, Feb. 2, 2001.

14   Ibid.

15   Bradsher, "Expert Says Car Weight Was Key in Tire Failures," *New York Times*, Feb. 3, 2001.

16   Ford Explorer product information from Ford's website: www.ford.com

17   Thomas.

18   Bradsher, "S.U.V. Tire Defects Were Known in '96 But Not Reported," *New York Times*, June 24, 2001, page A1.

19   Winerip, *New York Sunday Times* magazine cover story, Dec. 17, 2000.

20   "Firestone and Ford Place Blame," CBS News, Dec. 19, 2000.

21   "Firestone Announces New National Advertising Campaign; Ads to Focus on the Company's Action Plans for the Future, 'Making it Right'," Bridgestone/Firestone news release, April 5, 2001.

22   "Making It Right," Firestone print advertisement circa April 2001.

23 Shawn Zeller, "Blowout," *National Journal*, April 28, 2001.

24 Ibid.

25 Ibid.

26 Bradsher, "Ford is Said to Consider Seeking recalls of More Tires," *New York Times*, May 18, 2001.
http://query.nytimes.com/gst/fullpage.html?res=9506E6D8113AF93BA2 5756C0A9679C8B63&scp=4&sq=bradsher%20firestone%20ford%20re call&st=cse

27 Ibid.

28 Letter to Jac Nasser from John Lampe, faxed to CNN May 21, 2001.
http://money.cnn.com/2001/05/21/recalls/firestone/firestone_letter.htm

29 "Firestone Dumps Ford," CNN/Money May 21, 2001
http://money.cnn.com/2001/05/21/recalls/firestone/

30 Bradsher, "Ford Intends to Replace 13 Million Firestone Wilderness Tires," by Keith Bradsher, *New York Times*,
http://query.nytimes.com/gst/fullpage.html?res=9B07E3D7123DF930A1 5756C0A9679C8B63

31 Ibid.

32 Charles Gibson and Lisa Stark, "Ford and Firestone sever business ties amidst questions about vehicle and tire safety," ABC News: Good Morning America, May 23, 2001.

33 Bradsher, "Ford and Firestone Wrangle Over Rollovers and Tires," by *New York Times*, May 24, 2001.
http://query.nytimes.com/gst/fullpage.html?res=9B04E2D7103DF937A1 5756C0A9679C8B63

34 John Greenwald, et al, "Tired of Each Other," *TIME* magazine, June 4, 2001.
http://www.time.com/time/magazine/article/0,9171,1000025,00.html

35 Ibid.

36 Ibid.

37 Ibid.

38 Richard Parry-Jones presentation (PowerPoint), Ford news conference June 15, 2001.

39 Ibid.

Chapter Ten: Case Closed?

1 "Family Feud: Ford, Firestone Take Off the Gloves," consumeraffairs.com, May 28, 2001, http://www.consumeraffairs.com/news/family_feud.html

2 Bradsher, "House Committee Chairman Faults Inquiry On Firestone," *New York Times*, June 6, 2001. http://query.nytimes.com/gst/fullpage.html?res=9C03EFDF143EF93AA35755C0A9679C8B63&n=Top/Reference/Times%20Topics/Organizations/C/Congress

3 "It's Ford vs. Firestone in Congressional Battle," CBS news, June 20, 2001. http://www.cbc.ca/news/story/2001/06/19/FirestoneFord_010619.html

4 Ibid.

5 Ibid.

6 Tim Perry, "Ford Answers Firestone's Testimony," *Fleet Owner*, June 21, 2001. http://fleetowner.com/news/fleet_ford_answers_firestones/

7 Anitha Reddy, "Firestone to Close Illinois Factory, Decatur Plant Produced Most Recalled Tires," *The Washington Post*, June 28, 2001. http://pqasb.pqarchiver.com/washingtonpost/access/74805219.html?dids=74805219:74805219&FMT=ABS&FMTS=ABS:FT&fmac=&date=Jun+28%2C+2001&author=Anitha+Reddy&desc=Firestone+To+Close+Illinois+Factory%3B+Decatur+Plant+Made+Most+Recalled+Tires

8 Terril Yue Jones, "Bridgestone Rejects Wider Recall Request," *Los Angeles Times*, July 20, 2001

9 Ibid.

10 Ibid.

11 Ibid.

12 "NHTSA Announces Initial Decision That Additional Firestone Wilderness AT Tires Have a Safety Defect; Firestone Agrees to Recall Those Tires," NHTSA news release, Oct. 4, 2001. http://www.dot.gov/affairs/nhtsa5101.htm

13 "Firestone Pays Ford $240 Million for Defective Tires,"
MotorTrend.com Oct. 14, 2005.
http://www.indiacar.net/news/n15736.htm

14 NHTSA news release Oct. 4, 2001.

15 Alejandro Bodipo-Memba, "U.S. blames the tires, not Ford's Explorers,"
Detroit Free Press, Oct. 5, 2001.

16 Ibid.

17 Ibid.

18 Bodipo-Memba, "U.S. Clears Explorer," *Detroit Free Press*, Feb. 13, 2002.

19 PowerPoint presentation prepared for Richard Parry-Jones for use in Ford news conference June 15, 2001.

20 Lynn Sweet, "Firestone Admits Making Bad Tires," *Chicago Sun-Times*, Sept. 13, 2000.

21 Bradsher, "Firestone and Ford Make Progress on Tire Inquiries," *New York Times*, Dec. 15, 2000.
http://query.nytimes.com/gst/fullpage.html?res=9D05E7D81F3FF936A2
5751C1A9669C8B63&sec=&spon=&pagewanted=all

Chapter Eleven: Full Circle

1 Leslie Gaines-Ross, *CEO Capital*, (Hoboken, N.J.: John Wiley and Sons, 2003), p. 194.

2 John DiPietro, "Ford Explorer Features," Edmunds.com, May 15, 2003.
http://www.edmunds.com/insideline/do/Features/articleId=46006

3 Jim Kerr, "AutoTech: Airbags – advancing the technology,"
CanadianDriver, Sept. 4, 2000.
http://www.canadiandriver.com/2000/09/04/autotech-airbags-advancing-the-technology.htm

4 "2006 FORD EXPLORER SAFETY," Ford news release on Ford Truck Enthusiasts website: http://www.ford-trucks.com/specs/2006/2006_ford_explorer_4.html 5

5 Bradsher, *High and Mighty: The dangerous rise of the SUV*, (New York: Public Affairs, 2003), p. 272-73.

6 Ibid, p. 274.

7 Robyn Meredith, "What's Good for General Motors…," *Forbes.com*, October 29, 2001 http://www.forbes.com/forbes/2001/1029/052.html

8 Ibid.

9 Danny Hakim, "Ford Says New S.U.V.'s Less Fuel-Efficient than Old Ones," *New York Times*, July 18, 2003. http://www.mindfully.org/Energy/2003/Ford-SUV-Less-Efficient18jul03.htm

10 Jones, "Ford Board Deposes CEO Nasser," *Los Angeles Times*, Oct. 30, 2001. http://articles.latimes.com/2001/oct/30/business/fi-63216

11 Ibid.

12 "Biggest Layoffs 1993-2008," *BusinessWeek*, December 1, 2008. (Source: Challenger, Gray and Christmas).

13 Mark Truby, "Resilient Explorer Rides Again," *Detroit News*, Sept. 5, 2002.

14 Ibid.

15 Hakim, "Ford Backs Off Efficiency Pledge for Its S.U.V.'s," *New York Times*, April 18, 2003. http://query.nytimes.com/gst/fullpage.html?res=9C00EED8173AF93BA25757C0A9659C8B63&sec=&spon=&pagewanted=1

16 Eric Peters, "Activists Plan Ford Centennial Protest," *The Car Connection*, http://www.thecarconnection.com/article/1004881_activists-plan-ford-centennial-protest

17 "100-foot Dinosaur to Tower Over Ford Celebration," news release from Rainforest Action Network, June 13, 2003.

    http://www.commondreams.org/news2003/0613-07.htm

Epilogue

1 See: Healey and Kiley, "PR company comes up with 2 campaigns taking SUVs to task," *USA Today* Jan. 24, 2003.

    http://www.usatoday.com/money/autos/2003-01-23-suvattacks_x.htm

Appendix

1 "Ford Explorer and the Firestone Tire Replacement Program: Myths and Facts," can be found in numerous places on the web, including *Autochannel.com*.
http://www.theautochannel.com/news/2001/06/01/022275.html

2 "Venezuelan Police Raid Opposition Broadcaster," Associated Press, May 22, 2009. http://www.lucianne.com/thread/?artnum=471682

INDEX

273